## 32 *Prevailingly* Pink *Flowers*

## 20 *Prevailingly* Red *Flowers*

(*Continued on back endpapers*)

# The
# Guide to
# Garden Flowers

BOOKS BY NORMAN TAYLOR

TAYLOR'S ENCYCLOPEDIA OF GARDENING

FLIGHT FROM REALITY

CINCHONA IN JAVA

GUIDE TO THE WILD FLOWERS

COLOR IN THE GARDEN

FRAGRANCE IN THE GARDEN

THE PERMANENT GARDEN

HERBS IN THE GARDEN

THE EVERBLOOMING GARDEN

WILD FLOWER GARDENING

FRUIT IN THE GARDEN

MATHEWS' FIELD BOOK OF AMERICAN
WILD FLOWERS (*revision*)

TAYLOR'S GARDEN GUIDE

THE GUIDE TO GARDEN FLOWERS

# The
# Guide to
# Garden Flowers

*Their Identity and Culture*

## NORMAN TAYLOR

*with 324 species illustrated in color*
*and 88 in black and white*
*by*

### EDUARDO SALGADO

HOUGHTON MIFFLIN COMPANY BOSTON

The Riverside Press Cambridge

1958

# Preface

THIS book has two aims. The first is to make the identification of garden flowers as painless as possible. The second is to provide such cultural notes that growing them will be easy for all. Except for technical works there is no other book with these two targets — identity and culture. If its aim is good, the often puzzled amateur and even the initiated may find the answers to "What is that flower?" and "How do I grow it?"

As to that part of it having to do with identification the 36 color plates and 88 line cuts have all been drawn especially for this book by Eduardo Salgado, certainly one of the outstanding flower artists in America. Every one of the 412 species has an illustration.

N. T.

Elmwood
Princess Anne, Maryland
*Easter, 1957*

# Introduction

THE selection of material to include in this book and the rejection of plants to exclude has been the work of years. No plant is admitted which is not available from ordinary sources.

As a guide to these the following will be helpful:

All seeds, bulbs, tubers, corms, or roots are listed in the catalogues of *seedsmen,* of which there are many. It is urged that the reader get at least half a dozen catalogues before ordering.

All plants (ready to set out) are listed in the catalogues of *nurserymen,* of which there are scores. It is well to have a collection of such catalogues before ordering.

Not all seeds or plants are carried by every dealer, and a good many are so familiar that they are often to be picked up at roadside stands or at the various garden centers. If there is difficulty in finding any item the best source is: *The Plant Buyers Guide,* issued by the Massachusetts Horticultural Society, Horticultural Hall, Boston 15, Massachusetts. This lists, by species and varieties, the complete contents of the catalogues of 441 seedsmen and nurserymen. No other compilation is as valuable to the seeker of any plant mentioned in this book. Most of the plants are readily available, but for the few that are not so common — and are often more desirable — *The Plant Buyers Guide* should be consulted.

We here include all the common garden flowers likely to interest the amateur. It does not include shrubs or trees, no grasses or ferns or the few aquatic plants grown mostly by specialists. "Garden flowers," as here used, is confined to those that are hardy outdoors, except for a few summer-bedding plants

like Coleus, Fuchsia, and Lantana. It does not include greenhouse or house plants, which are not frost-hardy.

# How to Use This Book

There are 412 species described and illustrated in the book,
which would be a hopeless tangle without some system of dividing them into related groups.* The experts have a terrifying
terminology for the sequence and content of these groups, but it
is avoided here, since the aim is to help the seeker, not to sink
him in a morass of technicalities.

Plants, however, have definite organs, like ourselves, and the
seeker should become familiar with them, for the ultimate
identity of all plants depends upon various differences in these
organs. Root, stem, leaf, flower, fruit, and seed — it is upon
the modification of these that any system must be built.

The plants are grouped into families (with some exceptions),
since this is the simplest method of arranging them. These, and
the sequence of them has been dictated by the desire to bring
related plants together. The botanists, who invented plant families, are on sure ground here, for no grouping by color, height,
period of bloom, or any other grouping would lead to anything
but confusion. Plant families (each is briefly described) have
the advantage of putting related plants together, an asset to those
who want some vista of what the world of plant life really is.

# The Descriptions

Under each species will be found a brief note of what the plant
is and from what country it is derived. This is important, both
for interest and because the country of origin often dictates its
culture. Beneath are the boldface entries Color, Height, Flower-

* Also, there are 355 related plants, without illustrations, but with brief notes,
inserted to round out the garden plants that are available.

ing date, Varieties, and Culture. Each of these needs some amplification.

**Color:** The usual color is cited, always of the wild plant, and where hybridization or other horticultural skills have changed the color, these are noted at **Varieties.**

**Height:** The lowest and highest stature is cited, with the understanding that poor soil or a drought will upset the high figure. Average culture will usually produce a plant somewhere between the high and low points.

**Flowering date:** This indicates the earliest and latest date when the plant might be in bloom, taking as an average the latitude of New York City. Places north or south of this will be likely to produce flowers later or earlier than the specified dates. Also, proximity to the sea will retard the onset of spring, as will mountain elevations. Hence the dates are approximate and not a floral timetable.

**Varieties:** This is a puzzling term both to the amateur and many professionals. It is used here as a designation for named horticultural forms (such as Blue Gem, Silver Moon, Red Sunset, and thousands of others). The color of these, which is often quite different from the parent species, is always cited. Most of these named horticultural forms are unquestionably *cultivars,* a term dear to the pedantic but of little currency elsewhere. But under **Varieties** are also included forms of the species that originate naturally. These are *varieties* in the true botanical sense. Until the terms *variety* and *cultivar* become of unquestioned currency it seems best to use "Variety" as the inclusive term for both categories. *Clones* are also not designated as such, being classed, perhaps inappropritaely, as varieties.

**Culture:** The only terms needing definition are

*Annual* — a plant that lives but a single growing season, blooms and sets seed that year before it dies, and depends upon seeds for its perpetuation.

*Biennial* — a plant that lives only two years. It usually does not flower the first year but does the second, when it dies

after setting seed, upon which it depends for perpetuation.
*Perennial* — a plant that usually dies down to the ground each
fall but sends up new shoots in the spring from its under-
ground root or rootstock. Such plants may live for years.
A few perennials have evergreen or partially evergreen
leaves, and some perennials die out in a few years. All such
are noted.

# Contents

# Explanation of Key

A KEY *is designed to lead the seeker to the identity of a plant, without for the moment concerning himself with any other in the book. To eliminate all but the desired plant two major decisions must be made at the outset, and thereafter. As an illustration, take Categories I and II in the Key that follows:*

I. *Climbing Vines*

II. *Not Climbing Vines*

*All that is necessary here is to decide whether or not the plant in hand is a climbing vine. Assuming that it is not, then one must decide whether it comes under*

A. *Plants with parallel-veined leaves* (Garden Bulbs), *or*

B. *Plants with netted-veined leaves.*

*After deciding whether it comes under A or B, the next step would be* (under A, for example) *whether the plant has no stem, or has an obvious one, and so on throughout the Key. Mostly there are only two alternatives to choose from, rarely three. At each category there is a citation to a page number, where again smaller keys are inserted to direct the seeker to the plant in hand.*

*The Key below is what the botanists call a dichotomous key, because it nearly always presents us with two alternatives, and no more; hence* dichotomous (i.e., with two branches).

*No key is ever 100 per cent perfect, for three things constantly tend to make it imperfect: there is the amount of skill in the making of it, the competence of the user, and, most of all, the variability of plants in different regions and at different seasons. Any key is hence more of a* guide *to identity than a mathematical target at which one aims. Users of the Key, by constant reference to the text and illustrations, should find it helpful in identifying an unknown plant. It has no other use. In this book the characters upon which the Key is based apply only to the plants in the book —not to the many exceptions found in related plants not here included.*

# Key to
# Garden Flowers

# The Guide to Garden Flowers

## NOTE

All main *plant names* are cross-referenced to
the appropriate illustrations.
All *illustrations* are cross-referenced to the
plants to which they belong.

# Vines

## *Plants generally high-climbing; not prostrate or hugging the ground*

THE twelve garden vines below are all herbaceous. They send up a stem in the spring and die down to the ground in autumn. Some, like the Morning-Glory, are annuals and hence must be started from seeds every year. Others are perennial and come up each spring from their dormant roots or rootstocks. If woody plants were included in this book, here would come the wisteria, Virginia creeper, honeysuckle, bittersweet, and the grape.

The 12 vines are grouped thus:

*Leaves opposite each other. 3 species. See pp. 1–2.*
*Leaves alternate on the stem, 6 species. See pp. 3–8.*

## *With Opposite Leaves*

**BLACK–EYED SUSAN** (*Thunbergia alata*)                    p. 6
A tropical African perennial vine, the toothed leaves 2–3 inches long, the flowers long-stalked and solitary. **Color:** White, but purple, orange, or yellow in some forms, always darker in the center. **Height:** 3–8 feet, if given trellis support. **Flowering date:** July–frost, which will kill it in the North. **Varieties:** Aurantiaca (orange). **Culture:** In frostless regions it is a perennial, started from seed or purchased plants. In the North sow seed indoors (6 weeks before outdoor planting is safe). Transfer outdoors when warm weather arrives. Space them 3 feet apart, in full sun, and they bloom the first summer from seed.

**CLEMATIS** (*Clematis jackmani*)                                    p. 6
A very showy perennial, sometimes a woody vine, the flowers
often 4–6 inches wide; of hybrid origin and the parent of many
horticultural forms. **Color:** Violet-purple in the typical form,
but variously colored in some of the varieties noted below.
**Height:** 5–15 feet. **Flowering date:** July–frost. **Varieties:** There
are over 30. A half-dozen of the best are: Crimson King (red),
Elsa Spaeth (bright blue), Gypsy Queen (velvety purple), Prins
Hendrik (pale blue), Lord Neville (dark plum), and Ramona
(blue). All are hardy up to Canada. **Culture:** Start with purchased plants, set in an alkaline, cool, rich, well-drained soil.
If soil is not alkaline, use a tablespoonful of lime to each plant,
stirred into soil. Set 3–4 feet apart, in full sun. Will grow, but
not as well, in non-alkaline soil.

Related vines (not illustrated):

*Clematis ligusticifolia.* 10–15 feet. Flowers white.
*Clematis paniculata.* 20–30 feet. Flowers white.
*Clematis virginiana.* 10–18 feet. Flowers white.
*Clematis viticella.* 6–10 feet. Flowers rose-purple.

**CINNAMON VINE** (*Dioscorea batatas*)                              p. 6
A Chinese true yam (not a sweet potato) grown in China for its
huge edible tubers, but here only for its ornamental foliage and
small, spicy-fragrant, cinnamon-scented flowers. **Color:** White.
**Height:** 8–20 feet. **Flowering date:** June–July. **Varieties:** None.
**Culture:** Plant small, purchased bulblets 3 inches deep in sandy
soil in full sun. From Washington northward lift tubers for
winter storage in cool but frost-free place (no furnace heat). Replant in spring. In the South the tubers can be left out and will
become enormous. Space 3–4 feet apart. Blooms from tubers
the first season.

Related plant (not illustrated):

Air Potato (*Dioscorea bulbifera*). 8–12 feet. Flowers
greenish white.

# *With Alternate Leaves*

**MORNING–GLORY** (*Ipomoea purpurea*)                              p. 6
A quick-growing, tropical American annual vine, grown for its
showy, funnel-shaped flowers, which may be 3–5 inches wide.
**Color:** White, red, or blue. **Height:** 6–15 feet. **Flowering date:**
July–Sept. **Varieties:** Heavenly Blue (sky-blue), Blue-Star (blue,
with darker stripes), Pearly Gates (white), Scarlet O'Hara (rosy
red), Rose Marie (pink). **Culture:** Seeds are so hard they must
be nicked with a file or soaked in tepid water for 8–12 hours, before planting ½ inch deep, in any ordinary soil, in full sun,
when warm weather arrives. Space 2–3 feet apart, and the vines
need a trellis or other support. They will not stand frost. Seeds
may be saved and planted next year.
   Related plants (not illustrated):
      *Ipomoea hederacea*. Flowers blue or pale purple.
      *Ipomoea nil*. Flowers purple, blue, or rose-pink.
      *Ipomoea tricolor*. Flowers purplish blue, the tip red, the
      tube white.

**MOONFLOWER** (*Calonyction aculeatum*)                          p. 6
A tropical American perennial relative of the Morning-Glory,
grown for its large, handsome leaves and its night-blooming,
spicy-scented flowers, which may be 5 inches wide. **Color:** White,
pink, or violet. **Height:** 8–20 feet. **Flowering date:** July–Aug.
**Varieties:** Giant Pink (pink), Giant White (white), Evening
Glory (violet). **Culture:** Seeds hard, difficult to germinate.
Cover them with wet sand, kept moist, in a closed bell jar or
empty aquarium. Keep about 80° F. with an electric bulb, for
several days. When seeds sprout pot them up in a mixture of ½
loam and ½ sand, to grow until warm weather arrives. Then
plant seedlings outdoors in rich soil in full sun, spaced 3–5 feet
apart. Will bloom the first year from seed, but will not persist
outdoors in frosty regions.

**CARDINAL CLIMBER** (*Quamoclit sloteri*)                        p. 6
An annual hybrid vine derived from crossing two tropical Ameri-

can relatives of the Morning-Glory. It has deeply and finely divided leaves, the segments almost threadlike, and many small, tubular flowers. **Color:** Scarlet. **Height:** 10–15 feet. **Flowering date:** July–Aug. **Variety:** Hearts and Honey (scarlet with a yellow center). **Culture:** Sow seeds indoors (6 to 8 weeks before outdoor planting is safe). Transfer seedlings to permanent site when warm weather arrives. Plant in full sun in an open, well-drained soil, and space 2–4 feet apart. It will bloom from seed the first year but stand no frost. It needs a wire fence or trellis.

**BALLOON–VINE** (*Cardiospermum halicacabum*)                    p. 6
A tropical perennial vine, used here as an annual. Its rapid growth over trellises and low buildings and its clusters of flowers, followed by the inflated and papery pods, make it an interesting addition to any collection of vines. **Color:** White. **Height:** 8–12 feet. **Flowering date:** July–Aug. **Varieties:** None. **Culture:** Sow seeds outdoors when warm weather arrives, ½ inch deep, in any ordinary soil, in full sun, and space 2–4 feet apart. For earlier bloom plant indoors (6–8 weeks before outdoor planting is safe). Transfer seedlings outdoors when settled warm weather arrives. It will bloom from seed the first year, but will stand no frost. In frost-free regions it is a hardy perennial. It needs a trellis or wire for support.

**MADEIRA–VINE** (*Boussingaultia baselloides*)                    p. 6
A tropical American perennial vine, its small, very fragrant flowers in drooping clusters often 8–12 inches long. Leaves heart-shaped and taper-pointed. **Color:** White, turning black in age. **Height:** 10–12 feet. **Flowering date:** July–Aug. **Varieties:** None. **Culture:** Start from purchased bulbs, planted 2 inches deep in any ordinary soil, in full sun, after all danger of frost. Space 2–3 feet apart and provide a trellis. In frosty regions lift the bulbs in autumn before freezing weather and store in a cool, frost-free place (no furnace heat). South of Norfolk, Va., the vine may be left in the ground indefinitely, and sometimes north of it with a winter mulch. Often, for its fragrance, known as Mignonette-vine. It blooms the first year from bulbs. Small tubercles, produced at base of leafstalks, will produce new vines if planted in moist sand.

**BALSAM APPLE** (*Momordica balsamina*) p. 6
A quick-growing annual vine from the Old World tropics, its egg-shaped fruit orange and warty, related to the cucumber and with prominent tendrils. **Color:** Yellow, the center of the tube darker. **Height:** 4–6 feet. **Flowering date:** June–July. **Varieties:** None. **Culture:** Sow seed ½ inch deep in boxes or pots in the house (6 weeks before outdoor planting is safe). Transfer seedlings outdoors when settled warm weather has arrived. Space 1–2 feet apart and provide wires or a trellis.

Related plant (not illustrated):

Balsam Pear (*Momordica Charantia*). 5–10 feet. Flowers similar, but fruit larger and more showy.

**CUP–AND–SAUCER VINE** (*Cobaea scandens*) p. 6
A Mexican, tendril-bearing vine, often called Mexican Ivy, and much grown as an annual for its quick growth and showy bloom. In the tropics and deep South it is a perennial, woody vine. Flowers cup-shaped, nearly 2 inches long. **Color:** Violet or greenish purple. **Height:** 10–25 feet. **Flowering date:** July–Aug. **Varieties:** None. **Culture:** Sow seeds planted with edges down and scarcely covered, in boxes or pots indoors (5–6 weeks before outdoor planting is safe). They take 10–14 days to sprout. Move indoor seedlings outdoors as soon as settled warm weather arrives, spacing them 2–3 feet apart, in any ordinary soil, in full sun or half-shade, and provide a trellis or wires. Blooming from seed the first year, but killed by frost.

**HYACINTH BEAN** (*Dolichos lablab*) p. 6
A rampant or luxuriant vine of the Old World tropics, much grown for food and forage there, but here (mostly in the South) for its clustered, showy, pea-like flowers. **Color:** Purple or white. **Height:** 15–30 feet in the South, half that northward. **Flowering date:** June–July. **Varieties:** Giganteus (white). **Culture:** Sow seeds where wanted in any reasonably good soil, ½ inch deep, after warm weather arrives. Thin to 1–3 feet apart and provide trellis, or they will sprawl. They will bloom the first year from seed if season is warm. In the South they are perennial, but are killed by frost northward.

# GARDEN VINES

1. **Balsam Apple** (*Momordica balsamina*)                    p. 5
   Quick-growing annual, 4–6 feet high. Flowers yellow, bloom June–July. Start indoors before outdoor planting is safe.

2. **Hyacinth Bean** (*Dolichos lablab*)                    p. 5
   Luxuriant, quick-growing vine, 15–30 feet high, with pealike purple or white flowers in June–July. Not hardy northward.

3. **Cinnamon Vine** (*Dioscorea batatas*)                    p. 2
   Not frost-hardy northward, but growing 8–20 feet in a single season. Flowers white, cinnamon-scented, bloom June–July.

4. **Balloon-Vine** (*Cardiospermum halicacabum*)                    p. 4
   An annual vine in the North, 8–12 feet high. White flowers in midsummer. Needs a trellis.

5. **Black-eyed Susan** (*Thunbergia alata*)                    p. 1
   A tropical African vine, 3–8 feet high, to be started in the North from seed. Flowers white, purple, or orange, bloom July to frost.

6. **Clematis** (*Clematis jackmani*)                    p. 2
   A perennial or woody vine, 5–15 feet high, with large purple or blue flowers from July to frost.

7. **Morning-Glory** (*Ipomoea purpurea*)                    p. 3
   Annual vine, quick-growing, 6–15 feet high. Flowers blue, white, red, or pink, all summer. Seeds are hard and need treatment. See text.

8. **Cup-and-Saucer Vine** (*Cobaea scandens*)                    p. 5
   A quick-growing annual vine, 10–25 feet high, its violet or greenish-purple flowers in midsummer.

9. **Madeira-Vine** (*Boussingaultia baselloides*)                    p. 4
   Not frost-hardy northward, but growing 10–20 feet high in one season from spring-planted bulbs. Flowers white, fragrant.

10. **Moonflower** (*Calonyction aculeatum*)                    p. 3
    Difficult to grow but worth it. It grows 8–20 feet high in one season. Not frost-hardy. Flowers night-blooming, fragrant.

11. **Passion-Flower** (*Passiflora incarnata*)                    p. 8
    A native relative of mostly tropical vines, 15–25 feet high, perennial. Hardy up to New York City. Flowers white and purplish pink.

12. **Cardinal Climber** (*Quamoclit sloteri*)                    p. 3
    An annual vine, 10–15 feet high. Tubular flowers scarlet, bloom in midsummer. Start seeds indoors; 6–8 weeks before outdoor planting is safe.

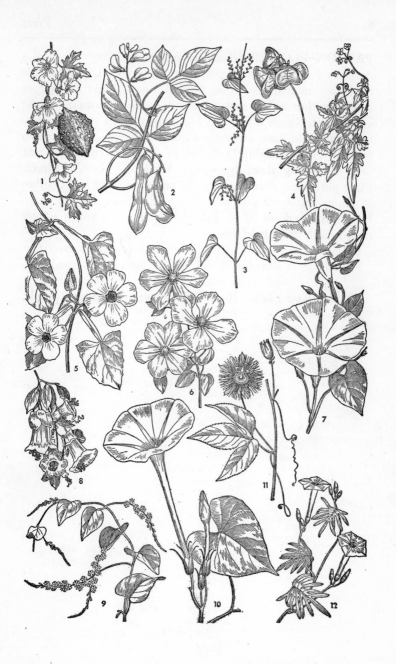

**PASSION–FLOWER** (*Passiflora incarnata*)                     p. 6
A native Passion-Flower, found from Va. to Texas, and the only
hardy representative of these tropical vines. Their flowers are
fringed within and to some suggest the crown of thorns of the
Crucifixion. Often called the Maypop, from its edible, yellow
fruit, and Wild Passion-Flower. **Color:** White, the fringed crown
purplish pink. **Height:** 15–25 feet in the wild; cultivated, half
this. **Flowering date:** June–July. **Varieties:** None. **Culture:**
Plant purchased, dormant roots in sandy loam, in early spring
in sun or half-shade, and provide a trellis. Space 2–3 feet apart.
Hardy as far north as New York City but needing a winter
mulch north of Philadelphia.

Related plants, only for frostless regions (not illustrated):

> *Passiflora caerulea*. 10–20 feet. Flowers white and pur-
> ple.
>
> *Passiflora edulis*. 10–15 feet. Flowers white and purple.

*If there are any vines in the plants that follow, they are sprawling or prostrate. This non-climbing habit applies to all the rest of the plants in the book (over 385). Looking through the pictures will help, but all of them are arranged in a simple scheme to make identification easy. The two major divisions of garden flowers are as follows:*

1. *Plants with the veins of the leaf parallel or essentially so. Parts of the flower (petals, etc.) in 3's or multiples of 3, hardly ever in 4's or 5's.*

    *This group includes all the common garden bulbs (tulip, hyacinth, crocus, iris, orchids, and many others). See pp. 9–52.*

2. *Plants with the veins of the leaf netted, crisscrossed, or reticulated; hardly ever parallel-veined. Parts of the flower (petals, etc.) in 4's or 5's, hardly ever in 3's.*

    *As this includes all the rest of the plants in the book, except the bulbous plants in group one and the high-climbing vines (see pp. 1–8), the identification of such a large residue is treated at p. 53.*

# Bulbs

THERE are over 60 garden plants grown as bulbs, although some of them grow from rootstocks like most irises and some orchids. For convenience they may be grouped thus:

*Flowers quite unsymmetrical and irregular, like the Canna, Gladiolus, and all the orchids. See pp. 48–52.*

*Flowers perfectly symmetrical, like the tulip or crocus. Among these some have an obvious stem that bears leaves and flowers, like the lily. For these see p. 26. All those below are stemless and may be divided into two groups:*

*Flowers borne in a cluster, like the Hyacinth or Lily-of-the-Valley. See pp. 19–26.*

*Only a single flower on each flower stalk (except the
Jonquil and Triplet Lily). Comprises the 13 species below.*

## Stemless: Flowers Usually Solitary, Symmetrical

**SPRING CROCUS** (*Crocus vernus*)                                          p. 12
A low, European bulbous plant, now in many varieties, best
planted in masses, making sheets of spring bloom. Leaves narrow and grasslike, with a silvery stripe in the middle. **Color:**
Various, see varieties below. **Height:** 3–5 inches. **Flowering date:**
March–April. **Varieties:** Striped Beauty (lavender-streaked), Al-
bion (white and purple), Pallas (violet, striped purple), Glad-
stone (reddish purple), Queen of the Blues (blue), Yellow
Mammoth (yellow), Mont Blanc (white). **Culture:** Plant purchased bulbs in Oct. or Nov. for next spring's bloom. Plant 2–3
inches deep, in quantities, in any ordinary garden soil, in sun or
shade, about 3 inches apart. After spring bloom do not mow until
leaves are withered, if naturalized in grassy places.
   Related plants, all spring-blooming (not illustrated):
      *Crocus aureus.* 3–5 inches. Flowers yellow.
      *Crocus imperati.* 4–6 inches. Flowers white or lilac,
         purple-striped.
      *Crocus susianus.* 4–6 inches. Flowers orange-yellow.

**SAFFRON CROCUS** (*Crocus sativus*)                                       p. 14
A bulbous herb from Anatolia popular for its fall bloom. Its
orange stigmas are the commercial source of saffron, and often
called Vegetable Gold. **Color:** White or lilac. **Height:** 3–5 inches.
**Flowering date:** Late Sept. and Oct. **Varieties:** None. **Culture:**
Plant purchased bulbs in late July or early Aug. for bloom 6–7
weeks hence. Plant 3 inches deep in any ordinary garden soil
and space 4 inches apart. It is not dependably hardy north of

New York City. Do not mow foliage the following spring. Left alone, it will spread and bloom for years.

Related plants all fall-blooming (not illustrated):

> *Crocus longiflorus*. 3–5 inches. Flowers lilac and yellow.
> *Crocus pulchellus*. 3–5 inches. Flowers lilac and fragrant.

## AUTUMN CROCUS (*Colchicum autumnale*) p. 12

Not related to the ordinary Spring Crocus or the Saffron Crocus, the Autumn Crocus has much larger and handsomer, fall-blooming flowers, followed the next spring by its narrow, grasslike leaves. It is from southern Europe and North Africa, and has no leaves when in bloom. **Color:** Rose-purple, but various in some varieties below. **Height:** 4–7 inches. **Flowering date:** Oct. and Nov. **Varieties:** Album (white), Roseum (rose), Atropurpureum (wine-red), Plenum (lilac), Lilac Wonder (lilac), Violet Queen (violet), Waterlily (pink and double-flowered). **Culture:** Plant purchased bulbs 3–4 inches deep, in rich soil, in late July or early Aug. for bloom 8–10 weeks later. Space 5–7 inches apart, and allow next spring's leaves to wither; do not cut them down. Left alone, the plant persists for years.

Related plants (not illustrated):

> *Colchicum bornmuelleri*. 5–8 inches. Flowers rose-lilac.
> *Colchicum speciosum*. 5–9 inches. Flowers lilac-purple,
> but white in variety *album*).

## SNOWDROP (*Galanthus nivalis*) p. 12

Planted in masses this Eurasian bulb, partial to cold, will make sheets of nodding bloom for many years; the first spring-blooming plant, often found among snow patches. **Color:** White, green tinged, or spotted. **Height:** 7–12 inches. **Flowering date:** Jan. to March, depending on site and distance southward. **Varieties:** Flore-pleno (white and double-flowered). **Culture:** Plant purchased bulbs in Aug. or Sept., 3 inches deep, in rich garden soil, partly or wholly shaded by shrubs or trees (not evergreens). Space 3–4 inches apart and leave them alone. Allow withered leaves to die down if you want the plants to spread and persist.

Related plant (not illustrated):

> *Galanthus elwesi*. 10–18 inches. Flowers white.

# GARDEN BULBS
### *(stemless; the flowers solitary)*

1. **Spring Crocus** (*Crocus vernus*)      **p. 10**
   Scores of varieties in many colors. Best planted in autumn for spring bloom.

2. **Autumn Crocus** (*Colchicum autumnale*)      **p. 11**
   Showy autumn-flowering bulb. Plant in late summer for bloom same fall.

3. **Snowflake** (*Leucojum vernum*)      **p. 14**
   Early-blooming bulb with nodding flowers. Plant in fall for spring bloom.

4. **Winter Daffodil** (*Sternbergia lutea*)      **p. 15**
   Yellow autumn-flowering bulb; crocus-like. Plant in late summer for bloom next year.

5. **Daffodil: Trumpet Narcissus** (*Narcissus pseudo-narcissus*)    **p. 17**
   In many varieties, mostly yellow and white. Easily grown from fall-planted bulbs.

6. **Poet's Narcissus** (*Narcissus poeticus*)      **p. 17**
   Fragrant, white-flowered, with central "eye" of red or orange. Plant in late summer.

7. **Snowdrop** (*Galanthus nivalis*)      **p. 11**
   Earliest of spring-blooming bulbs, often while snow is still evident. Plant in late summer.

8. **Zephyr Lily** (*Zephyranthes grandiflora*)      **p. 15**
   Not hardy in the North. Summer-blooming. Plant in fall for next season's bloom.

9. **Dogtooth Violet** (*Erythronium americanum*)      **p. 16**
   Spring-blooming native suited only to shady wild garden.

# GARDEN BULBS
## *(stemless; the flowers clustered)*

1. **Bluebell of England** (*Scilla nonscripta*)　　　　p. 20
   Easily grown squill, useful in masses. Plant in fall for bloom next April.

2. **Grape Hyacinth** (*Muscari botryoides*)　　　　p. 20
   Spring-blooming bluebell for mass effects. Plant in fall for next season's flowers.

3. **Hardy Amaryllis** (*Lycoris squamigera*)　　　　p. 24
   Not really hardy northward. Summer-blooming. Plant in midsummer, 6–8 inches deep.

4. **Summer Hyacinth** (*Galtonia candicans*)　　　　p. 23
   Summer-blooming giant hyacinth. Plant in May for same season's bloom. Not hardy northward.

5. **Lily-of-the-Valley** (*Convallaria majalis*)　　　　p. 21
   Fragrant, shade-enduring perennial. Plant in fall or early spring for May bloom.

6. **Lily-of-the-Nile** (*Agapanthus africanus*)　　　　p. 24
   Not hardy northward. Summer-blooming. Best grown in pots north of Philadelphia.

7. **Siberian Squill** (*Scilla sibirica*)　　　　p. 20
   A low squill thriving under dense shade of evergreens. Plant in Oct. for April bloom.

8. **Hyacinth** (*Hyacinthus orientalis;* Lady Derby)　　　　p. 22
   Very fragrant, spring-blooming, prevailingly blue. Plant in autumn for April or May bloom.

9. **Glory-of-the-Snow** (*Chionodoxa luciliae*)　　　　p. 21
   Useful for mass effects in moist sites. Plant in fall for March–April bloom.

**SNOWFLAKE** (*Leucojum vernum*)                              p. 12
Related to the Snowdrop, but the flowers are later, larger, fragrant,
bell-shaped, and have hollow stalks. The Snowflake is an early-
blooming bulb from southern Europe with nodding, rather heavy
flowers and leaves broader than grasslike. **Color:** White, but
green-tipped. **Height:** 9–12 inches. **Flowering date:** March–April.
**Varieties:** Carpathicum (petals tipped with yellow). **Culture:**
Plant purchased bulbs 4–5 inches deep and 4 inches apart in Oct.
or early Nov. for next spring's bloom. Choose sandy loam, preferably somewhat moist in full sun or half-shade of shrubs or trees
(no evergreens). Allow foliage to wither and they will persist
for years. Best planted in masses.

Related plants (not illustrated):
> *Leucojum aestivum.* 9–12 inches. Flowers white but green-
> tipped. Early spring.
> *Leucojum autumnale.* 7–9 inches. White but red-tinged.
> Late autumn.

Left: Spring Meadow Saffron (*Bulbocodium vernum*), p. 15. Right:
Saffron Crocus (*Crocus sativus*), p. 10.

## SPRING MEADOW SAFFRON
(*Bulbocodium vernum*) p. 14
A crocus-like European plant, its flowers practically stalkless and hugging the ground. Its narrow, nearly grasslike leaves follow the bloom, which appears quite naked. **Color:** Purple. **Height:** 3–5 inches. **Flowering date:** April. **Varieties:** None. **Culture:** Plant purchased bulbs in Sept. or Oct. in a good but gritty soil, 3 inches deep and 3–4 inches apart. Best planted in masses in full sun or partial shade. Allow foliage to wither and the plant persists for years.

## WINTER DAFFODIL (*Sternbergia lutea*) p. 12
This Eurasian bulb is sometimes called Lily-of-the-Field, a name more appropriate, since its crocus-like flowers have nothing to do with a Daffodil. It is much grown for its late bloom. **Color:** Yellow. **Height:** 4–6 inches. **Flowering date:** Sept–Oct. **Varieties:** None. **Culture:** Plant purchased bulbs 4 inches deep, as early in Aug. as possible, in a good, gritty soil, preferably against a south-facing wall. Space 4 inches apart and leave undisturbed until foliage has withered. It is not very persistent and may need re-planting every third or fourth year. Not dependably hardy north of New York City.

## ZEPHYR LILY (*Zephyranthes grandiflora*) p. 12
A tropical American bulbous herb, much grown in pots for its summer bloom, or outdoors from Washington, D.C., southward. It has flat, narrow leaves and funnel-shaped, handsome flowers on a hollow stalk. **Color:** Pink or pinkish red. **Height:** 6–10 inches. **Flowering date:** July–Aug. **Varieties:** None. **Culture:** Plant purchased bulbs in Oct. or early Nov., in light or sandy loam, 3 inches deep and 3–4 inches apart, in full sun. Not reliably hardy north of Washington, D.C. If planted northward, put on south side of house, and cover with a winter mulch of straw or salt hay and remove it in late March.

Related plants (not illustrated):

Atamasco Lily (*Zephyranthes atamasco*). 9–12 inches. Flowers white.

*Zephyranthes rosea*. 3–6 inches. Flowers pink. **Aug.–Sept.**

**TRIPLET LILY** (*Brodiaea laxa*)                                       p. 18
Attractive bulbous plants, mostly from Calif., the Triplet Lily
one of the few safely hardy in the East. Flowers solitary or in
lax clusters, the leaves narrow, grasslike, and soon withering
after the plant blooms. **Color:** Blue, purple, or white. **Height:**
12–18 inches. **Flowering date:** May–June. **Varieties:** No named
ones, but a yellow variety is offered. **Culture:** Not reliably hardy
north of Washington, D.C., unless in sheltered place. Plant
purchased bulbs in full sun, in loose, gritty soil, 3–4 inches deep,
in early autumn. In the East lift bulbs after spring bloom, and
when leaves are withered, for summer storage in cool, dry place.
The Triplet Lily does not thrive in moist, hot summers, but does
well outdoors on the Pacific Coast.

   Related plants (not illustrated):
      Blue Dicks (*Brodiaea capitata*). 15–20 inches. Flowers blue.
      Pretty-Face (*Brodiaea ixioides*). 10–18 inches. Flowers
         salmon-yellow, purple-streaked.
      Wild Hyacinth (*Brodiaea lactea*). 10–18 inches. Flowers
         white or lilac.

**DOGTOOTH VIOLET** (*Erythronium americanum*)          p. 12
Beautiful American woodland plant, often called Yellow Ad-
der's-Tongue or Trout Lily, with brownish-mottled, handsome
leaves and nodding, showy lily-like flowers. **Color:** Yellow.
**Height:** 6–8 inches. **Flowering date:** May. **Varieties:** None.
**Culture:** Plant purchased bulbs, 3 inches deep in partial or full
shade (not under evergreens), in rich woodland soil with plenty
of humus, but not acid. Space 3–4 inches apart. A wild garden
plant not suited to open garden, and best planted in masses.

   Related plants, mostly for Pacific Coast and not reliably hardy
      in the East (not illustrated):
         Fawn Lily (*Erythronium californicum*). 7–12 inches.
         Flowers cream-white.
      Adam-and-Eve or the Chamise Lily (*Erythronium grandi-
         florum*). 18–24 inches. Flowers yellow.
      *Erythronium tuolumnense.* 9–12 inches. Flowers golden
         yellow.

**DAFFODIL:** Trumpet Narcissus
  (*Narcissus pseudo-narcissus*) p. 12
The showiest and most easily grown of the innumerable species and varieties of the genus *Narcissus,* which includes not only the Daffodil but the Poet's Narcissus and the Jonquil (treated at the next two entries), and many others. They are bulbous plants, mostly European, with flat or rushlike and roundish leaves and very handsome flowers. In the Daffodil the central "trumpet" is as long as or longer than the petals. **Color:** Prevailingly yellow or sometimes white, but see under varieties below. **Height:** 8–15 inches. **Flowering date:** April–May. **Varieties:** Aerolite (primrose yellow), Beersheba (white), Mrs. R. O. Backhouse (petals white, trumpet pink), Lord Wellington (petals yellow, trumpet orange-yellow), King Alfred (yellow), White Monarch (white), Pink Fancy (petals white, trumpet pink), Magnificence (deep golden yellow), President Lebrun (petals white, trumpet golden yellow). **Culture:** Plant purchased bulbs in late Aug. or Sept., in full sun, 5–6 inches deep in well-drained, rich garden soil, for bloom the following and successive springs. Do not cut off leaves until they wither. After 3–4 years lift bulbs in Sept. and replant to prevent crowding which causes poorer and fewer flowers. The Trumpet Narcissus, or Daffodil, is sometimes incorrectly called a Jonquil. Can be grown indoors in pebbles and water.
  Related plants (not illustrated):
    *Narcissus leedsi.* 8–15 inches. Flowers (in some varieties) white, yellow, and greenish yellow.
    *Narcissus incomparabilis.* 8–12 inches. Variously colored.

**POET'S NARCISSUS** (*Narcissus poeticus*) p. 12
A beautifully fragrant narcissus, which has a central "crown," but no trumpet, the crown usually of different color from the petals. It has flat, grasslike leaves, is a native of southern Europe, and much cultivated for its delightful odor and starlike flowers. **Color:** Prevailingly white, but the central crown reddish, or orange-red. **Height:** 12–18 inches. **Flowering date:** April–May. **Varieties:** Actaea (petals white, crown yellow but red-edged),

Recurvus (petals white, crown orange-red), Pheasant's-Eye
(petals white, crown orange but red-edged), Sarchedon (petals
white, crown crimson), Dulcimer (petals white, crown yellow
with red edge), Red Rim (petals white, crown yellow with broad
red margin). **Culture:** Plant purchased bulbs in late Aug. or
Sept., 3–4 inches deep, in well-drained, rich garden soil, in full
sun. Space 4–5 inches apart. Cover with winter mulch of straw
or salt hay and remove it in March. Do not cut off leaves until
they wither. When plants become too crowded for first-class
bloom (3–4 years) lift bulbs in Sept. and replant. This and the
Trumpet Narcissus are fine for naturalizing in masses. Can be
grown indoors in pebbles and water.

**JONQUIL** (*Narcissus jonquilla*)                                    below
A delightfully fragrant bulbous plant from southern Europe and
North Africa, with terete, rushlike leaves, and with the central

Left: Triplet Lily (*Brodiaea laxa*), p. 16. Right: Jonquil
(*Narcissus jonquilla*), above.

cup or crown of the flower less than half the length of the petals. The flowers are sometimes only one on a stalk, more often in loose, lax few-flowered clusters. **Color:** Yellow. **Height:** 8–12 inches. **Flowering date:** April–May. **Varieties:** Golden Scepter (petals yellow, cup golden), Trevithian (lemon yellow), Odorus Plenus (flowers double, yellow), Orange Queen (orange), Simplex (yellow). **Culture:** Plant purchased bulbs 3–4 inches deep in rich, well-drained garden soil, in full sun, in Sept. Space 4–5 inches apart. Provide winter mulch of straw or salt hay and remove it in March. Do not cut leaves until they wither. If crowding (after 3–4 years) reduces amount and quality of bloom, lift bulbs and replant in Sept. The name Jonquil is often, incorrectly, applied to the Daffodil or Trumpet Narcissus. The Jonquil can be grown indoors in pebbles and water.

Related plants (not illustrated):

*Narcissus juncifolius.* 3–6 inches. Flowers yellow.

Campernelle Jonquil (*Narcissus odorus*). 8–12 inches. Flowers yellow.

# *Stemless: Flowers Clustered, Symmetrical*

Bulbs without a true stem that bears leaves and flowers (as in the lily), although the flower stalk may be stem-like and often mistaken for a stem.

THE 14 bulbous plants without a true stem, treated below, differ from those on pp. 10–19 because the flowers are in clusters, never one to a stalk. These clustered-flowered bulbs may be separated thus:

*Plants generally 9 inches high or less. 7 species. See pp. 20–22.*

*Plants mostly 10 inches high or more, sometimes considerably more. 7 species. See pp. 22–26.*

**GRAPE HYACINTH** (*Muscari botryoides*) p. 13
One of the bluebells of Europe and widely planted in masses for its early spring bloom, resembling a miniature hyacinth. The individual urn-shaped flower is drooping and the leaves are narrow and grasslike. **Color:** Typically blue, but see varieties below. **Height:** 3–7 inches. **Flowering date:** April. **Varieties:** Album (white), Carneum (pink), Heavenly Blue (blue). **Culture:** Plant purchased bulbs, in quantity for mass effects, 3 inches deep in Oct., in any ordinary garden soil or in the lawn. Space 2–3 inches apart, and leave alone, since they do not tend to become crowded. Sometimes called the Starch Hyacinth.

Related plants (not illustrated):

Musk Hyacinth (*Muscari moschatum*). 6–9 inches. Flowers greenish yellow, fragrant.

*Muscari armeniacum.* 4–5 inches. Flowers blue.

Tassel Hyacinth (*Muscari comosum*). 6–9 inches. Flowers violet-blue.

Feather Hyacinth (*Muscari comosum monstrosum*). 6–9 inches. Flowers violet-blue, feathered.

**BLUEBELL OF ENGLAND** (*Scilla nonscripta*) p. 13
One of the many Eurasian squills and an easily grown bulb for mass effects. It has small, bell-like, fragrant flowers in lax clusters, and narrow grasslike leaves. **Color:** Typically blue, but see varieties below. **Height:** 6–9 inches. **Flowering date:** April. **Varieties:** Blush Queen (pink), Alba (white), Rosea (pink). **Culture:** Plant purchased bulbs, in masses for effective bloom, in Oct., 4–5 inches deep, in rich sandy soil, preferably in half-shade. Space 3–5 inches apart and leave alone to permit spreading. This bluebell is often offered under the incorrect name of *Scilla nutans,* and is sometimes called the Wood Hyacinth.

Related plant (not illustrated):

Spanish Bluebell (*Scilla hispanica,* but often offered under the incorrect name of *Scilla campanulata*). 8–10 inches. Flowers blue, pink, or white.

**SIBERIAN SQUILL** (*Scilla sibirica*) p. 13
Related to the Bluebell of England, but lower and thriving under

dense evergreen shade where little else will grow. Leaves not grasslike, nearly ½ inch wide, the flowers nodding. **Color:** Blue or white. **Height:** 4–6 inches. **Flowering date:** April. **Varieties:** Alba (white), Azurea (light blue). **Culture:** Plant purchased bulbs in Oct., in rich garden soil, under shade (even under evergreens), 3–4 inches deep. Space 3–4 inches apart, and leave alone to permit spreading.

Related plant (not illustrated):

Star Hyacinth (*Scilla amoena*). 4–6 inches. Flowers purplish blue.

**GLORY–OF–THE–SNOW** (*Chionodoxa luciliae*)     p. 13
Early-blooming bulbous plant from Asia Minor, with narrow, grasslike leaves and profuse clusters of tiny flowers, the lowest in the cluster nodding. Useful for mass effects. **Color:** Blue, with a white center or "eye." **Height:** 2–3 inches. **Flowering date:** March–April. **Varieties:** Alba (white). **Culture:** Plant purchased bulbs in Oct., 3 inches deep and 3 inches apart, in sandy or gritty loam in full sun, and preferably in a moist but not wet site. Do not disturb and in a few years it will provide sheets of bloom.

Related plant (not illustrated):

*Chinodoxa sardensis*. 2–3 inches. Flowers gentian-blue.

**LILY–OF–THE–VALLEY** (*Convallaria majalis*)     p. 13
An exceptionally fragrant Eurasian plant, perhaps native also in the higher Alleghenies from Va. to Tenn., and much cultivated for its delicious odor. Flowers bell-shaped, nodding; the fine glossy leaves persistent but not evergreen. **Color:** Typically white, but see varieties below. **Height:** 6–8 inches. **Flowering date:** May. **Varieties:** Albo-striata (yellow-banded leaves), Florepleno (flowers double), Rosea (pink). **Culture:** Not a true bulb, and purchased plants or "pips" (a bulblike rootstock) should be planted 2–3 inches deep in rich woods soil or garden soil with plenty of humus, in partial shade, late in autumn or in early April. Space 6–8 inches apart. Cover the bed in winter with old rotted manure. Respace after 3–4 years if plants are so crowded that bloom is reduced.

**COW–TONGUE** (*Clintonia borealis*)                        p. 23
An American woodland plant, suited only to the wild garden
and often known as Bluebead or Corn Lily. It is a perennial
growing mostly in deep shady woods and is attractive also for its
bright blue fruits. It has thickish, long-oval leaves, and a lax
terminal cluster of only 3–8 flowers. **Color:** Greenish yellow.
**Height:** 6–9 inches. **Flowering date:** May. **Varieties:** None.
**Culture:** Start with purchased plants set in rich woods soil, or
in sphagnum moss, late in autumn or early in April, in a cool
shaded site (not on the warm coastal plain). Space 6–8 inches
apart and do not cultivate or disturb it.
    Related plant (not illustrated):
        *Clintonia umbellata.* 6–9 inches. Flowers white.

**STAR OF BETHLEHEM**
    (*Ornithogalum umbellatum*)                             p. 23
A starry-flowered herb from the Mediterranean region, now
widely escaped in North America and cultivated often under the
names of Summer Snowflake or Sleepy Dick. It is a close relative
of the florists' Chinkerichee, and has narrow, grasslike leaves.
Left to itself it may spread so much as to become a nuisance.
**Color:** White. **Height:** 6–9 inches. **Flowering date: May. Varieties:** None. **Culture:** Start with purchased bulbs, planted 1–2
inches deep in any soil and in shade or sun. Next to impossible
to kill it, and often it becomes a pest in lawns or borders.

**HYACINTH** (*Hyacinthus orientalis*)                       p. 13
A deliciously fragrant bulbous plant from Greece and Turkey
widely grown for its many-flowered clusters of spring bloom, and
available in numerous horticultural varieties. **Color:** Typically
blue or white, but some of its varieties red, pink, pinkish orange,
or violet. **Height:** 10–15 inches, the flowering stalk stiff. **Flowering date:** April–May. **Varieties:** Roi des Belges and La Victoire
(red), Lady Derby and Queen of the Pinks (pink), Purity and
L'Innocence (white), and scores of others. **Culture:** Plant purchased First-sized bulbs in late Oct. for bloom next spring and
thereafter. Put 5–6 inches deep in rich soil and in full sunlight,
8–10 inches apart. Cover with light mulch of straw or manure in

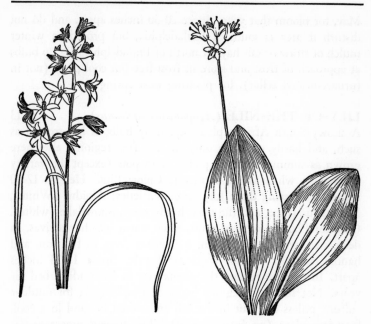

Left: Star of Bethlehem (*Ornithogalum umbellatum*), p. 22. Right:
Cow-Tongue (*Clintonia borealis*), p. 22.

severe winters. Do not cut flowering truss if bloom is wanted
second and third year. Start with fresh bulbs every third or
fourth year. For forcing indoors use Exhibition-sized bulbs.
Related plants (not illustrated):

> Roman Hyacinth (*Hyacinthus orientalis albulus*). 8–12
> inches. Flowers blue or white. Early spring.
>
> *Hyacinthus ciliatus* (often called *Hyacinthus azureus*).
> 4–6 inches. Flowers pale blue. Early spring.

**SUMMER HYACINTH** (*Galtonia candicans*)          p. 13
This summer-blooming, South African bulbous plant is often
called Giant Summer Hyacinth from its great height. It has
basal, strap-shaped leaves and a tall, prolific cluster of narrowly
bell-shaped flowers. **Color:** White. **Height:** 2–3½ feet. **Flowering date:** July–Aug. **Varieties:** None. **Culture:** Plant purchased
bulbs 5–6 inches deep in full sun, in any ordinary garden soil, in

May, for bloom that year. Space 20–30 inches apart, and do not disturb if area is south of Philadelphia, but provide a winter mulch of straw or salt hay. If north of Philadelphia, dig up bulbs at approach of frost and store in frost-free but cool place (not in furnace-heated cellar), for planting next spring.

**LILY–OF–THE–NILE** (*Agapanthus africanus*)                    p. 13
A showy South African plant, not truly bulbous but treated as such, and hardy outdoors only in frost-free regions; elsewhere grown as summer bedding plants or in pots (except the variety *mooreanus,* which is the hardiest). **Color:** Blue. **Height:** 12–20 inches. **Flowering date:** July–Aug. **Varieties:** Albidus (White), Mooreanus (blue, and the most hardy sort), Snowflake (white). **Culture:** Plant purchased roots, after warm weather arrives, in deep, rich, well-drained loam, 4–5 inches deep, in full sun, and handle carefully because roots are brittle. Space 18–24 inches apart. In frostless regions the plants may be left undisturbed for years. Not suited to regions north of Philadelphia for outdoor culture, unless dug out in the fall and stored in sand in a cool, frost-free place (no furnace heat). The variety *mooreanus* is hardy, with a winter mulch as far north as Wilmington, Del. The Lily-of-the-Nile is often called the African Lily and is offered by some dealers as *Agapanthus umbellatus.*

**HARDY AMARYLLIS** (*Lycoris squamigera*)                    p. 13
Asiatic and very showy garden plant, with a large terminal cluster (umbel) of fragrant flowers on a tall solid stalk, its basal strap-shaped leaves developing before the flowers appear. Of chief interest as the only amaryllis-like plant suited to outdoor culture as far north as Wilmington, Del.; northward only as a pot plant or for sumer bedding. **Color:** Lilac-pink. **Height:** 18–30 inches. **Flowering date:** Aug.–Sept. **Varieties:** None. **Culture:** Plant purchased roots in early Aug. or late July, 6–8 inches deep in rich, loamy garden soil, well drained, and in full sun. Space 15–20 inches apart. South of Washington, D.C., they should be left undisturbed, but northward to Wilmington, or even to Philadelphia, apply a winter mulch of straw or salt hay.

Left: Lily Leek (*Allium moly*), p. 26. Center: Wild Onion (*Allium stellatum*), below. Right: Striped Squill (*Puschkinia scilloides*), p. 26.

It is a rich feeder, and manure or fertilizer should be applied every other year at the rate of a forkful of well-rotted manure or a cupful of commercial fertilizer per plant, well dug in. Sometimes sold under the incorrect name of *Amaryllis hallii*.

Related plants (not illustrated):

*Lycoris aurea*. 12–20 inches. Flowers yellow.

*Lycoris radiata*. 12–20 inches. Flowers red.

(Both are unsuited to frosty regions.)

**WILD ONION** (*Allium stellatum*)                    above

A rather showy wild onion from the central U.S., often cultivated for its handsome cluster (umbel) of onion-scented flowers, and hardy everywhere. Leaves narrow, strap-shaped, and nearly flat, decidedly onion-scented. **Color:** Pink. **Height:** 12–18 inches. **Flowering date:** June–July. **Varieties:** None. **Culture:** Plant purchased bulbs, 3–4 inches deep in almost any soil, in Oct. or

April, in full sun. Space 4–6 inches apart. It may spread to become a nuisance, and needs little attention except to prevent spreading.

**LILY LEEK** (*Allium moly*)                                        p. 25
An onion-scented bulbous plant from southern Europe, often grown for its compact cluster (umbel) of flowers, it being the only cultivated allium with yellow flowers. It has broad, flat, pointed leaves, decidedly onion-scented when bruised. **Color:** Yellow. **Height:** 9–14 inches. **Flowering date:** July. **Varieties:** None. **Culture:** Plant purchased bulbs in Oct. or April, in any reasonably good garden soil, preferably partly shaded, 3–4 inches deep. Space 4–5 inches apart, and leave alone. Useful for the open border or rock garden.

**STRIPED SQUILL** (*Puschkinia scilloides*)                        p. 25
A tidy little border plant from Asia Minor, closely related to the true squills and cultivated for its early bloom. It has strap-shaped leaves nearly as long as the flower stalk, and is much planted for its charming, if modest flowers. **Color:** Blue. **Height:** 9–12 inches. **Flowering date:** April. **Varieties:** Alba (white). **Culture:** Plant purchased bulbs 3–4 inches deep, in Oct., in a relatively sandy loam, in full sun or partial shade. Space 3–4 inches apart, and for best effects plant in masses. They should be left alone unless crowding prevents bloom, when they must be dug up and respaced after the leaves wither.

## *Bulbs with an Obvious Stem*

ALL of the bulbous plants already treated (see pp. 10–26) are without a true stem, although many of them have a flower stalk that is often mistaken for a stem. All those below, however, have true stems that bear leaves and flowers, of which the lily and trillium are common examples. For convenience this group of garden bulbs (some bear rootstocks instead of bulbs but are treated as bulbs culturally) can be divided thus:

*Relatively tall plants, usually 24 inches high or more, some-*

*times much more. 17 species. See pp. 37–48.*
*Shorter plants, mostly not over 20 inches high, except the*
*Japanese Iris. 14 species. See below.*

# TULIPS

Garden tulips are so numerous and so diverse that they are divided into several different classes, in each of which are scores or even hundreds of varieties. Only three classes can be treated here. Darwin Tulips, Triumph Tulips, and Cottage Tulips, leaving for more encyclopedic works the less known classes. All of the three groups below have been derived by selection and hybridization of original species from Turkey, mostly in Holland.

**DARWIN TULIP** (*Tulipa* hybrids)                          p. 28
The tallest and finest of the garden tulips, grown by the million for spring bloom and for cut flowers. Its thick, fleshy leaves are borne on a short stem usually much exceeded by the flower stalk. The flowers are nearly rectangular toward the base, the squarish blunt tips of the petals slightly incurved. **Color:** Various, see below. **Height:** 10–20 inches. **Flowering date:** May. **Varieties:** Hundreds are listed of which the following will provide a good selection. RED OR ROSE: Masterpiece, City of Haarlem, Scarlet O'Hara. PINK: Peach, Smiling Queen. YELLOW: Yellow Giant, Helen Gahagan, Niphetos. WHITE: Glacier, White Giant, Zwanenburg. PURPLE: Faust, Storm King, La Tulipe Noire (almost black). LILAC: Mme. Butterfly, Blue Ribbon, Insurpassable. **Culture:** Plant purchased bulbs in Oct. or Nov., 5–8 inches deep in rich garden soil, well manured below the base of the bulb, but the manure separated from the bulb by ½–¾ inch of unmanured soil. Plant in full sun and space 7–10 inches apart, and in severe climates provide a winter mulch of straw or salt hay. After plants bloom allow leaves to wither before lifting the bulbs if space is needed for other plants. Most amateurs should start with fresh bulbs each autumn, unless they can dust the dried bulbs with sulphur and provide a cool, dry place for summer storage until fall planting.

# GARDEN BULBS
*(with true stem; mostly 20 inches or less)*

1. **Tall Bearded Iris** (*Iris* hybrids)                    p. 31
   Easily grown perennial with stout rootstock; in hundreds of varieties.

2. **Cottage Tulip** (*Tulipa* hybrids; White City)          p. 30
   May-flowering tulip in scores of varieties. Plant in Oct.–Nov. for next season's bloom.

3. **Darwin Tulip** (*Tulipa* hybrids; Smiling Queen)        p. 27
   Aristocrats of the tulip world; in hundreds of varieties. Plant in fall for May bloom.

4. **Triumph Tulip** (*Tulipa* hybrids; Bruno Walter)        p. 30
   Taller than Darwin Tulips and blooming a fortnight earlier. Plant in fall for spring bloom.

5. **Large-flowered Trillium** (*Trillium grandiflorum*)     p. 30
   Splendid native perennial for rich, shady wild garden. May-blooming.

6. **Guinea-Hen Flower** (*Fritillaria meleagris*)           p. 34
   Lily-like, nodding flowers in May–June. Plant in early fall for next season's bloom.

7. **White Mariposa Lily** (*Calochortus venustus*)          p. 33
   Not hardy northward, mostly suited to western gardens, especially Calif.

8. **Plantain-Lily** (*Hosta plantaginea*)                   p. 33
   Popular edging perennial with late summer bloom and of easy culture.

9. **Japanese Iris** (*Iris kaempferi*)                      p. 32
   Saucer-wide, showy flowers in June–July. Plant rootstocks in moist site in early spring.

# GARDEN BULBS
*(with a true stem; mostly 24 inches or more)*

1. **Royal Lily** (*Lilium regale*)      **p. 39**
   Enormous, fragrant flowers in midsummer. Plant deep, in late
   Nov. for next season's bloom.

2. **Montbretia** (*Tritonia crocosmaeflora*)      **p. 42**
   Summer-blooming relative of Gladiolus, but taller. Not hardy
   northward. Plant bulbs in May.

3. **Madonna Lily** (*Lilium candidum*)      **p. 39**
   An early summer-flowering lily, often 3–4 feet high. Plant bulbs
   in Nov. for next season's bloom.

4. **Daylily** (*Hemerocallis* hybrids)      **p. 40**
   A protean group of perennials of easy culture. Flowers from
   June to Sept., according to varieties.

5. **Asphodel** (*Asphodeline lutea*)      **p. 43**
   An old-time favorite, not often grown today, and flowering in
   July. Plant roots in April or Oct.

6. **Red-hot Poker** (*Kniphofia uvaria grandiflora*)      **p. 42**
   African perennial, not quite hardy northward. Midsummer-
   blooming, 3–4 feet high.

7. **Foxtail Lily** (*Eremurus elwesi*)      **p. 41**
   The aristocrat of all bulbous plants, 10–12 feet high and of exacting culture.

8. **Peruvian Lily** (*Alstroemeria aurantiaca*)      **p. 40**
   Not reliably hardy northward. Summer-blooming. Plant in May,
   but lift roots for winter storage north of Washington, D.C.

9. **Tiger-Flower** (*Tigridia pavonia*)      **p. 43**
   Iris-like, but tender, bulbous plant, grown outdoors safely only
   south of Richmond, Va.

**TRIUMPH TULIP** (*Tulipa* hybrids)                                                    p. 28
This recently developed class of tulips closely resembles the
Darwins, and in part was derived from crossing the latter with
earlier-flowering sorts. The Triumph Tulips are a little taller
than the Darwins and flower 10–14 days earlier. **Color:** Various,
see below. **Height:** 12–24 inches. **Flowering date:** Early May or
late April. **Varieties:** Bruno Walter (orange-yellow), Tele-
scopium (violet-rose); Kantara (white), Korneforos (red),
Elmus (cherry-red), Mr. Zimmerman (rose-pink), Rhineland
(yellow), Red Giant (scarlet). **Culture:** Exactly the same as for
Darwin Tulips (see preceding).

**COTTAGE TULIP** (*Tulipa* hybrids)                                                   p. 28
A race of tulips, with innumerable varieties, generally with
cylindrical flowers, the pointed petals of which are scarcely
incurved as they are in the Darwins. But some Cottage Tulips
have flowers with swollen bases and the petals are rounded at the
tip. While the race is thus rather ill-defined it comprises some of
the most treasured tulip varieties in cultivation. All bloom about
the same time as the Darwins. **Color:** Various, see below. **Height:**
10–20 inches. **Flowering date:** May. **Varieties:** Very numerous,
but the following selection will provide for most needs —
Advance (scarlet), Belle Jaune (dark yellow), Carrara (white),
Golden Harvest (light yellow), G. W. Leak (red), Mongolia
(chrome-yellow), Mrs. John T. Scheepers (pale yellow), Rosa-
bella (bright rose), President Hoover (orange-scarlet), White
City (white). **Culture:** Exactly the same as outlined under
Darwin Tulip (see p. 27).

# SHORT BULBOUS PLANTS WITH AN OBVIOUS STEM
(Except Tall Bearded and Japanese Iris)

**LARGE-FLOWERED TRILLIUM**
   (*Trillium grandiflorum*)                                                            p. 28
The most handsome and widely cultivated of all our native
trilliums, its 3 leaves borne at the summit of the stem, crowned

by a solitary waxy, ultimately nodding flower. The plant is not truly bulbous but treated as such. **Color:** White, fading to pink. **Height:** 8–12 inches. **Flowering date:** May. **Varieties:** None. **Culture:** Suited only to the wild garden. Plant purchased rootstocks in Oct. or early April, under partial shade, 4–5 inches deep, in rich woods soil with plenty of humus; not too acid. Space 5–7 inches apart. Do not cultivate and leave alone for years. Provide a permanent mulch of dried leaves (not pine needles). Unsuited to ordinary garden soil; often called Wakerobin.

Related plants (not illustrated):

Purple Trillium (*Trillium erectum*). 12–15 inches. Flowers brownish purple to pink.

Painted Trillium (*Trillium recurvatum*). 12–15 inches. Flowers white, streaked crimson.

**YELLOW TRILLIUM** (*Trillium viride luteum*)          p. 35

Our only yellow trillium and sometimes offered as *Trillium luteum,* and generally only by dealers in woodland plants. **Color:** Yellow. **Height:** 9–15 inches. **Flowering date:** May–June. **Varieties:** None. **Culture:** Suited only to the wild garden. Plant purchased rootstocks in Oct. or April, under partial shade, 4–5 inches deep, in rich woods soil, not too acid, and 5–7 inches apart. Cover with a permanent mulch of dried leaves (not pine needles). Unsuited to ordinary garden soil.

**TALL BEARDED IRIS** (*Iris* hybrids)          p. 28

The most popular of all irises and commonly (before World War I) called German Iris, and still so called by many. It has thousands of named forms or varieties. All have a stout, creeping rootstock, sword-shaped stiffish leaves arising in one plane, and extremely showy flowers. Flower segments 6, 3 of which are reflexed (called the "falls"), while the 3 inner ones are erect (called the "standards"); usually prominently bearded. **Color:** Nearly all colors; see below. **Height:** 12–20 inches, sometimes more. **Flowering date:** May–June; also some fall-flowering forms. **Varieties:** Over 2000 named varieties are offered, many of them essentially duplicates. Grouped by color a good selection

could include the following. WHITE (prevailingly): White God-
dess, Snow Belle, Katherine Fay, Mount Cloud, Minnie Colquitt.
BLUE or VIOLET: Great Lakes, West Point, Amigo, Nightfall,
Sable, Indian Hills. PINK to REDDISH PURPLE: Frieda Mohr,
California Peach, Harriet Thoreau, Melanie, Action Front.
YELLOW: Golden Fleece, Berkeley Gold, Elsa Sass, Ming Yellow,
Ola Kala. BLENDS (mostly with the falls or standards with red,
brown, yellow, bronze or purple in contrasting colors): City of
Lincoln, China Maid, Copper Rose, Mulberry Rose, Tobacco
Road. **Culture:** Difficult to kill, since the stout rootstocks can
be planted almost any time except when the plant is in flower.
Thrives in all garden soils, except wet ones, in full sun, and just
cover lightly the rootstocks. Do not buy expensive novelties unless
you have more money than brains, for many of them are minor
variants of the well-tried varieties listed above.

Related plants (not illustrated):

Blue Flag (*Iris versicolor*). 15–25 inches. Flowers blue.
Water Flag (*Iris pseudacorus*). 15–25 inches. Flowers
yellow.

## JAPANESE IRIS (*Iris kaempferi*)                          p. 28

Taller than the Tall Bearded Iris, with a larger, beardless flower
and blooming a month later, now in many forms but all derived
from a Japanese ancestor that grew "with one foot in the water."
The flowers are often 4–6 inches in diameter, very showy, and
flattish in contour; many are double-flowered. **Color:** Various,
see below. **Height:** 18–30 inches, or even more. **Flowering date:**
Late June–July. **Varieties:** Blue Bird (blue), Columbia (white
and yellow), Dominator (blue and white), Pyramid (violet-
purple and white), Eleanor Parry (claret, fading to blue), Purple
and Gold (violet-purple). There are no true yellows. **Culture:**
Plant purchased rootstocks in early spring, 2–3 inches deep, in
rich moist (but not wet) soil, in full sun or half-shade. Replant
every 4–5 years, since they tend to crowd each other and reduce
the number and quality of bloom.

## CRESTED IRIS (*Iris cristata*)                            p. 36

A delightful, low, early-blooming native American iris, useful for edging beds or borders. It is almost stemless, and its small flowers are without a beard, but are crested. **Color:** Light blue. **Height:** 3–5 inches. **Flowering date:** April. **Varieties:** None. **Culture:** Plant rootstocks 2–3 inches deep, in Oct., in any ordinary garden soil, in full sun. Space 3–5 inches apart, and allow them to spread. They will soon make a continuous edging or a dense mat.

Related plant (not illustrated):

*Iris pumila.* 3–5 inches. Red, yellow, blue, or white according to variety.

Related bulbous irises (not illustrated):

English Iris (hybrids). 18–24 inches. Colors various.

Spanish Iris (hybrids). 15–20 inches. Colors various.

Dutch Iris (hybrids). 6–12 inches. Colors various.

**WHITE MARIPOSA LILY** (*Calochortus venustus*)     p. 28
A beautiful Californian bulbous plant with grasslike but somewhat fleshy leaves, which die down soon after the flowers bloom. Unfortunately the plant does not thrive well in the East, except by following the directions for culture below. **Color:** Pale, lilac, the center reddish brown. **Height:** 8–12 inches. **Flowering date:** June. **Varieties:** Superbus (large-flowered), Roseus (rose-spotted), Citrinus (yellow). **Culture:** Plant purchased bulbs 3–4 inches deep in a loose, gritty or sandy soil, after the first fall frost and cover with a mulch of straw or salt hay at least 6 inches thick. The drainage must be free, since they rot from winter slush in the East. If the site is too flat, raise the bed 4–5 inches. Take off mulch in early April and north of Philadelphia lift the bulbs for summer storage after leaves have withered. Also called Globe Tulip.

Related plants (not illustrated):

White Globe Lily (*Calochortus albus*). 15–20 inches. Flowers white and purple.

*Calochortus luteus.* 15–24 inches. Flowers yellow, brown-spotted.

**PLANTAIN–LILY** (*Hosta plantaginea*)     p. 28
An old garden favorite from China (or Japan) often cultivated

under its old name of *Funkia*. It has broad, pointed leaves with prominent ribs and a loose terminal cluster of bell-shaped, fragrant flowers. **Color:** White. **Height:** 10–12 inches. **Flowering date:** Aug.–Oct. **Varieties:** None. **Culture:** Plant purchased roots (it bears no bulbs) in late Oct. or early April, 3–5 inches deep, in full sun, in any ordinary garden soil. Space 5–8 inches apart. It needs little subsequent care and will spread rapidly.

Related plants (not illustrated):

> *Hosta caerulea*. 18–24 inches. Flowers blue.
>
> *Hosta sieboldiana*. 12–18 inches. Flowers pale lilac.
>
> *Hosta japonica*. 18–24 inches. Flowers lilac (a variegated-leaved form is offered).

## GUINEA–HEN FLOWER (*Fritillaria meleagris*) p. 28

A beautiful Eurasian bulbous plant closely related to the crown imperial, and grown for its checkered flowers, hence its other names of Checkered Lily, Toad Lily, or Snake's-Head. It has only a few, oblongish leaves, and many varieties with bell-shaped nodding, lily-like flowers that are 2–3 inches wide. **Color:** Purplish or maroon but see below. **Height:** 12–18 inches. **Flowering date:** May–June. **Varieties** (all are checkered): Alba (white), Purpurea (purple); Aphrodite (white), Purple King (purple), also an unnamed yellow variety. **Culture:** Plant purchased bulbs in Sept. or early Oct. 3–4 inches deep, in rich but light sandy loam, preferably in a moist but not wet site. Space 6–8 inches apart and cover with a winter mulch of straw or salt hay or old rotted manure. Do not disturb, and replant only when crowding makes it necessary (3–5 years).

Related plants (not illustrated):

> Yellow Fritillary (*Fritillaria pudica*). 6–9 inches. Flowers yellow.
>
> Scarlet Fritillary (*Fritillaria recurva*). 15–30 inches. Flowers scarlet, yellow-spotted.
>
> Crown Imperial (*Fritillaria imperialis*), see p. 37.

## BELLWORT (*Uvularia grandiflora*) p. 35

A rather inconspicuous native American woodland plant suited only to the wild garden, with slender, tube-shaped flowers borne in lax, terminal, few-flowered clusters, the leaves appearing as if perforated by the stem. **Color:** Greenish yellow. **Height:** 12–18 inches. **Flowering date:** May–June. **Varieties:** None. **Culture:** Purchased plants (it bears no bulbs) should be set 3–4 inches deep in a rich woodland soil, in partial or full shade, and spaced 6–8 inches apart. Maintain a permanent mulch of dried leaves, and do not disturb. Not suited to ordinary garden conditions.

Left: Bellwort (*Uvularia grandiflora*), p. 34. **Right:** Yellow Trillium (*Trillium viride luteum*), p. 31.

**LILY TURF** (*Ophiopogon japonicus*) p. 36

This turflike relative of the lily from Japan is often sold under the incorrect name of *Mondo,* and few plants excel it as a ground cover under the shade of trees, although its small flowers are scarcely ornamental. Leaves evergreen, grasslike but much thicker, about 8 inches long, growing so densely as to suggest turf. **Color:** Lilac. **Height:** 8–10 inches. **Flowering date:** July–Aug. **Varieties:** None. **Culture:** Plant purchased bulbs 2–3 inches

Left: Spiderwort (*Tradescantia virginiana*), below. Center: Lily Turf (*Ophiopogon japonicus*), p. 35. Right: Crested Iris (*Iris cristata*), p. 32.

deep, in any garden soil, in Oct. or Nov., preferably under shade, although it will grow in the open. Plant in masses to cover shady places, and space 3–4 inches apart. It needs no subsequent attention and is safely hardy up to New York City and beyond along the coast.

Related plant (not illustrated):

Lily Turf (*Liriope muscari*). 12–15 inches. Flowers blue.

**SPIDERWORT** (*Tradescantia virginiana*)　　　　　　　above
A delicate, watery-juiced perennial from eastern North America, little grown outside the wild garden. Stems and leaves flaccid or softly succulent and the rather showy flowers soon withering if picked. **Color:** Blue or purple. **Height:** 8–15 inches. **Flowering date:** May–Aug. **Varieties:** Alba (white). **Culture:** Plant purchased rootstocks, 2–3 inches deep in moist, shady place, in any ordinary garden soil. Space 5–6 inches apart. It will easily root

from the readily separable joints of the stem if these are placed in wet sand.

# TALL BULBOUS PLANTS WITH AN OBVIOUS STEM

The plants treated in this section are generally higher, some much higher, than in the bulbs on pp. 30–36. There are 17 different plants in this group, which comprises some very handsome garden flowers. Some of them do not bear bulbs but for cultural reasons are usually treated as such. They may be divided thus:

*Mostly spring-blooming. 3 species. See pp. 37–39.*
*Generally summer-blooming. 11 species. See pp. 39–46.*
*Fall-blooming. 3 species. See pp. 47–48.*

## SPRING-BLOOMING

**CROWN IMPERIAL** (*Fritillaria imperialis*) p. 38
Rather a stout, somewhat strong-smelling, Persian bulbous plant, with numerous leaves, some in a terminal cluster above the nodding, lily-like and bell-shaped flowers, the petals of which are veined. **Color:** Reddish purple. **Height:** 2–4 feet. **Flowering date:** May. **Varieties:** Lutea Maxima (yellow), Orange Brilliant (orange), Maxima Red (red), Sulphurion (yellow). **Culture:** Plant purchased bulbs 6–8 inches deep in sandy, well-drained loam to which a teaspoonful of lime is added per bulb, in a partially shaded place, or in full sun, in late Sept. or early Oct. Space 8–10 inches apart and provide a winter mulch of compost or well-rotted manure. Do not disturb unless crowding makes resetting necessary (in 3–5 years).

For related plants see p. 34.

**CAMASS** (*Camassia quamash*) p. 38
A Pacific Coast bulbous plant, the edible bulbs used as food by the Indians. It has narrow, grasslike or strap-shaped basal leaves, and a tall, terminal cluster of flowers the petals of which are

separate (not tube-like or bell-shaped). **Color:** Whitish blue.
**Height:** 2–3 feet. **Flowering date:** June. **Varieties:** None. **Cul-ture:** Plant purchased bulbs, preferably in masses, 4–5 inches
deep, in a moist but not wet, rich but somewhat sandy loam, in
partial shade or in the open, in Oct. Space 6–8 inches apart, pro-vide winter mulch of well-rotted manure or compost, and do not
disturb, unless crowding makes resetting necessary.

Left: Jack-in-the-Pulpit (*Arisaema triphyllum*), below. Center: Crown
Imperial (*Fritillaria imperialis*), p. 37. Right: Camass (*Camassia qua-mash*), p. 37.

## JACK–IN–THE–PULPIT (*Arisaema triphyllum*)          above

A popular wild flower of the forests of the eastern states grown
only in the wild garden. Its "flower" consists of a central stalk-like spadix (upon which the tiny, real flowers are crowded) sur-rounded by a mostly fluted, tubular spathe (the "pulpit") the
pointed tip of which overlaps the spadix. Fruits brilliant scarlet.
**Color:** Greenish. **Height:** 24–36 inches. **Flowering date:** May–

June. **Varieties:** None. **Culture:** Dig wild plant from the woods, after it withers, being careful to get all its turnip-like root (10–15 inches deep) and plant at once in moist shady place in woods soil where it can remain undisturbed. Space 8–10 inches apart and leave it alone. Also suited to ordinary garden soil if there is shade.

Related plant (not illustrated):

> Green Dragon (*Arisaema dracontium*). 2–3½ feet. Flowers greenish.

## Summer-blooming

**MADONNA LILY** (*Lilium candidum*)  p. 29

One of the most handsome of over 40 species of lily cultivated in American gardens. It is a tall Eurasian lily, its basal leaves persisting over the winter and its showy flower erect and bell-shaped. Its stem leaves are scattered, narrow, and pointed. The terminal flower cluster is open, lax, but usually many-flowered. **Color:** White. **Height:** 2½–4 feet. **Flowering date:** June–July. **Varieties:** None. **Culture:** Plant purchased bulbs 2–3 inches deep in rich garden soil in full sun, in late Nov. (if ground is likely to freeze, protect it with temporary mulch). Space 12–15 inches apart. It produces a basal rosette of leaves which should be covered with a light strawy mulch over the winter. Each spring mulch the plant with well-rotted manure. It will die out in a few years and must be replaced with new bulbs. Also called Annunciation Lily.

Related plants (not illustrated):

> Easter Lily (*Lilium longiflorum,* and its forms, among which is the Croft Lily). 2–3 feet. Flowers white. Not reliably hardy in the East.
>
> Star Lily (*Lilium concolor*). 3–4 feet. Flowers red.
>
> Canada Lily (*Lilium canadense*). 3–5 feet. Flowers orange-yellow, brown-spotted.

**ROYAL LILY** (*Lilium regale*)  p. 29

A Chinese lily with enormous fragrant flowers, its funnel-shaped corolla often 6 inches long. Leaves many, scattered, narrow,

pointed and rather drooping. Flowers not erect, nearly hori-
zontal, borne in a few-flowered, terminal cluster. **Color:** Lilac or
purplish white outside, white inside the cup, but the base yellow,
the ribs strongly veined in deeper purple. **Height:** 4–5 feet.
**Flowering date:** July–Aug. **Varieties:** None (excluding doubtful
ones). **Culture:** Plant purchased bulbs in deep, rich garden soil,
8–9 inches deep, in full sun or partial shade, in late Nov. (if
ground is likely to freeze protect it with temporary mulch).
Space 15–20 inches apart and provide winter mulch of straw or
salt hay. Each spring mulch with well-rotted manure. Replace
by new bulbs every few years, as it tends to die out.

Related plants (not illustrated):

>    *Lilium auratum.* 4–6 feet. Flowers white, crimson-spotted
>    and with central band of yellow.
>    *Lilium henryi.* 7–9 feet. Flowers orange, brown-spotted.
>    *Lilium superbum.* 5–9 feet. Flowers orange-red, brown-
>    spotted.

**PERUVIAN LILY** (*Alstroemeria aurantiaca*)                p. 29
A South American, somewhat tender, tuberous-rooted plant, with
a great profusion of narrow leaves, often in dense clusters under
the tight flower cluster, which is terminal, and sometimes
branched. The flowers are of separate petals — not tubular or
bell-shaped. **Color:** Yellow but green-tipped and brown-spotted.
**Height:** 2–4 feet. **Flowering date:** July–Aug. **Varieties:** None.
**Culture:** Plant purchased roots (it has no bulbs) in mid-May, in
deep, rich garden soil, 6–8 inches deep, and space 8–10 inches
apart, in full sun. South of Washington, D.C., the plants can be
left undisturbed. North of this dig up roots in mid-Oct., and
store in a cool, frost-free place (no furnace heat) in boxes of sand
and with some of the soil clinging to the roots. Replant each
year, north of Washington, D.C., although some mulched and
sheltered plants survive the cold as far north as New York City.

**DAYLILY** (*Hemerocallis* hybrids)                        p. 29
An enormous group of hybrid perennials mostly derived from
Japanese and Chinese species that are little grown. The hybrids,
many of which have only trivial differences, are very popular

among gardeners because of ease of culture and range of color. All have tall, strap-shaped, or grasslike keeled leaves and a terminal, few-flowered cluster of lily-like flowers. **Color:** Various, see below. **Height:** 2–4 feet. **Flowering date:** June–Sept., according to variety. **Varieties:** Over 1500, of which the following provide a good selection. YELLOW: Devon Cream, Gold Cargo, Golden West, Jewell Russell, Golden Triangle. ORANGE: Glowing Gold, Cibola, Golden Hours, Joanna Hutchins, Golden Orchid. PINK: Marie Wood, Laurel, Salmon Sheen, Ruth Lehman, Brulée. RED: Knighthood, Morocco, Tejas, Dominion, Scarlet Sunset. TWO-COLORED OR BANDED: Myone, Camet, Constance, Cathedral Towers, Nashville. **Culture:** Easily grown and sometimes difficult to eradicate the more rampant varieties. Plant rootstocks 4–6 inches deep in any garden soil, in Oct. or April, in full sun, and leave them alone. Space 1–2 feet apart. Only the weakest need staking.

**FOXTAIL LILY** (*Eremurus elwesi*) p. 29

A garden aristocrat, perhaps the tallest hardy perennial, probably of hybrid origin, but its parentage almost certainly Himalayan. Leaves all basal, rather narrow, and from this rosette springs the huge flowering stalk, upon the upper part of which are hundreds of tiny bell-shaped flowers. It is not easy to grow and the cultural directions below must be followed carefully. **Color:** Pink. **Height:** 10–12 feet. **Flowering date:** July–Aug. **Varieties:** Albus (white). **Culture:** Prepare ground weeks before planting by excavating 18 inches deep and filling with a mixture of ⅓ rich loam, ⅓ rotted cow manure, and ⅓ chopped peat, all thoroughly mixed. Site in full sun. Into this bed plant the extremely fragile (and expensive) roots, 6–8 inches deep, in Oct., and spread them so that none are broken. Provide winter mulch of straw or salt hay. In early spring, when shoots appear, protect with a box or bagging from night frosts. Provide plenty of manure as topdressing in spring. Do not disturb, and keep cultivator teeth or a hoe away from the roots. It is a most striking garden plant that does better if shaded from wind rather than planted in the open.

Related plants (not illustrated):
   *Eremurus bungei.* 3–5 feet. Flowers yellow.
   *Eremurus robustus.* 8–10 feet. Flowers pink.
   *Eremurus himalaicus.* 6–8 feet. Flowers white.

**RED–HOT POKER** (*Kniphofia uvaria grandiflora*)          p. 29
A not quite hardy, African perennial of the Lily Family, much
grown for its striking habit and gorgeous color. It has a mass of
narrow, basal leaves from which springs the stiff flower stalk,
crowded at the spike-like summit by scores of tubular, down-
ward pointing flowers. **Color:** Red and yellow (but see below).
**Height:** 3–4 feet. **Flowering date:** July–Aug. **Varieties:** Gold-
mine (golden yellow), Lemon Belle (pale yellow), White Fairy
(white), Star of Baden (straw yellow), Pfitzer hybrids (in many
shades of pink, red, yellow or white). **Culture:** Plant purchased
roots (it bears no bulbs) in Oct. or April, 5–6 inches deep in a
rich sandy loam, avoiding low or wet places, in full sun. Space
10–15 inches apart. North of Philadelphia provide a winter mulch
of salt hay or straw and see that it does not pack down. Not
reliably hardy in regions of bitter winters. It will not thrive if
too much water or slush covers the roots in winter. Often called
Torch Lily and sometimes incorrectly called *Tritoma.*

**MONTBRETIA** (*Tritonia crocosmaeflora*)                     p. 29
A hybrid bulbous plant, both its parents South African, not unlike Gladiolus, but the tubular or bell-shaped flower nearly symmetrical. Leaves sword-shaped and much shorter than the flowering spike, which is clothed with sheathing bracts from between
which emerge the flowers. **Color:** Red and yellow, but see below.
**Height:** 3–4 feet. **Flowering date:** July–Aug. **Varieties:** Apricot
Queen (apricot), Lemon Queen (light yellow), Red Knight
(red), Rose Queen (pink), White Beauty (white), Fire King
(scarlet), Queen Alexandra (golden-orange), Rheingold (golden
yellow). **Culture:** Plant purchased bulbs in late May, 3–4 inches
deep and 4–5 inches apart, in rich but sandy, well-drained loam,
in full sun. From New York City northward lift bulbs in autumn
and store in cool, frost-free place (no furnace heat). Often hardy
from New York City southward to Washington, D.C., if cov-

ered with a winter mulch of straw or salt hay. South of Washington can be left in the ground indefinitely. Called by some *Crocosmia crocosmiiflora.*

**TIGER–FLOWER** (*Tigridia pavonia*) p. 29

Central American somewhat iris-like bulbous plant grown like Gladiolus as it is not hardy outdoors in frosty regions. Leaves sword-shaped, basal, much shorter than the flowering stalk which, from between sheaths, bears showy rather fugitive flowers often 3–5 inches wide. **Color:** Red, but spotted. **Height:** 2–3 feet. **Flowering date:** July–Aug. **Varieties:** Several white, yellow, and scarlet varieties are offered, but their names are uncertain. **Culture:** Plant purchased bulbs 3–5 inches deep, in late May, in full sun, in any ordinary garden soil. Space 5–6 inches apart. Before frost, dig and store bulbs in frost-free but cool place (no furnace heat). South of Richmond, Va., hardy outdoors with a light mulch of straw or salt hay.

**ASPHODEL** (*Asphodeline lutea*) p. 29

A European perennial plant found also in North Africa, the Asphodel of the ancients, cultivated more for interest than for beauty, but common in old gardens. Its mostly basal leaves are also scattered on the flowering stalk, which is crowned with a finger-shaped cluster of small, narrow, funnel-shaped or tubular flowers. **Color:** Yellow. **Height:** 2–3 feet. **Flowering date:** July. **Varieties:** None. **Culture:** Easy in any ordinary garden soil, in sun or partial shade; plant roots in Oct. or April, 3–4 inches deep. Space 5–6 inches apart.

**BLACKBERRY LILY** (*Belamcanda chinensis*) p. 46

An Asiatic perennial often running wild in the northeastern states, with iris-like leaves, and a terminal, lax cluster of rather showy flowers. The capsule, as it splits, reveals the cluster of blackberry-like seeds. **Color:** Orange, but magenta-spotted. **Height:** 2–3 feet. **Flowering date:** July–Aug. **Varieties:** None. **Culture:** Easy in any ordinary garden soil. Plant rootstocks in Oct. or April, 2–3 inches deep, in full sun and space 6–8 inches apart. Not commonly cultivated as its close relative, the iris, is far more desirable.

# GARDEN BULBS

*(some have rootstocks but are treated as bulbs;
flowers irregular or unsymmetrical)*

1. **Yellow Lady's-Slipper**
   (*Cypripedium calceolus pubescens*)                    **p. 51**
   A native perennial, 10–20 inches high, and one of the easiest
   orchids to grow.

2. **Canna** (*Canna* hybrid; Yellow King Humbert)          **p. 48**
   A green-leaved, showy, tender bedding plant. Summer-blooming.

3. **Acidanthera** (*Acidanthera bicolor*)                 **p. 51**
   A fragrant relative of Gladiolus, 2–4 feet high. Summer-blooming.

4. **Gladiolus** (hybrid form)                             **p. 49**
   Tender African plant with mostly scentless flowers. For many
   other varieties and culture see text.

5. **Antholyza** (*Antholyza aethiopica*)                  **p. 50**
   Related to Gladiolus and grown like it. Summer-blooming.

6. **Night-blooming Gladiolus** (*Gladiolus tristis*)      **p. 50**
   Beautifully night-fragrant relative of the common Gladiolus.

7. **Showy Orchis** (*Orchis spectabilis*)                 **p. 52**
   Our showiest spring-blooming native orchid, 8–12 inches high.
   Fit only for rich woods.

8. **Canna** (*Canna* hybrid; America)                     **p. 48**
   A bronze-leaved variety, 3–4 feet high and tender. For culture
   see text.

9. **Copper-Tip** (*Crocosmia aurea*)                      **p. 50**
   Related to the Montbretia and often 3½ feet high. Summer-
   blooming.

# IMMORTELLES, EVERLASTINGS, STRAWFLOWERS

**1. Love-Lies-Bleeding** (*Amaranthus caudatus*)  **p. 57**
An annual suited to poor, sandy soil. Summer-blooming. Foliage
brightly colored. Will stand heat and drought.

**2. Immortelle** (*Xeranthemum annuum*)  **p. 55**
An annual with ashy foliage, good for light sandy soils. Flower
heads chaffy, good for winter bouquets.

**3. Swan River Everlasting** (*Helipterum manglesi*)  **p. 54**
One of the best annual everlastings. Sow seeds in sandy soil only
when warm weather arrives.

**4. Strawflower** (*Helichrysum bracteatum*)  **p. 54**
Flower heads chaffy, and long-lasting; one of the best annuals
for winter bouquets.

**5. Pearly Everlasting** (*Anaphalis margaritacea*)  **p. 54**
A weedy perennial, easily dug from the wild, its button-like heads
long-lasting.

**6. Globe Amaranth** (*Gomphrena globosa*)  **p. 56**
An annual, its globular, chaffy flower heads much used for winter
bouquets.

**7. Winged Everlasting** (*Ammobium alatum grandiflorum*)  **p. 55**
An ashy-leaved perennial, the flower heads long-lasting if picked
when immature.

**8. Blue Succory** (*Catananche caerulea*)  **p. 56**
A perennial, and useful as one of the only blue flowers among
the everlastings.

**9. Edelweiss** (*Leontopodium alpinum*)  **p. 55**
Chiefly of interest as perennial alpine from Switzerland, much
sought by mountaineers. Not very showy.

**ADAM'S–NEEDLE** (*Yucca filamentosa*)                          below
One of a small group of semidesert plants, which culminate in
the fantastically branched Joshua tree (*Yucca brevifolia*) of
southwestern deserts. The Adam's-Needle has a short or practically no stem, and a basal cluster of stiff, sword-shaped leaves,
thready on their margins, and much shorter than the stalk of the
flower cluster. Flowers cup-shaped, fragrant, and nodding.
**Color:** White. **Height:** 8–10 feet. **Flowering date:** July–Aug.
**Varieties:** None. **Culture:** Plant young offsets, which are freely
produced by old plants, in a light, gritty, or sandy soil, in full
sun, 4–5 inches deep, and space 1–2 feet apart. The site must not
be wet. Thrives in pure sand and in spite of great summer heat.
Not reliably hardy north of Boston.

Related plant (not illustrated):

Spanish Dagger (*Yucca gloriosa*). 6–8 feet. Flowers
greenish white or reddish.

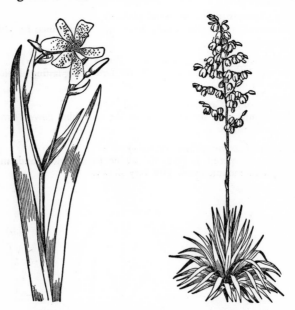

Left: Blackberry Lily (*Belamcanda chinensis*), p. 43.
Right: Adam's-Needle (*Yucca filamentosa*), above.

# Fall-blooming

**TUBEROSE** (*Polianthes tuberosa*)                    below
Perhaps the most fragrant commonly cultivated plant. Thousands of acres of this Mexican bulbous herb are grown in France for its perfume. It has basal, rather flabby and weak, strap-shaped leaves, and a lax, few-flowered, terminal cluster of waxy flowers. **Color:** White. **Height:** 24–36 inches. **Flowering date:** Sept.–Oct. **Varieties:** None (except an uncertainly named pink, double-flowered form). **Culture:** Plant purchased, guaranteed-flowering bulbs, in late May, 3 inches deep and 6–8 inches apart, in full sun, in any ordinary garden soil. Before the first autumnal frost dig and store the bulb with its numerous attached bulblets. These, if grown the second year, will not bloom, so that it is better to start with fresh bulbs each year unless the small bulblets can be grown along to the flowering stage (3–4 years).

Left: Toad Lily (*Tricyrtis hirta*), p. 48. Center: Feather-Fleece (*Stenanthium gramineum*), p. 48. Right: Tuberose (*Polianthes tuberosa*), above.

**TOAD LILY** (*Tricyrtis hirta*)                                    p. 47
A Japanese perennial with branching rootstock (no bulbs) grown
for its late bloom of spotted flowers, but not very popular and
not hardy outdoors north of Richmond, Va., without protection.
**Color:** White, spotted purple. **Height:** 2–3 feet. **Flowering date:**
Oct. **Varieties:** None. **Culture:** Plant purchased clumps in partial shade, in May, 3–5 inches deep, in a somewhat acid, peaty
soil. Space 4–6 inches apart. North of Washington, D.C., dig
and store the roots in moist sand for winter protection, in a frost-
free, cool place (no furnace heat). From Washington southward
it will survive outdoors with a winter mulch of straw or salt hay,
or often with no mulch if in a sheltered place. For another plant
called Toad Lily, see p. 34

**FEATHER–FLEECE** (*Stenanthium gramineum*)              p. 47
A tall leafy-stemmed perennial of the eastern U.S., grown only
in a fairly acid, moist site in the wild garden. Leaves very
narrow, grasslike or thready, the tall terminal flowering cluster,
with very numerous small flowers, often 2 feet long. **Color:**
Greenish white. **Height:** 3–4 feet. **Flowering date:** Late Aug.
and Sept. **Varieties:** None. **Culture:** Plant purchased roots
(from a dealer in wild flowers), 3–5 inches deep, in a sandy,
moist, fairly acid soil, in April, in full sun. Space 1–2 feet apart
and leave alone. Perfectly hardy but not suited to ordinary
garden soils. Often called Featherbells and usually offered under
its old, and incorrect name of *Stenanthium robustum*.

## *Irregular or Unsymmetrical Flowers*

Garden bulbs with highly irregular flowers, which are
unsymmetrical, lopsided, or otherwise irregular; never
symmetrical like a Tulip or Lily-of-the-Valley. Common
examples of plants with irregular flowers are the Canna,
Gladiolus, and all the orchids, of which only a few are
garden plants.

**CANNA** (*Canna* hybrids)                                        p. 44
One of the most colorful of all summer bedding plants, originally

of tropical American ancestry, but its hundreds of named forms and hybrids of uncertain parentage. They have tuberous roots, nowhere hardy except in very mild climates, immense, prominently veined leaves with sheathing leafstalks. The highly irregular flowers, often 4–5 inches wide, are borne in a stout terminal cluster, extremely showy, and impart a tropical aspect to any garden. Many of its varieties can be divided into two types — bronzy-leaved or green-leaved. **Color:** Various, see below. **Height:** 4–6 feet. **Flowering date:** July–Aug., often later. **Varieties:** Legion, and best sorted as bronzy- or green-leaved. Bronzy-leaved: America (dark red), Apricot (apricot), King Humbert (scarlet), Mrs. Alfred Conard (salmon-pink), Caliente (scarlet), Copper Giant (madder red), Wyoming (cherry red). Green-leaved: Yellow King Humbert (yellow), Richard Wallace (canary yellow), Rigoletto (pale yellow), Salmon Beauty (salmon pink), President (scarlet), Eureka (white). **Culture:** Plant purchased tubers 3–4 inches deep, in rich garden loam, preferably in a moist but not wet place, in late May. Space 1–2 feet apart, and water them if the season is dry. Use well-rotted manure or balanced fertilizer as top-dressing, since they are rich feeders. After first frost cut off stems, leaving about 6 inches attached to each tuber, which must be dug and stored in moist sand or the soil in which they grew, in a cool but frost-free place (no furnace heat). Hardy outdoors in the far South.

**GLADIOLUS** (*Gladiolus* hybrids) p. 44

A protean group of very popular garden plants all derived by selection and hybridization of a few South African species, but most of them of uncertain parentage. They have rather flabby, sword-shaped leaves, mostly basal, and a tall terminal spike of showy flowers from between sheathing bracts, and bloom from the bottom upward. **Color:** Various, see below. **Height:** 20–36 inches. **Flowering date:** July–Aug. **Varieties:** Over 2000, some estimates up to 3500. A reasonable dozen could include: Picardy (salmon-pink), Minuet (lavender), Commander Koehl (red), Burma (deep rose), Ethel Cave Cole (pink), Dieppe (salmon-red), Margaret Beaton (white, red "eye"), Abu Hassan (violet-

blue), Spic and Span (pink), Gold Dust (yellow), Elizabeth
the Queen (lavender and rose), General Eisenhower (rose-pink).
There is also a race or strain of so-called Miniature Gladiolus,
which are lower and come in many colors. **Culture:** Plant purchased bulbs 4–6 inches deep in rich, well-drained garden loam
in late May, in full sun. Space 8–12 inches apart and stake the
tall varieties if in a windy place. Plant a second or third lot of
bulbs at 10-day intervals if bloom is wanted until frost. Before
the first hard frost dig bulbs, dry them, and store in a cool, dark,
frost-free place (no furnace heat). In the far South, hardy outdoors if the site is not too wet.

## NIGHT–BLOOMING GLADIOLUS
(*Gladiolus tristis*)                                                    p. 44
A small species of Gladiolus from South Africa of interest only
for its night-blooming, very fragrant flowers (the large showy
relatives are usually scentless). **Color:** Yellowish white. **Height:**
18–24 inches. **Flowering date:** Aug.–Sept. **Varieties:** Concolor
(pure white). **Culture:** Same as for the showy Gladiolus (see
above).

## ANTHOLYZA (*Antholyza aethiopica*)                    p. 44
A gladiolus-like African bulbous plant, not much grown, but
showy and handsome. It differs from Gladiolus in having longer
and more slender, tubular flowers. The leaves are long and
sword-shaped and are much shorter than the terminal spike of
flowers, which appear from between membranous or leafy
sheaths. **Color:** Red and yellow. **Height:** 3–4 feet. **Flowering
date:** July–Aug. **Varieties:** None. **Culture:** Plant purchased
bulbs 4–6 inches deep, in rich garden soil, in late May, in full
sun. Space 8–12 inches apart, and stake them if site is windy.
Before first hard frost dig bulbs, dry them, and store in a cool,
dark, frost-free place (no furnace heat). Called by some
*Chasmanthe aethiopica*.

## COPPER–TIP (*Crocosmia aurea*)                          p. 44
A South African bulbous plant related to the Montbretia (see
p. 42) and not very common in ordinary gardens. Its dried

flowers soaked in water have a saffron odor. It is related to Gladiolus, but not so showy. Grown chiefly for interest. **Color:** Orange-yellow. **Height:** 2½–4 feet. **Flowering date:** July–Aug. **Varieties:** None. **Culture:** Plant purchased bulbs in rich but somewhat sandy soil, 3–4 inches deep, in late May, in full sun. Space 4–6 inches apart. Before first frost dig up bulbs, dry and store in a dark, cool, frost-free place (no furnace heat). It is often offered as *Tritonia aurea.*

**ACIDANTHERA** (*Acidanthera bicolor*)                          p. 44
A widely grown relative of Gladiolus, popular for its fragrant flowers, and a native of Africa. It bears a leafy terminal spike of long-tubed flowers. Leaves mostly basal, few and sword-shaped. **Color:** White, but brownish inside. **Height:** 12–20 inches. **Flowering date:** July–Aug. **Varieties:** None. **Culture:** Plant purchased bulbs 3–5 inches deep, in rich but rather sandy soil, in full sun, late May. Space 5–7 inches apart. Before first frost dig and dry bulbs, and store in a dark place with a winter temperature of 55°–60°.

**YELLOW LADY'S–SLIPPER**
    (*Cypripedium calceolus pubescens*)                          p. 44
For the wild gardener the easiest and most satisfactory of all the lady's-slippers to grow in a shady, moist nook, but quite unsuited to ordinary garden soil. It is a leafy-stemmed perennial from the forests of the eastern U.S. with sac- or pouch-like flower. **Color:** Yellow. **Height:** 12–20 inches. **Flowering date:** June. **Varieties:** None. **Culture:** Relatively easy. Purchase stout clumps (from dealer in wild flowers) in April, and plant in cool, shaded place in rich woods soil having plenty of humus. Mulch with dried leaves, do not cultivate it, and in a few years it will spread. Once it is established, do not move it unless absolutely necessary. In many catalogues it is listed under its old name of *Cypripedium pubescens.*

    Related plant (not illustrated):
        Pink Lady's-Slipper or Moccasin-Flower (*Cypripedium acaule*). 12–15 inches. Flowers pink. Almost impossible to grow.

**SHOWY ORCHIS** (*Orchis spectabilis*)                                    p. 44

Perhaps the most beautiful of all our native orchids, found in rich woods in eastern North America, and often grown in the wild garden, but unsuited to ordinary garden soil. It has only 2 thick, shining, basal leaves, and a few-flowered cluster of highly irregular flowers. **Color:** White and magenta. **Height:** 5–10 inches. **Flowering date:** May–June. **Varieties:** None. **Culture:** Plant roots (purchased from a wild-flower nursery), 3–4 inches deep, in early April, in a rich woods, rather acid soil, and under the shade of trees. Space 4–6 inches apart, and mulch with dried leaves. If necessary to water, use rain water. Neither disturb nor cultivate it, and do not move unless essential. It is one of the few native orchids relatively easy to grow.

# Everlastings

*Immortelles, Everlastings, Strawflowers, Edelweiss, Cockscomb, Thrifts, and other Chaffy-Flowered Plants*

A SMALL group of garden plants, quite unrelated, all having flowers or foliage so chaffy, membranous or papery that they hold their color even when dry. The following 15 are thus most popular as dried flowers and for winter decoration. All except two are natives of the Old World, and mostly summer-blooming. They may be distinguished thus:

*Those with globular or daisy-like heads. 9 species. See below.*

*Flowers not in daisy-like or globular heads. 6 species. See pp. 57–62.*

# Daisy-like or Globular Flower Heads

**SWAN RIVER EVERLASTING**
(*Helipterum manglesi*)                                                    p. 45
An Australian annual, sometimes offered as *Acroclinium* or
*Rhodanthe,* grown for its nearly everlasting flowers and ashy
foliage. **Color:** White or pink, the center yellow. **Height:** 8–15
inches. **Flowering date:** July–Aug. **Varieties:** One, unnamed,
has red-spotted leaflets beneath the flower head. **Culture:** Sow
seed indoors ½ inch deep, 8 weeks before trees leaf out. Transplant outdoors when warm weather arrives, in full sun, in light,
somewhat sandy soil. Space 6–8 inches apart. If later bloom is
desired sow seed directly outdoors after warm weather arrives.
For other plants in this family see pp. 241–285.
      Related plants (not illustrated):
            *Helipterum humboldtianum.* 8–18 inches. Flowers yellow.
            *Helipterum roseum.* 12–20 inches. Flowers white or rose.

**STRAWFLOWER** (*Helichrysum bracteatum*)                    p. 45
An Australian annual with narrow toothless leaves, and chaffy,
showy flower heads much prized for dry bouquets, although
they can be cut for fresh flowers when in full bloom. **Color:**
Yellow, orange, red, pink, or white. **Height:** 12–30 inches.
**Flowering date:** July–Aug. **Varieties:** Snowball (white), Salmon
Queen (salmon), Fire Ball (crimson), and Golden Ball (golden
yellow). **Culture:** For early bloom sow seed indoors (6–8 weeks
before outdoor planting is safe). When trees leaf out set the
seedlings 10–15 inches apart in warm, light soil, in full sun. For
other plants in this family see pp. 241–285.
      Related plant (not illustrated):
            *Helichrysum petiolatum.* 20–30 inches. Flowers yellow.

**PEARLY EVERLASTING** (*Anaphalis margaritacea*)      p. 45
A rather weedy perennial, wild over much of North America,
and cultivated only for its pearly white, chaffy, button-like,
faintly spicy flower heads, which are in lax terminal clusters
above the narrow, ashy white leaves. **Color:** Pearl-white. **Height:**

18–30 inches, the stem wandlike and weak. **Flowering date:** July–Aug. **Varieties:** None. **Culture:** Will grow anywhere, preferably in a somewhat sandy soil. Plants dug from the wild are easy to establish; otherwise they must be purchased, since seedsmen do not carry them. Space 9–12 inches apart. For other plants in this family see pp. 241–285.

**IMMORTELLE** (*Xeranthemum annuum*) p. 45
The most widely grown everlasting, usually so called but often under the name Immortelle. It is a hardy annual herb from the Mediterranean region, with white-felty foliage, and solitary, long-stalked chaffy flower heads. **Color:** Pink, purple, or white. **Height:** 2–3 feet. **Flowering date:** July–Aug. **Varieties:** Many, but mostly unnamed. **Culture:** Sow seed about ¼ inch deep, in a light, preferably sandy soil, in full sun whenever warm weather has arrived, either broadcast or in rows 8–10 inches apart. Space 10–15 inches apart. The silky flower heads, if for winter bouquets, should be cut before the head is really open. For other plants in this family see pp. 241–285.

**WINGED EVERLASTING**
   (*Ammobium alatum grandiflorum*) p. 45
A perennial Australian everlasting with white-woolly leaves and a branching habit, the faintly spicy flower heads solitary and the branches prominently winged. **Color:** Heads yellow, but the bracts beneath them brilliantly white. **Height:** 1–3 feet. **Flowering date:** June–July. **Varieties:** None. **Culture:** Sow seeds ¼ inch deep, broadcast or in rows, in a light, sandy soil, in full sun, and space 10–15 inches apart. For earlier bloom start seedlings indoors 6–8 weeks before outdoor planting is safe, transplanting seedlings to the open ground when trees leaf out. For winter decoration cut the flowers well before the heads are fully open. For other plants in this family see pp. 241–285.

**EDELWEISS** (*Leontopodium alpinum*) p. 45
A romantic perennial alpine plant from Switzerland and the Pyrenees, the unwitting cause of several mountain tragedies when venturesome climbers have sought its not particularly

handsome bloom. It has white-woolly foliage, but the wool is shed by midsummer. **Color:** Yellow, but beneath the head a row of gray or pearly white, very woolly bracts. **Height:** 5–7 inches. **Flowering date:** June. **Varieties:** None. **Culture:** Confine it to the rock garden, preferably in a gritty, loose soil, in full sunlight. Start from purchased plants in Oct. spaced 6–8 inches apart. Unless there is heavy snowfall give it a light strawy winter mulch (no manure), removing it in March or April. For other plants in the family see pp. 241–285.

**BLUE SUCCORY** (*Catananche caerulea*)                                    p. 45
A European perennial often known as Cupid's-Dart, the mostly basal leaves densely hairy, but not ashy gray, and narrow. **Color:** Blue. **Height:** 12–18 inches. **Flowering date:** June–Aug. **Varieties:** Alba (white), Bicolor (blue and white). **Culture:** Sow seed outdoors in early spring, ¼ inch deep broadcast or in rows 1 foot apart in any ordinary garden soil. Thin to 9–12 inches apart. Some prefer to plant annually because of its tendency to die out. Sometimes known as Cupidone. Holds its color a little less permanently than most everlastings. For other plants in this family see pp. 241–285.

**GLOBE AMARANTH** (*Gomphrena globosa*)                              p. 45
An erect, branched, Old World tropical annual much grown for its persistently colored, chaffy, dense, clover-like heads that are usually solitary or in sparse clusters, the heads about ¾ inch wide. **Color:** Red, pink, white, or orange. **Height:** 12–20 inches. **Flowering date:** July–Aug. **Varieties:** Many but mostly unnamed. **Culture:** Sow seed ¼ inch deep in boxes or pots, indoors (6 to 8 weeks before outdoor planting is safe). Transfer outdoors when trees leaf out. Space 9–12 inches apart in any ordinary but not too rich soil, in full sunlight. If blooms are wanted for winter use, pick when thoroughly mature, mostly around mid-August.

# *Flower Heads Not Globular*

**LOVE–LIES–BLEEDING** (*Amaranthus caudatus*)    p. 45
A rather coarse tropical annual grown for its brilliantly colored foliage and its long, drooping, often branched clusters of minute chaffy flowers, the terminal cluster often suggesting a rat's tail. **Color:** Red, but horticultural forms are pink, green, or yellow. **Height:** 12–30 inches. **Flowering date:** July–Aug. **Varieties:** None, or doubtfully distinct. **Culture:** Sow outdoors when trees are leafing out, about ¼ inch deep, in rows 18 inches apart, or broadcast in poor, sandy, never rich soil. Space 12–15 inches apart. Seedsmen have a number of confusing Latin names for Love-Lies-Bleeding such as *elegantissima, superbus,* etc.

Related plants (not illustrated):

> Joseph's-Coat (*Amaranthus tricolor*). 2–4 feet. Variously colored foliage.
>
> Prince's-Feather (*Amaranthus hybridus hypochondriacus*). 3–4 feet. Flowers and foliage red.

**COCKSCOMB** (*Celosia argentea cristata*)    p. 58
A tropical Asiatic annual grown only for its grotesque clusters of tiny, chaffy flowers, crowded in monstrosities like a giant cock's comb (the commonest sort), plumes, spires, and many other distorted but extremely colorful clusters. All of them make good decorative material for winter bouquets. **Color:** Prevailingly red, but bronze, gold, yellow, or silvery in some forms. **Height:** 1–2½ feet. **Flowering date:** July–Aug. **Varieties:** Empress (dwarf, crimson-purple), Rose Beauty (rose-pink), Maple Gold (heads globular, golden), Golden Fleece (plumes golden). **Culture:** Sow seeds ¼ inch deep outdoors in a reasonably rich garden soil, about May 15 (6 weeks earlier in the house, if bloom is to be hastened), broadcast or in rows, and space at least 18 inches apart. They need a reasonable amount of moisture, unlike many other everlastings, which thrive in poor soil.

Related plants (not illustrated):

*Celosia floribunda.* 8–10 feet (tender in the North). Flower red, yellow, or orange.

*Celosia* (horticultural forms). Plants related to the Cockscomb but generally taller, the clusters plume-like and in many colors.

Left: Summer Cypress (*Kochia scoparia trichophila*), below. **Center:** Honesty (*Lunaria annua*), p. 59. Right: Cockscomb (*Celosia argentea cristata*), p. 57.

**SUMMER CYPRESS** (*Kochia scoparia trichophila*)          above
Often called Burning Bush or Belvedere Cypress, this Eurasian annual is grown mostly for its finely cut, handsomely colored foliage, but not for the inconspicuous flowers. **Color:** Red or yellow foliage, the minute flowers greenish. **Height:** 20–36 inches. **Flowering date:** July–Sept. **Varieties:** None. **Culture:** Start seeds indoors in pots or boxes, 6 weeks before outdoor planting is safe. Transfer to the open border when trees leaf out. Space 15–20 inches apart in moderately rich garden soil, full

sunlight, and see that they do not dry out. For dried material cut the foliage in mid-Aug. and dry as quickly as possible (no artificial heat), since the Summer Cypress does not hold its color as well as some other everlastings.

## HONESTY (*Lunaria annua*) p. 58

A Eurasian annual, often called Satinpod or Moonwort. Its not very showy flowers are borne in a loose sparse cluster followed by the thin, silvery, round, parchment-like pod 1½ inches in diameter for which Honesty is grown, because the pods make fine winter decoration. **Color:** Flowers purplish, fruits silvery white. **Height:** 18–30 inches. **Flowering date:** June–July; fruits July–Aug. **Varieties:** None. **Culture:** Sow seeds in June–July in reasonably good garden soil, preferably in partial shade, where the plants are to remain, since they do not take kindly to transplanting. Space 10–18 inches apart. Cover the young seedlings during the first winter with a light strawy mulch. They will bloom and set seeds during the second season. Once established, it will generally perpetuate itself by self-sown seeds. For other plants in this family see p. 97.

Related plant (not illustrated):

> *Lunaria rediviva.* 18–30 inches and perennial. Pods oblong, not so showy as Honesty.

## THRIFT (*Armeria maritima*) p. 62

This is one of the best of the everlastings and a perennial from Europe, northern North America, and the Andes of Chile. It has small, basal, evergreen leaves in a rosette, from which springs a stiff flower stalk crowned with a head of chaffy flowers. **Color:** Pink, purple, or white. **Height:** 8–12 inches. **Flowering date:** June–July. **Varieties:** Laucheana, dwarf (4–6 inches), and pink; Alba (white) and nearly 12 inches high. **Culture:** Start with purchased plants, set 7–12 inches apart, in a light sandy or even gritty soil, in full sunlight, in Oct. or April; or seeds can be sown about ¼ inch deep in early spring, to be transplanted where wanted. Cover during winter with a light mulch of straw, strawy manure or salt hay. For related plants in this family see p. 176.

# PINK FAMILY
## (*Caryophyllaceae*)

# BUTTERCUP FAMILY
## (*Ranunculaceae*)

1. **Marsh Marigold** (*Caltha palustris*)  p. 84
   A spring-blooming perennial suited only to wet or moist places.

2. **Winter Aconite** (*Eranthis hyemalis*)  p. 84
   A tuberous Eurasian plant, 3–8 inches high, often blooming under the snow.

3. **Love-in-a-Mist** (*Nigella damascena*)  p. 84
   A free-blooming annual, 8–10 inches high, flowering in midsummer.

4. **Peony** (*Paeonia* hybrids)  p. 83
   Stout, free-blooming perennials, 2–3 feet high of many colors. June-flowering.

5. **Japanese Anemone** (*Anemone japonica*)  p. 81
   A fall-blooming perennial, 18–30 inches high, its leaves dissected.

6. **Snowdrop Windflower** (*Anemone sylvestris*)  p. 82
   A Eurasian perennial, 5–9 inches high and May-blooming. For rock garden or wild garden.

7. **Globeflower** (*Trollius europaeus*)  p. 82
   A stout, spring-blooming perennial, 12–20 inches high. Prefers a moist shady place.

8. **Pasque-Flower** (*Anemone Pulsatilla*)  p. 81
   A European perennial, blooming in April. Not over 12 inches high.

9. **Christmas Rose** (*Helleborus niger*)  p. 83
   A winter-blooming European perennial, 5–8 inches high; flowers generally pure white. Its roots contain a violent poison.

Related plants (not illustrated):

>   *Armeria juniperina.* 2 inches. Flowers pink or purple. A
>   rock garden plant.
>
>   *Armeria plantaginea.* 12–20 inches. Flowers pink, purple,
>   crimson, or white.

**PRICKLY THRIFT** (*Acantholimon glumaceum*)          below
A southern European perennial closely related to the common
Thrift, with similar basal, evergreen small leaves, but the tiny
chaffy faintly fragrant flowers in an open, 1-sided cluster. **Color:**
Rose-pink. **Height:** 4–6 inches. **Flowering date:** July–Aug. **Varieties:** None. **Culture:** Same as for the common Thrift (above)
but space plants only 3–5 inches apart. Even more than the
Thrift, it needs a sandy or gritty soil; best suited to the rock
garden, although it can be grown in the open border. For related
plants in this family see p. 176.

Left: Sea Lavender (*Limonium latifolium*), p. 63. Center: Thrift (*Armeria maritima*), p. 59. Right: Prickly Thrift (*Acantholimon glumaceum*), above.

**SEA LAVENDER** (*Limonium latifolium*) p. 62
Closely related to the common sea lavender of our salt marshes.
It is a Eurasian perennial with a basal rosette of broad, oblongish
leaves and minute faintly spicy flowers in a much branched
hairy cluster, which looks from a distance like a faint blue haze.
The plant is often but incorrectly listed as a *Statice*. **Color:** Blue,
but the calyx white. **Height:** 15–24 inches. **Flowering date:**
Aug.–Sept. **Varieties:** Album (white). **Culture:** Purchased
plants should be spaced 10–15 inches apart in a light sandy soil
in full sunshine in April or Oct. They increase easily by division
of the roots in spring, or after the bloom in the fall. The hairy,
branching flower clusters are especially fine for the feathery trimming of winter bouquets. For related plants in this family see
p. 176.

# Flowers with Petals Separate

THESE plants with separate petals contain over 100 garden
flowers, among them such popular favorites as Poppy, Sweet
William, all the pinks, and many others. Some have perfectly
regular flowers, like a Poppy, while others have highly irregular
flowers like the Sweet Pea, Violet, or Columbine. To simplify
their arrangement they are here divided into two groups:

*Flowers highly irregular, 1-sided, lopsided, or otherwise unsymmetrical. See p. 142.*

*Flowers regular, i.e., the petals not pea-like, violet-like, or otherwise unsymmetrical. The group comprises all the plants below and up to p. 141. For convenience they are here grouped according to the sequence most likely to be helpful.*

# Flowers Regular

## FOUR O'CLOCK FAMILY
### (*Nyctaginaceae*)

A CHIEFLY tropical and small family of shrubs and trees, including the gorgeous *Bougainvillaea,* but only a handful of garden flowers suited to temperate regions. Of these only the two following are included here. They have no true petals but the sepals are colored and petal-like, and the leaves are oppositely arranged in both.

**FOUR O'CLOCK** (*Mirabilis jalapa*) p. 66
A tropical American perennial plant, grown in the North as an annual and usually from self-sown seed, persisting from year to year, often weedy and invasive, especially south of Washington, D.C. Leaves opposite, ovalish. Flowers opening in late afternoon (or all day if cloudy), tubular, mostly solitary on the branches. **Color:** Red, yellow, lavender, or white. **Height:** 15–30 inches. **Flowering date:** July–frost. **Varieties:** None, except unnamed color forms. **Culture:** Sow seeds in mid-May, ¼ inch deep, in any ordinary garden soil, in full sun or partial shade. Space 6–9 inches apart. For earlier bloom sow seeds indoors 6–8 weeks before outdoor planting is safe, and transfer seedlings outdoors when trees leaf out. South of Richmond, Va., it is often a persistent perennial. Northward, plant seed each year.

**SAND VERBENA** (*Abronia umbellata*)                                    below
A Pacific Coast perennial, but since it blooms from seed the first
year is generally treated as an annual. It is more or less prostrate,
has slightly inequilateral leaves, and small, very fragrant flowers
crowded in a close cluster, suggesting a verbena. Whole plant
rather sticky. **Color:** Pink. **Height:** 5–8 inches. **Flowering date:**
June–July. **Varieties:** None. **Culture:** Sow seeds (the husk of
which should be removed) in mid-May, ¼ inch deep, in light,
somewhat sandy loam, in full sun. Space 12–15 inches apart.

Left: Ice-Plant (*Mesembryanthemum crystallinum*), p. 67. Center: Sand
Verbena (*Abronia umbellata*), above. Right: Four O'Clock (*Mirabilis
jalapa*), p. 65.

For earlier bloom sow seed indoors (6–8 weeks before outdoor
planting is safe). Transfer seedlings outdoors when trees leaf
out. Seeds slow to germinate (15–20 days). For the true Garden
Verbena see p. 203.

# CARPET-WEED FAMILY
## (*Aizoaceae*)

MOSTLY desert herbs, many from South Africa, and comprising over 500 species. Several are grown in Calif., but the only one included here is the Ice-Plant, since it is quite generally cultivated throughout the country. Many of the Aizoaceae have glistening foliage. In the one below the petals are numerous and the flower starlike. Leaves alternately arranged, flat and fleshy.

**ICE–PLANT** (*Mesembryanthemum crystallinum*)  p. 66
One of hundreds of South African relatives grown in warm regions as a perennial, but mostly as an annual. Often called Fig Marigold, and Sea Marigold (in Calif., where it runs wild on seaside cliffs). Foliage thick and fleshy, covered with white, glistening, ice-like dots. Flowers solitary, nearly stalkless, showy, glistening, and daisy-like from its numerous petals. **Color:** White or pink. **Height:** Prostrate; less than 5 inches. **Flowering date:** July–Aug. **Varieties:** None. **Culture:** Sow seed outdoors in mid-May, in open sun, ¼ inch deep, in a sandy or gritty loam. Space 6–8 inches apart. For earlier bloom, and if north of Philadelphia, sow seeds indoors (6–8 weeks before outdoor planting is safe). Transfer seedlings outdoors when trees leaf out. Needs, in the east, a long, hot summer to bloom freely, and does best in the rock garden.
   Related plant (not illustrated):
   *Mesembryanthemum criniflorum*. Prostrate. Flowers red, white, or pink.

# PURSLANE FAMILY
## (*Portulacaceae*)

A MEDIUM-SIZED family, mostly from tropical America, and garden subjects of minor interest. Contains the pernicious "pusley," one of our worst weeds. Portulacaceae has somewhat fleshy leaves and flowers that are rather fleeting. Of over 150 species, only the Rock Purslane, the Bitter-root, and Rose Moss are included here.

**ROCK PURSLANE** (*Calandrinia grandiflora*)          below
A Chilean perennial, grown here as an annual, since it blooms
from seed the first year. It has pointed, ovalish leaves narrowed
to a stalk, and rather ephemeral flowers that close at night but
open the next morning. **Color:** Light purple. **Height:** 4–6 inches,
essentially prostrate or spreading. **Flowering date:** July–Aug.
**Varieties:** None. **Culture:** Sow seeds in sandy or gritty loam,
¼ inch deep, in full sun, around mid-May. Space 6–8 inches
apart. For earlier bloom, or if north of Philadelphia, sow seeds
indoors (6–8 weeks before outdoor planting is safe). Transfer
seedlings outdoors when trees leaf out. Needs a long, hot summer
for free blooming and does best in the rock garden.

   Related plant (not illustrated):

>    *Calandrinia umbellata.* 4–7 inches. Flowers red or ma-
>    genta.

Left: Rose Moss (*Portulaca grandiflora*), p. 69. **Center:** Rock Purslane
(*Calandrinia grandiflora*), above. **Right:** Bitter-Root (*Lewisia rediviva*),
p. 69

**BITTER–ROOT** (*Lewisia rediviva*) p. 68
A Rocky Mountain fleshy perennial, suited only to the rock garden, with a fleshy, starchy, edible root much used as food by the Indians until midsummer, after which it becomes very bitter. Plant practically stemless, comprising a rosette of basal leaves and a solitary, essentially stalkless flower. **Color:** Rose-pink to white. **Height:** Prostrate. **Flowering date:** June–July. **Varieties:** None. **Culture:** Put purchased plants in April or Oct. in light, gritty or sandy soil, in full sun. Space 3–6 inches apart. After flowering, the plant is so inconspicuous it may be weeded out. Keep winter slush and rain from roots. It is the state flower of Montana.

**ROSE MOSS** (*Portulaca grandiflora*) p. 68
An extremely popular Brazilian annual, much prized for its ease of culture and profusion of bloom, which opens only in sunlight. It is a prostrate plant with thickish, spoon-shaped leaves, and showy, terminal, solitary flowers about 1 inch wide. **Color:** Red, pink, white, yellow, or salmon. **Height:** Prostrate. **Flowering date:** July–Aug. **Varieties:** Many unnamed color forms and one series double-flowered, in various colors. **Culture:** Sow seeds broadcast, about ¼ inch deep, in full sun, in mid-May, in light loam or any ordinary garden soil, for it tolerates a variety of conditions. Left alone, without spacing, it will produce sheets of midsummer color.

# PINK FAMILY
## (*Caryophyllaceae*)

A HUGE family (over 1000 species) of herbs all having opposite toothless leaves and swollen joints, which are conspicuous in the carnation. Among the many species are such garden favorites as the pinks, carnation, baby's-breath, catchfly, and the campions. Of these the best liked and most popular in cultivation are the 19 below. All have (except in double-flowered forms) 5, often notched, tattered, or fringed petals. Some of the flowers are spicily fragrant.

# PINK FAMILY
## (*Caryophyllaceae*)

1. **Baby's-Breath** (*Gypsophila paniculata*)                    p. 75
   Popular, rather fragile perennial with clouds of tiny white flowers
   in June–July. Easily grown anywhere.

2. **Bouncing Bet** (*Saponaria officinalis*)                    p. 75
   Weedy perennial grown only for its night-fragrant white flowers
   in June–July. Easily grown anywhere.

3. **Rose-of-Heaven** (*Lychnis coeli-rosa*)                    p. 80
   An easily grown annual from southern Europe. Its profuse pink
   bloom June–July. Also blue varieties.

4. **Evening Campion** (*Lychnis alba*)                    p. 79
   Night-blooming and night-fragrant perennial, 12–20 inches high.
   Flowers white, bloom in June. Easy to grow.

5. **Saxifrage Pink** (*Tunica Saxifraga*)                    p. 78
   Fragile little perennial, 5–9 inches high. Its small pink flowers
   bloom May–June. Easy to grow.

6. **Maltese Cross** (*Lychnis chalcedonica*)                    p. 79
   Asiatic perennial, 2–3 feet high. Its flowers bloom in June
   and are bright scarlet. Can be grown anywhere.

7. **Snow-in-Summer** (*Cerastium tomentosum*)                    p. 78
   Ashy-leaved, prostrate perennial, 3–5 inches high and mat-
   forming. Flowers white, midsummer.

8. **Rose Campion** (*Lychnis coronaria*)                    p. 79
   A white-woolly perennial, 15–24 inches high. Flowers crimson,
   bloom June–July. Culture not difficult.

9. **Sandwort** (*Arenaria montana*)                    p. 78
   A tiny European perennial, 3–4 inches high, fit mostly for rock
   garden or pavement planting. Flowers white, spring-blooming.

**HARDY CARNATION** (*Dianthus Caryophyllus*)          p. 60
Similar to the florist's carnation but treated as an annual, the
flowers a little smaller than the greenhouse kind, but more spicily
fragrant. Although they bloom from seed in a single season,
they are not hardy outdoors in regions of severe frosts, and north
of Washington, D.C., are best treated as annuals. South of this
they may be biennials or perennials and should persist. All have
wandlike stems, bluish-gray leaves and much doubled flowers.
**Color:** Red, scarlet, white, pink, purple, yellow, and not green
(St. Patrick's Day carnations are dyed!). **Height:** 12–18 inches.
**Flowering date:** Aug.–frost. **Varieties:** Very numerous, mostly
unnamed color forms, but the Bizarres have 2–3 stripes of contrasting colors on the petals; the Picotees have the petals edged
with a contrasting color; and the Flukes are striped with only one
color. **Culture:** For certainty of bloom, plant seeds indoors (6–8
weeks before outdoor planting is safe), ½ inch deep in shallow
boxes or pans. Transfer seedlings outdoors when trees leaf out.
Space 8–10 inches apart, in full sun, in any ordinary garden soil
except an acid one. If soil is acid, add a teaspoonful of lime to
each plant, thoroughly mixed with the soil. For best bloom take
off all flower buds, leaving only one to a plant. The Clove Pink
is a variety of the Hardy Carnation, little known here.

**SWEET WILLIAM** (*Dianthus barbatus*)          p. 60
A Eurasian biennial but, in some of its horticultural forms, grown
as an annual, since it will bloom from seed if the growing season
is long enough. Leaves green, flat, and broader than in the carnation. Flowers showy, in dense heads, not at all fragrant. **Color:**
Various, see below. **Height:** 12–20 inches. **Flowering date:** June–
July or Aug.–frost. **Varieties:** Atrococcineus (scarlet), Giant
White (white), Nigricans (dark red), Sutton's Scarlet (scarlet),
Pink Beauty (pink), Copper Red (bronzy red), Newport Pink
(pink). **Culture:** As an annual, sow seeds indoors (6–8 weeks
before outdoor planting is safe). Transfer seedlings when trees
leaf out, to any ordinary garden soil, in full sun. Space 8–10
inches apart. Such plants will be in bloom by Aug. As a biennial, sow seeds outdoors, ¼ inch deep in good soil, in full sun, in

June or July. In Aug. space the seedlings 8–10 inches apart and cover with a winter mulch of straw. Such plants will bloom the following May or June, and then die. Often persistent in the South from self-sown seeds.

**GRASS PINK** (*Dianthus plumarius*) p. 60

A large group of so-called border pinks, originally a Eurasian perennial, but now much hybridized and comprising many old garden favorites. It is a mat-forming plant with bluish-gray foliage and rather stiffish, often forked flower stalks. Flowers not numerous, but showy, fragrant, and with fringed petals. **Color:** Various, see below. **Height:** 10–15 inches. **Flowering date:** May–Aug. **Varieties:** Many, a good selection including Crimson Glow (dark red), Evangeline (rose), Moon Mist (white), Salmon Unique (salmon-pink), The Bishop (purple), Bristol Purity (white), Her Majesty (double, white), Rose Cushion (pink), Pheasant's Eye (white-eyed but pink). **Culture:** Set out purchased plants in Oct. or early April, in any ordinary garden soil, in full sun and space 8–10 inches apart. Perfectly hardy everywhere.

**CHINA PINK** (*Dianthus chinensis*) p. 60

Originally an Asiatic perennial, but by hybridizing is the source of several annual pinks of various colors. The China Pink is an almost scentless *Dianthus* with green foliage and tends to grow in tufts or clumps. The stems are erect and stiffish, crowned with a single flower (rarely a few), nearly 1 inch wide. **Color:** Red, pink, white, or lilac. **Height:** 12–18 inches. **Flowering date:** July–Aug. **Varieties:** Heddewigi (double), Laciniatus (petals fringed), Salmon Queen (salmon-pink). **Culture:** Set out purchased plants in Oct. or April, in any garden soil, in full sun, and space 8–10 inches apart. Of easy culture anywhere.

**MAIDEN PINK** (*Dianthus deltoides*) p. 60

A mat-forming pink, from Eurasia, its tiny green leaves carpeting the ground. From them springs a forked flower stalk crowned with small dainty flowers scarcely ¾ inch wide. The plant is often called Spink, and is a perennial. **Color:** Red or pink,

or white with a crimson eye. **Height:** 4–9 inches. **Flowering
date:** May. **Varieties:** Albus (white), Brilliant (red), Burgundy
Red (red). **Culture:** Set out purchased plants in Oct. or early
April, in full sun, in a somewhat sandy garden soil and space
4–7 inches apart. In a few years it covers the ground like a
green mat, dotted with a profusion of flowers.

**FIRE–PINK** (*Silene virginica*)                                    p. 60
A showy, but little known perennial relative of the catchfly,
grown in the wild garden or in shady borders for its neat habit.
Native in eastern North America, it grows naturally in open
woods or in clearings in the forest. Leaves few and weak, the
terminal flower cluster loose, the petals cleft at the tip. **Color:**
Scarlet. **Height:** 6–10 inches. **Flowering date:** May–June. **Varieties:** None. **Culture:** Set purchased plants (from a wild-flower
dealer) in Oct. or early April, in a somewhat sandy, decidedly
acid soil, in partial shade. Space 4–6 inches apart and leave alone
when once established. If it needs water when planted, use rain
water. Not certainly hardy north of New York City.

**SWEET WILLIAM CATCHFLY** (*Silene Armeria*)      p. 60
A European annual with bluish-gray foliage, often running wild
in fields and thickets, but not much grown in gardens even
though its flowers are rather showy. **Color:** Pink. **Height:** 1–2
feet. **Flowering date:** July–Aug. **Varieties:** None. **Culture:** Sow
seeds ¼ inch deep in any ordinary garden soil in mid-May, in
full sun. Space 8–12 inches apart, and it will often persist from
self-sown seed. Often called None-So-Pretty.

**ALPINE CATCHFLY** (*Silene alpestris*)                          p. 60
A lovely little rock garden perennial from the mountains of
Europe and not suited to hot dry sites. It has rather sticky,
sprawling stems and loose clusters of satiny flowers. **Color:**
White. **Height:** 3–6 inches. **Flowering date:** June. **Varieties:**
None. **Culture:** Set purchased plants (from a rock garden dealer)
in gritty or sandy soil, preferably in a rock garden, in Oct. or
April, in full sun. It needs perfect drainage, and little or no
standing water or slush in winter. If not protected by snowfall,

provide a winter mulch of straw or salt hay. Not suited to ordinary garden soil, nor to hot, dry places.

**MOSS CAMPION** (*Silene Schafta*) p. 60
A tiny little perennial from the Caucasus, useful in the rock garden, for pavement planting or on dry walls. Stems sprawling, hairy, the small leaves in rosettes. **Color:** Rose or purple. **Height:** 3–6 inches. **Flowering date:** June–frost. **Varieties:** None. **Culture:** Set purchased plants in Oct. or April in somewhat sandy loam, in full sun, and preferably in the rock garden between cracks in pavement or in pockets on dry walls. It does not like slush or standing water at its roots in winter. If not covered by snow, should be provided winter mulch of straw or salt hay.

**BABY'S–BREATH** (*Gypsophila paniculata*) p. 70
This most popular florist's flower, used for trimming bouquets, is an easily grown perennial from Eurasia, and is an old garden favorite. It has a widely branching habit, small leaves, and so many minute white flowers that it is often called Mist. **Color:** Typically white, but pink in one variety. **Height:** 18–30 inches. **Flowering date:** June–July. **Varieties:** Bristol Fairy (white and double-flowered), White Queen (white). **Culture:** Set purchased plants in Oct. or April in any ordinary garden soil (not acid; if so, lime it with a teaspoonful of lime per plant), in full sun, and space 2–3 feet apart. Of the easiest culture and making great masses of bloom. There are also annual varieties of Baby's-breath, to be sown each year, where wanted.

Related plants (not illustrated):

> *Gypsophila elegans grandiflora.* 10–18 inches, and annual. Flowers white or pinkish.
>
> *Gypsophila repens.* 6–8 inches and perennial. Flowers white or pinkish.

**BOUNCING BET** (*Saponaria officinalis*) p. 70
An Asiatic perennial, common as a weed along railway tracks and roadsides throughout North America, and treasured as a garden plant only for its beautifully night-fragrant flowers (it is essentially odorless in sunshine). **Color:** White. **Height:** 1–2

76

# POPPY FAMILY
## (*Papaveraceae*)

1. **Bloodroot** (*Sanguinaria canadensis*)       p. 97
   Woodland perennial, 6–8 inches high, blooming in April or May.
   Fine for shady wild garden.

2. **Prickly Poppy** (*Argemone grandiflora*)       p. 96
   A Mexican annual, 2–3 feet high. Summer-blooming.

3. **California Poppy** (*Eschschlotzia californica*)       p. 95
   One of the finest annuals from the Pacific Coast, 8–12 inches
   high. Blooms July to Oct.

4. **Welsh Poppy** (*Meconopsis cambrica*)       p. 96
   A European perennial, 1–2 feet high, its foliage divided. Summer-blooming.

5. **Plume Poppy** (*Macleaya cordata*)       p. 95
   A striking perennial, 4–6 feet high, the summer-blooming flower
   cluster about 1 foot long.

6. **Iceland Poppy** (*Papaver nudicaule*)       p. 95
   A hardy perennial, its June-flowering bloom fragrant. Only
   8–12 inches high.

7. **Golden Cup** (*Hunnemannia fumariaefolia*)       p. 96
   A Mexican plant best grown as an annual; 12–20 inches high,
   blooming July to Oct.

8. **Oriental Poppy** (*Papaver orientale*)       p. 94
   Hairy perennial, 2½–4 feet high, now in many varieties. Blooms
   June–July.

9. **Cream Cups** (*Platystemon californicus*)       p. 97
   A Californian annual, 6–12 inches high, the flowers summer-
   blooming.

# MUSTARD OR CRESS FAMILY
## (*Cruciferae*)

1. **Gold-Dust** (*Alyssum saxatile compactum*)     **p. 98**
   A fine perennial for pavement planting. May-blooming. Prefers sandy loam.

2. **Wallflower** (*Cheiranthus cheiri*)     **p. 99**
   Better suited to the Pacific Coast than the East. Not suited to wet, slushy winters, but a fine spring-blooming perennial.

3. **Stone Cress** (*Aethionema grandiflorum*)     **p. 102**
   A rock garden perennial partial to lime. Flowers in June–July. Rather apt to die out in a year or so.

4. **Sweet Alyssum** (*Lobularia maritima*)     **p. 98**
   A fine edging perennial grown as an annual. Summer-flowering, the heads small but profuse.

5. **Dame's Rocket** (*Hesperis matronalis*)     **p. 100**
   A perennial with night-fragrant, midsummer bloom. Best treated as a biennial, since it tends to die out.

6. **Ten-Weeks Stock** (*Mathiola incana annua*)     **p. 101**
   Variously colored, profuse bloom and preference for alkaline soil. Start from seeds sown indoors.

7. **Night-scented Stock** (*Mathiola bicornis*)     **p. 101**
   One of the finest of night-scented plants; an annual easily grown in any ordinary garden soil.

8. **Purple Rock Cress** (*Aubretia deltoidea*)     **p. 100**
   A mat-forming, rock garden perennial with early spring bloom. Avoid hot, dry places.

9. **Candytuft** (*Iberis umbellata*)     **p. 99**
   An annual relative of the Perennial Candytuft, and more freely blooming. Flowers from June to frost. Flowers also white.

feet. **Flowering date:** June–July. **Varieties:** Flore-pleno (double-flowered and not so fragrant as the common sort). There is also a double-flowered pink variety, to be avoided if scent is sought. **Culture:** Set purchased plants in Oct. or April, in any soil, in sun or shade (the plant is weedy and hard to kill!). Space 10–15 inches apart.

Related plant (not illustrated):

*Saponaria ocymoides.* Prostrate. Flowers pink.

### SAXIFRAGE PINK (*Tunica Saxifraga*)                              p. 70

The most delicate, fragile, and one of the most beautiful of all the Pink Family, this little perennial from Europe is prized for its small leaves and its wiry, stiff stem, crowned with a small cluster of flowers that are scarcely ½ inch wide. **Color:** Pink. **Height:** 5–9 inches. **Flowering date:** May–June. **Varieties:** Alba (white), Rosea (rose pink), Flore-pleno (double-flowered). **Culture:** Set purchased plants in Oct. or April, in any ordinary garden soil, in full sun. Space 5–6 inches apart. Also easily started from seed sown indoors in March, ¹⁄₁₆ inch deep, and the seedlings transferred to the open in late May. Often called Tunic Flower or Coat Flower.

### SNOW–IN–SUMMER (*Cerastium tomentosum*)                    p. 70

An ashy-leaved prostrate perennial from Europe, often forming large patches and a fine ground cover for open sandy places. It has tiny crowded leaves that are white-woolly and a cluster of flowers that stand above the general carpet of foliage. **Color:** White. **Height:** 3–5 inches. **Flowering date:** July–Aug. **Varieties:** None. **Culture:** Set purchased plants, in Oct. or April in any ordinary garden soil but preferably a sandy loam, in full sun. Space 4–6 inches apart, and in a year or two it will carpet the ground, and the profusion of its flowers look like snow on an ashy carpet.

### SANDWORT (*Arenaria montana*)                                   p. 70

A sand- or grit-loving, tiny European perennial, usually growing in tufts, and often forming ground-covering mats. It has very small but numerous leaves, and small but profuse silvery flowers.

It is a fine plant for edging and for the rock garden. **Color:** White. **Height:** 3–4 inches. **Flowering date:** May–June. **Varieties:** None. **Culture:** Set purchased plants in full sun, in Oct. or April, in a gritty or sandy soil, and space 3–5 inches apart. Do not let winter rainfall or slush puddle the plants.

Related plants (not illustrated):

Mountain Sandwort (*Arenaria groenlandica*). 3–4 inches. Flowers white.

*Arenaria verna.* 3–4 inches. Flowers white.

### EVENING CAMPION (*Lychnis alba*) p. 70

A deliciously night-fragrant and night-blooming European herb with sticky, oblong or ovalish leaves and a small cluster of flowers, about 1 inch wide, the petals deeply cleft. Below the flower is a swollen, pouchlike striped calyx which ultimately encloses the pod. **Color:** White. **Height:** 12–20 inches. **Flowering date:** June. **Varieties:** None. **Culture:** Easy, since it has escaped as a roadside weed over much of the eastern states. Set purchased plants, or those dug from the wild, in any garden soil, in Oct. or April, in full sun, and space 9–12 inches apart. Often called White Campion.

### ROSE CAMPION (*Lychnis coronaria*) p. 70

Dusty Miller and Mullein Pink are also common names for the Rose Campion because of its white-woolly foliage. It is a perennial from southern Europe, with ovalish or oblong leaves, and a single flower to each stalk, the blossom about 1 inch wide, the petals cleft or notched. **Color:** Crimson. **Height:** 15–24 inches. **Flowering date:** June–July. **Varieties:** Alba (white), Atrosanguinea (dark red), Bicolor (white and red). **Culture:** Set purchased plants in Oct. or April, in any ordinary garden soil, in full sun and space 8–10 inches apart. It often blooms from seed the first season, in midsummer if seeds are sown where wanted, ½ inch deep, in mid-May. Often offered under the incorrect name of *Agrostemma coronaria.*

### MALTESE CROSS (*Lychnis chalcedonica*) p. 70

Originally named for the fabled Chalcedon, once near Istanbul,

**and** dedicated to the Knights of Malta, who fought in the Crusades. It is now known from much of western Asia and is a popular garden perennial grown for its dense clusters of brilliantly colored flowers. Because of its color it is often called Scarlet Lightning or Jerusalem Cross. **Color:** Scarlet. **Height:** 2–3 feet. **Flowering date:** June. **Varieties:** Flesh (pink), Alba (white). **Culture:** Set purchased plants in Oct. or April, in full sun, in any ordinary garden soil, and space 10–15 inches apart.

**ROSE–OF–HEAVEN** (*Lychnis coeli-rosa*)                          p. 70
Often offered under the incorrect names of *Agrostemma coeli-rosa* or *Viscaria,* this delightful annual from southern Europe is a popular garden plant. It has very narrow leaves and a single flower to each stalk, the blossom about one inch wide. It is loosely branched and covered with a profusion of flowers. **Color:** Typically rose-pink, but see below. **Height:** 12–18 inches. **Flowering date:** June–July. **Varieties:** Blue Gem (blue), Rose Gem (pale rose), Blue Pearl (blue), Oculata (red, with darker center). **Culture:** Sow seeds ¼ inch deep in any ordinary garden soil, but preferably a little sandy, in full sun, in early May. Space 12–15 inches apart. It thrives best in cool sites, since it does not like hot summer nights.

Related plant (not illustrated):

> *Lychnis haageana.* 8–12 inches. Flowers orange-red or crimson.

**PEARLWORT** (*Sagina subulata*)                                p. 91
A Corsican, tiny, perennial herb, with minute evergreen leaves, the plant practically prostrate, and from its mosslike foliage springs a profusion of very small flowers. **Color:** White. **Height:** 1–3 inches. **Flowering date:** July–Aug. **Varieties:** None. **Culture:** Set purchased plants in a somewhat sandy loam, in full sun, in Oct. or April and space 2–3 inches apart. It will soon form a mat if winter rains and slush are kept from standing at its roots. Not widely grown.

# BUTTERCUP FAMILY
## (*Ranunculaceae*)

THERE are over 1200 species in this huge family of plants that are scattered all over the North Temperate Zone, mostly in the cooler parts of it. Besides the Buttercup it contains such old garden favorites as the Peony, anemones, Hepatica, Love-in-a-Mist, and many others. All those below have regular, symmetrical flowers, but some members of it have highly irregular or unsymmetrical flowers like the Columbine, Monkshood, and Delphinium or Larkspur. For these see pp. 152–153.

Those below, all with regular and symmetrical flowers, comprise those most likely to be found in gardens.

**JAPANESE ANEMONE** (*Anemone japonica*)     p. 61
A deservedly popular Asiatic perennial, grown in many gardens for its fall bloom. It is a stout, branching herb, its leaves divided into segments; its flowers nearly 2½ inches wide and very showy. It is hardy throughout the country and has many varieties. **Color:** Pink or white, but see below. **Height:** 18–30 inches. **Flowering date:** Sept.–frost. **Varieties:** Alba (white), September Charm (silvery pink), Alice (rose-pink), Prince Heinrich (deep pink), Rubra (red), Marie Manchard (white). **Culture:** Set purchased plants only in early spring, in rich garden loam, preferably in half-shady place, in the lee of north winds. Space 15–20 inches apart and leave them alone, since they do not like to be moved.
Related plants (not illustrated):
> *Anemone hupehensis.* 12–20 inches. Flowers mauve.
> Poppy Anemone, the anemone of the florists (*Anemone coronaria*). 6–12 inches. Flowers red, blue, or white. Not hardy outdoors except in Deep South and Calif.

**PASQUE–FLOWER** (*Anemone Pulsatilla*)     p. 61
This European perennial is, or should be, primarily a plant for the rock garden, as it is apt to grow more foliage than flowers in ordinary garden soil. It is a showy plant, even after blooming, its flowers succeeded by long feathery plumes. In the center of the

flower is a mass of golden stamens. **Color:** Lilac or purple.
**Height:** 7–12 inches. **Flowering date:** April. **Varieties:** Alba
(white). **Culture:** Set purchased plants, only in Oct., in a gritty
mixture of sandy loam and crushed limestone, in the rock garden
in full sun. Space 6–8 inches apart and do not move them unless
absolutely necessary. Often sold under its old name of *Pulsatilla
vulgaris.*

   Related plant (not illustrated):

   American Pasque-Flower (*Anemone patens*). 4–6 inches.
   Flowers bluish purple.

## SNOWDROP WINDFLOWER (*Anemone sylvestris*)    p. 61

A Eurasian, woodland perennial, and best suited to the wild garden. It has mostly basal, divided leaves and solitary (or a few),
fragrant, nodding showy flowers nearly 2 inches wide, and with
waxlike sepals (there are no petals). **Color:** White. **Height:**
5–9 inches. **Flowering date:** May. **Varieties:** None. **Culture:**
Set purchased plants, only in Oct., in partial or complete shade
of trees (not evergreens) in a soil rich in humus or made so by
the addition of chopped peat. Space 5–7 inches apart and maintain a permanent mulch of leaves. Do not cultivate the soil and
do not move the plants unless necessary.

   Related plant (not illustrated):

   Wood Anemone or Windflower (*Anemone quinque-
   folia*). 5–7 inches. Flowers white.

## GLOBEFLOWER (*Trollius europaeus*)                p. 61

The globe-shaped flower of this European perennial has only inconspicuous petals as these are replaced by the colored sepals that
are handsome and showy. It is a stout, bushy plant with deeply
cut leaves, and a solitary flower at the tip of the branches. **Color:**
Yellow. **Height:** 12–20 inches. **Flowering date:** May. **Varieties:**
Orange Globe (orange), Lemon Queen (lemon yellow). **Culture:** Set purchased plants in Oct., in a partially shaded place in
good garden loam and in a moist but not wet site. Space 10–15
inches apart and do not disturb. It is a good plant for edges of
pools or shady moist ravines.

Related plants (not illustrated):
> *Trollius ledebouri.* 18–30 inches. Flowers yellow.
> *Trollius laxus.* 12–20 inches. Flowers greenish yellow.

**PEONY** (*Paeonia* hybrids)                                    p. 61

Magnificent garden plants, now in hundreds of varieties, but all stemming from a Chinese perennial and unknown in cultivation here or in Europe before 1800. They have large, much divided leaves, and huge, globe-shaped flowers, now much doubled and with numerous waxy petals, in every color but yellow. The roots of all peonies are fleshy and brittle and must be handled with care. **Color:** Various, see below. **Height:** 15–36 inches. **Flowering date:** June. **Varieties:** Over 3000, many of them duplicates. Of these a reasonable selection could include among DOUBLE-FLOWERED: Felix Crousse (red), Festiva Maxima (white), Lady Alexandra Duff (pink), Marie Crousse (salmon pink), Mons. Martin Cahuzac (purple-garnet), Solange (white, tinged with orange), Walter Faxon (pink), Thérèse (violet-rose). SINGLE-FLOWERED: Eva (lilac-crimson), Jacqueline (white), Mikado (red), Cleopatra (red), Kinsui (salmon-pink), Nippon Beauty (garnet-red). **Culture:** Easy only if the directions are carefully followed. Dig out bed 18 inches deep and fill bottom 9 inches with well-rotted manure. Fill the hole with good garden loam and plant the purchased roots (which are fragile), not over 2 or 3 inches from top of root to surface of soil. Plant only in late Oct. and space 2–3 feet apart. The site can be partly shady and shade in the afternoon improves quality of bloom. Never disturb, since replanting and your initial planting will retard bloom from 1 to 3 years. A good Peony clump may thrive for 25 years if left undisturbed.

Related plants (not illustrated):
> Tree Peony (*Paeonia suffruticosa*). 4–6 feet and shrubby.
>> Flowers red or white.
> *Paeonia lutea.* 2–3 feet. Flowers yellow.

**CHRISTMAS ROSE** (*Helleborus niger*)                          p. 61

Blooming under the snow or in patches free of it, this European perennial — according to its site and the season — may be in bloom any time from mid-Dec. to Feb. It has thick, fibrous roots (easily broken) and mostly basal, long-stalked, divided leaves. Flowers solitary on each stalk, rarely a few, nearly 2½ inches wide. **Color:** White. **Height:** 5–8 inches. **Flowering date:** Dec.–Feb. **Varieties:** None. **Culture:** Set purchased roots (which are fragile and violently poisonous if eaten) in a rich garden soil in April or Sept., planted about 3 inches deep in a moist but not wet site and in partial shade. Handle roots carefully or they will break. Space 4–6 inches apart and leave alone.

**WINTER ACONITE** (*Eranthis hyemalis*)                              p. 61

A tuberous-rooted, winter-blooming Eurasian perennial, with basal leaves much cut into fine segments. Flower solitary, not very showy but welcome when so few plants are in bloom. **Color:** Yellow. **Height:** 3–6 inches. **Flowering date:** Dec.–Feb., often under the snow. **Varieties:** None. **Culture:** Plant purchased tubers in Aug. or Sept., 3 inches deep, in partial shade (it does well on a wooded bank) and space 3–4 inches apart. If left alone it seeds freely and should soon spread. The plant dies down in summer and cannot be found then, all its growth beginning in October.

**LOVE–IN–A–MIST** (*Nigella damascena*)                              p. 61

This is also called, in southern Europe, Devil-in-the-Bush, both common names reflecting the fact that the handsome double flowers are nestled in a mass of fine, lacy, threadlike leaves. It is an annual of easy culture, and very popular everywhere. **Color:** Typically blue, but white in an unnamed variety. **Height:** 8–10 inches. **Flowering date:** July–Aug. **Varieties:** Only an unnamed white one. **Culture:** Plant seeds ⅛ inch deep, in mid-May, in any ordinary garden soil, in full sun. Thin to 9 inches apart and leave alone.

**MARSH MARIGOLD** (*Caltha palustris*)                              p. 61

A swamp plant of eastern North America, buttercup-like, but coarser and with much more handsome flowers. It is a perennial with kidney-shaped leaves and showy flowers on hollow stalks. **Color:** Golden yellow. **Height:** 10–20 inches. **Flowering date:** April. **Varieties:** None. **Culture:** Plants dug from the swamps are easily established in moist or wet places, either in sun or shade. It will even grow in ordinary garden soil if the place is reasonably moist and in partial shade. Space 8–12 inches apart. Often (incorrectly) called Cowslip; also King-Cup, May-Blob, and Gools.

**SPRING ADONIS** (*Adonis vernalis*)                              p. 86
A sparsely cultivated perennial from Europe grown mostly in the rock garden, but not necessarily. It has very finely divided, almost fernlike foliage and a solitary flower nearly 3 inches wide. **Color:** Yellow. **Height:** 6–9 inches. **Flowering date:** March–April. **Varieties:** None. **Culture:** Set purchased plants, only in Oct., in sandy loam, in full sun or partial shade. Space 5–8 inches apart and leave alone. It does not like too much moisture.
   Related plants (not illustrated):
      *Adonis annua.* 12–18 inches. Flowers red, dark-centered.
      *Adonis amurensis.* 7–12 inches. Flowers golden yellow.

**HEPATICA** (*Hepatica americana*)                                p. 86
An early spring flower of eastern North America, often called Liver-Leaf, from the shape of the evergreen leaves, and frequently sold under its old name of *Hepatica triloba*. It has basal leaves that develop after the plant blooms. Flowers solitary on each stalk, its sepals petal-like, since it bears no true petals. Suited only to the wild garden. **Color:** Bluish lavender or pinkish. **Height:** 4–6 inches. **Flowering date:** March–April. **Varieties:** None. **Culture:** Set purchased plants, only in Oct., in rich woods soil, not too acid, under partial or complete shade of trees (not evergreens). Space 4–6 inches apart and provide a permanent mulch of leaves. Do not cultivate it or move it unless absolutely necessary. Often called Mayflower.
   Related plant (not illustrated):
      *Hepatica acutiloba.* 4–6 inches. Flowers bluish lavender.

**BLACK COHOSH** (*Cimicifuga racemosa*)                           p. 86
This striking woodland plant of eastern North America is locally called Black Snakeroot, and is a stately perennial with much divided leaves and a huge branching flower cluster, the

## BUTTERCUP FAMILY (*Ranunculaceae*), 1–3, 5–7
## BARBERRY FAMILY (*Berberidaceae*), 4, 8, and 9

**1. Spring Adonis** (*Adonis vernalis*)     **p. 85**
Not well known here, but an attractive perennial, 6–9 inches high, with yellow flowers in March–April.

**2. Rue Anemone** (*Anemonella thalictroides*)     **p. 88**
Shy woodland perennial, 5–7 inches high, with white flowers in May. Fit only for shaded, windless places in the wild garden.

**3. Meadow Rue** (*Thalictum aquilegifolium*)     **p. 88**
A stately perennial, 2–4 feet high, the flowers pinkish purple, in June–July. Prefers partial shade and moist site.

**4. Twin-Leaf** (*Jeffersonia diphylla*)     **p. 90**
Native perennial, 8–12 inches high, its solitary, waxy, white flower in May–June. Suited only to the wild garden.

**5. Hepatica** (*Hepatica americana*)     **p. 85**
Early spring-flowering native perennial, 4–6 inches high, its flowers bluish lavender. Try with care in the wild garden.

**6. Black Cohosh** (*Cimicifuga racemosa*)     **p. 85**
Striking native woodland perennial, 4–6 feet high, its white flower spike 9–20 inches long; midsummer. Only for the wild garden.

**7. Creeping Buttercup** (*Ranunculus repens*)     **p. 89**
An invasive, prostrate perennial, useful as a ground cover, but hard to confine. Flowers yellow, bloom May–June.

**8. Mayapple** (*Podophyllum peltatum*)     **p. 89**
Showy but evil-smelling perennial, 10–18 inches high. Flowers in May, white and waxy. For the wild garden.

**9. Blue Cohosh** (*Caulophyllum thalictroides*)     **p. 90**
Native perennial, 18–30 inches high, its greenish-purple flowers in May. Best suited to the wild garden.

ultimate spike of which may be 9–20 inches long. It is suited only
to the wild garden. **Color:** White. **Height:** 4–6 feet. **Flowering
date:** July–Aug. **Varieties:** None. **Culture:** Set purchased plants
in a mixture of ½ rotted sods and ½ black leafmold (not acid),
in April or Oct., under partial or complete shade of trees (not
evergreens). Space 20–30 inches apart and leave alone with a
permanent mulch of leaves. Needs a reasonably moist but not
wet site. Very handsome in bloom.

Related plant (not illustrated):

*Cimicifuga americana.* 1–3 feet. Flowers white.

**MEADOW RUE** (*Thalictrum aquilegifolium*)                    p. 86
The male and female flowers of this Eurasian perennial are on
separate plants and the male plants are the more showy. It is
well to have both. It is a tall stately plant the ultimate segments
of its much divided leaf like the Columbine. Flowers grouped
in terminal, branching clusters, without petals, but the stamens
showy. **Color:** Pinkish purple. **Height:** 2–4 feet. **Flowering
date:** June–July. **Varieties:** Pink, purple, and white are offered,
but they are unnamed. **Culture:** Set purchased plants, in Oct. or
April, in any good rich garden soil, in full sun or partial shade,
and preferably in a moist but not wet site. Space 1–2½ feet
apart, or even more in rich soil, because the tops are branchy and
spreading.

Related plant (not illustrated):

*Thalictrum glaucum.* 3–4 feet. Flowers yellow.

**RUE ANEMONE** (*Anemonella thalictroides*)                    p. 86
One of the most charming, shy woodland perennials of the eastern U.S., impatient of wind and sun and hence only for the most
sheltered place in the wild garden. It is low, has leaves like the
Meadow Rue and fragile flowers on weak stalks. Hence it should
never be picked, for it wilts quickly. **Color:** White. **Height:**
5–7 inches. **Flowering date:** May. **Varieties:** None. **Culture:**
Set purchased plants in a wind-free, sheltered, half-shady place,
in rich woodland soil (not acid), in Oct. or late March. Space
5–7 inches apart and do not disturb. It will not thrive in full
sun nor in a windy place, although it is one of the windflowers.

**CREEPING BUTTERCUP** (*Ranunculus repens*)          p. 86
A coarse, rampant, ground-covering perennial from Europe. It has nothing to do with the florists' ranunculus, which cannot be grown outdoors over most of the country. The Creeping Buttercup is invasive and may become a nuisance unless restricted. It has coarse leaves and many flowers, which are usually double and profuse. **Color:** Yellow. **Height:** 10–12 inches. **Flowering date:** May–June, often later. **Varieties:** A double-flowered form is commoner than the original single-flowered species. **Culture:** Easy; start from purchased plants any time, in any soil, under partial shade or full sun, and space 1–2 feet apart. It will soon cover the ground, often at the expense of better plants!

# BARBERRY FAMILY
## (*Berberidaceae*)

THE Barberry Family, so rich in splendid Chinese and Himalayan shrubs, some of them evergreen, is rather weak in the number of garden perennials or annuals. Only the 4 below are likely to be met in American gardens, and even these are relatively rare in cultivation, although the first 3 are common as wild plants in many of our woods in the eastern states. The family is closely related to the Buttercup Family and differs from it only in technical characters.

**MAYAPPLE** (*Podophyllum peltatum*)          p. 86
Often called Mandrake, although it has nothing to do with the fabled mandrake of the Orient. It is a stout perennial, often growing in large patches in the woods of eastern North America, with leaves nearly a foot in diameter, and a solitary waxlike, short-stalked, nodding, rather evil-smelling flower. **Color:** White. **Height:** 10–18 inches. **Flowering date:** May. **Varieties:** None. **Culture:** Set purchased plants (from wild-flower dealer) in rich woods soil, in Oct., in partial or complete shade of trees (not evergreens). Space 10–15 inches apart and choose a moist but not wet site rather than a dry one. Roots, seeds, and foliage poisonous if eaten, but the lemon-yellow berry is eaten by some.

**BLUE COHOSH** (*Caulophyllum thalictroides*)          p. 86
The young foliage of this woodland plant of eastern North
America is a beautiful pale bluish green, turning green in
midsummer when the large, much divided leaves become mature.
It has a few-flowered terminal cluster of not very showy flowers,
followed by handsome, berry-like blue fruit. **Color:** Greenish
purple. **Height:** 18–30 inches. **Flowering date:** May. **Varieties:**
None. **Culture:** Set purchased plants (from a wild-flower dealer)
in Oct., in rich woods soil (not particularly acid) in partial or
complete shade of trees (not evergreens). Space 12–15 inches
apart and leave alone. Suited only to shady wild garden.

**TWIN–LEAF** (*Jeffersonia diphylla*)                    p. 86
A curious inhabitant of the woods of the eastern U.S., its broad
leaf so evenly divided into 2 equal lobes that it looks like two
leaves — hence its name. It has a single waxy flower about an
inch wide. Sometimes called Rheumatism Root, for its reputed
efficacy in that disease. **Color:** White. **Height:** 8–12 inches.
**Flowering date:** May–June. **Varieties:** None. **Culture:** Set
purchased plants (from a wild-flower dealer) in rich woods soil,
not especially acid, in partial or full shade of trees (not evergreens) in Oct. or April. Space 7–10 inches apart and leave
alone.

**BARRENWORT** (*Epimedium pinnatum colchicum*)      p. 91
This half-evergreen, almost woody perennial from Persia and
the Caucasus is apt to be offered under the incorrect name of
*Epimedium pinnatum sulphureum*. Leaves much divided, the
ultimate segments fine-toothed on the margin. It is grown mostly
in the rock garden, but suited to the border if given proper
conditions. It spreads rapidly from its woody rootstocks. **Color:**
Yellow and slightly red. **Height:** 8–12 inches. **Flowering date:**
May–June. **Varieties:** None. **Culture:** Set purchased plants in
partial shade, in Oct. or April, in any ordinary garden soil,
preferably fairly rich in humus, and in a moist but not wet site.
Space 6–9 inches apart. If covered with a light, strawy winter
mulch its leaves may stay green all winter. If left alone it makes
an agreeable ground cover in a few years.

Related plant (not illustrated):

    *Epimedium grandiflorum.* 6–9 inches. Flowers red, violet, and white. Often offered under the incorrect name of ***Epimedium macranthum.***

**Left:** Pearlwort (*Sagina subulata*), p. 80. **Right:** Barrenwort (*Epimedium pinnatum colchicum*), p. 90.

## POPPY FAMILY
### (*Papaveraceae*)

Gorgeous garden plants including besides the poppies several other widely cultivated flowers, among them the dreaded Opium Poppy, the only source of morphine and heroin. All have a some-what milky, often colored juice, and the flowers of most either quickly wither if picked or the petals drop off naturally while still on the plant. Of over 100 species in the family, the following 9 are most likely to be found in American gardens, comprising

## MUSTARD OR CRESS FAMILY (*Cruciferae*), 1–5
## CAPER FAMILY (*Capparidaceae*), 6
## STONECROP FAMILY (*Crassulaceae*), 7 and 8
## MIGNONETTE FAMILY (*Resedaceae*), 9

1. **Siberian Wallflower** (*Erysimum asperum*)  p. 99
   An ephemeral perennial best grown as a biennial; flowering in July–Aug. and showy.

2. **Wall Cress** (*Arabis albida*)  p. 103
   Pale-foliaged perennial, thriving only in gritty or sandy soils. May-blooming and fragrant.

3. **Alpine Wallflower** (*Erysimum linifolium*)  p. 100
   A somewhat rare Spanish perennial, with grayish foliage and May-blooming flowers.

4. **Bladder-Pod** (*Vesicaria utriculata*)  p. 102
   A rock garden perennial grown as much for its inflated pods as its early-blooming yellow flowers.

5. **Whitlow Grass** (*Draba aizoides*)  p. 102
   A tiny rock garden perennial 3–4 inches high, suited only to gritty or sandy alkaline soils.

6. **Spiderflower** (*Cleome spinosa*)  p. 103
   An unpleasantly scented annual with showy terminal flowers. Easily grown in open sun.

7. **Houseleek** (*Sempervivum tectorum*)  p. 106
   A fleshy perennial with basal rosette of thick leaves and terminal cluster of summer bloom.

8. **Sedum** (*Sedum sieboldi*)  p. 106
   One of finest of all the sedums, blooming from Oct. to frost. Stands drought, but not slushy winters.

9. **Mignonette** (*Reseda odorata*)  p. 104
   Sweet but ephemerally scented annual, to be sown where wanted, since it transplants poorly.

## STONECROP FAMILY (*Crassulaceae*), 1–3
## SAXIFRAGE FAMILY (*Saxifragaceae*), 4–9

1. **Worm-Grass** (*Sedum album*)                              **p. 106**
   A prostrate, mat-forming perennial useful as a ground cover, with small, July-blooming flowers.

2. **Wall Pepper** (*Sedum acre*)                              **p. 105**
   A prostrate, ground-covering perennial with small but profuse bloom, mostly in May or June.

3. **Stonecrop** (*Sedum spectabile*)                          **p. 105**
   A stout perennial with thick, fleshy leaves and showy bloom from Aug. to frost.

4. **Foam Flower** (*Tiarella cordifolia*)                     **p. 111**
   Native woodland perennial, spring-flowering, suited only to rich woods soil in the wild garden. Flowers generally white.

5. **Rockfoil** (*Saxifraga aizoon*)                           **p. 107**
   Its basal rosette of leaves are more noteworthy than the flower cluster. Summer-blooming.

6. **Coral Bells** (*Heuchera sanguinea*)                      **p. 111**
   A popular border perennial, with June-flowering bloom. Prefers partial shade.

7. **London Pride** (*Saxifraga umbrosa*)                      **p. 110**
   An old-fashioned perennial more popular in England than here. Prefers cool moist sites.

8. **Siberian Tea** (*Bergenia crassifolia*)                   **p. 110**
   Early-blooming perennial with large coarse leaves, and showy, terminal flower clusters.

9. **Saxifraga** (*Saxifraga decipiens*)                       **p. 110**
   A tufted rock garden perennial to be grown in gritty or sandy alkaline soil. Spring-flowering.

besides the poppies, the Golden Cup, and Cream Cups (both from Calif. and Mexico), and the Bloodroot from eastern woodlands. All plants in the family have rather brittle roots.

**ORIENTAL POPPY** (*Papaver orientale*)                    p. 76
*The* garden poppy, now found in scores of varieties, all originating from this stout perennial of the eastern Mediterranean region. It has huge, bisected, hairy leaves, often up to 18 inches long, and an immense solitary, long-stalked, vividly colored flower (some are 6–8 inches wide) with 5 petals, the center often deeper-colored than the margin of the flower. All tend to wither quickly when picked. **Color:** Prevailingly scarlet, but see varieties below. **Height:** 2½–4 feet. **Flowering date:** June–July. **Varieties:** Over 140 are offered, many of them duplicates. Of these the following dozen comprise a reasonable selection. Beauty of Livermore (crimson and black), Helen Elizabeth (pink), Indian Chief (mahogany), May Sadler (salmon-pink), Mrs. Perry (orange-apricot), Perry's White (white), Barr's White (white), Cavalier (scarlet-red), Enchantress (lilac-rose), Olympia (scarlet), Fairy (pale pink), Toreador (carmine-red). **Culture:** Set purchased plants in Oct. in full sun, in a soil especially prepared, being careful not to injure the brittle roots. Dig out existing soil 18 inches deep, and fill 3–4 inches of cinders or gravel to provide perfect drainage. Fill rest of hole with a mixture of ½ good garden soil and ½ humus or well-rotted compost, but no manure. Roots should be 2 inches below the surface of soil. Space 20–30 inches apart and leave alone, since they resent being moved. In light sandy loams the layer of cinders or gravel can be omitted. Stake all plants if site is windy. Mulch each winter with 2–3 inches of well-rotted manure (no fresh manure), and dig it in in the spring. They need watering in dry spells.

Related plants (not illustrated):

Alpine Poppy (*Papaver alpinum*). 1–2 feet. Flowers white or yellow.

Opium Poppy (*Papaver somniferum*). 3–4 feet. Flowers variously colored. It will not produce opium in the U.S., and growing it is illegal.

**ICELAND POPPY** (*Papaver nudicaule*)                    p. 76
A hardy perennial from the arctic regions, much grown for its
fragrant flowers that are not as showy as the Oriental Poppy,
but more delicate in coloring. Leaves cut into equal lobes, and
its solitary flowers rarely more than 1–2 inches wide, and keeping,
when cut, much longer than the Oriental Poppy. **Color:** Practically all colors. **Height:** 8–12 inches. **Flowering date:** June.
**Varieties:** Many, but mostly unnamed and in a variety of colors;
named sorts are Gibson's Orange (orange), Gartford Art Strains
(many colors), Yellow Emperor (yellow), Yellow Wonder
(yellow). **Culture:** While a true perennial, it will bloom from
seed the first year. Sow seeds indoors in Feb., scarcely covering
the seed. Transfer seedlings outdoors when trees leaf out, being
careful not to break roots. Space 12–15 inches apart in a good
sandy loam. They do not like regions of much humidity and
hot nights.
   Related plant (not illustrated):
      Corn and Shirley Poppies (*Papaver rhoeas*). 15–30
      inches. Flowers in nearly all colors. Both annuals.

**PLUME POPPY** (*Macleaya cordata*)                    p. 76
This handsome, bushy perennial from eastern Asia with large
bluish-gray leaves is often offered under the incorrect name of
*Bocconia*. Its leaves are almost white on the underside and deeply
lobed. Flowers in a showy terminal cluster nearly 1 foot long,
the individual flowers without petals but with many handsome
stamens. **Color:** White. **Height:** 4–6 feet. **Flowering date:** June–
July. **Varieties:** None. **Culture:** Set purchased plants in a good,
rich garden soil, in full sun, in Oct. or April. Space 3–5 feet
apart, or even more, since the plant is bold and spreading.

**CALIFORNIA POPPY** (*Eschscholtzia californica*)                    p. 76
A showy perennial from the Pacific Coast, mostly grown as an
annual, but a perennial in Calif. and the South. Leaves feathery,
dusty green. Flowers solitary, long-stalked, and quickly withering if picked, often 3–4 inches wide. **Color:** Prevailingly orange-
yellow, but see below. **Height:** 8–12 inches. **Flowering date:**
July–frost. **Varieties:** Many unnamed ones, with colors vary-

ing from yellow, through orange to pink, apricot, and even red.
**Culture:** Treat as an annual, since it is transplanted with difficulty. Sow seeds in full sun, in mid-May, in a warm sandy loam,
or even in a definitely sandy place. Scatter seeds where wanted
and cover very lightly. Thin out to 8–10 inches apart. Often
persisting over the winter south of Richmond, Va.

**WELSH POPPY** (*Meconopsis cambrica*)                              p. 76
A European, somewhat hairy perennial, its leaves cut feather-
fashion and decidedly pale on the underside. Flowers solitary,
about 2 inches wide, and borne far above the finely cut foliage,
the juice of which is yellow. **Color:** Yellow. **Height:** 12–30
inches. **Flowering date:** July–Aug. **Varieties:** None. **Culture:**
Set purchased plants in good garden soil, in Oct. or April, in a
moist but not wet place, under partial shade. Set 2–3 feet apart,
and avoid places with too much summer heat and scant rainfall. Water if drought occurs.

**PRICKLY POPPY** (*Argemone grandiflora*)                          p. 76
A rather showy but not widely grown Mexican annual, with
large white-veined leaves that are faintly prickly on their
toothed margins, their juice yellow. Flowers nearly 3 inches
wide, usually solitary or a few together. **Color:** White or yellowish. **Height:** 2–3 feet. **Flowering date:** July–Aug. **Varieties:**
None. **Culture:** Sow seeds in mid-May, ¼ inch deep, in full sun
in a sandy loam or in a definitely sandy place. Thin out to 2–3
feet apart. It does best in warm, dry regions, and will not thrive
in a moist, wet, or cool place.

**GOLDEN CUP** (*Hunnemannia fumariaefolia*)                        p. 76
This Mexican perennial, usually grown as an annual because it
blooms from seed the first year, is also called the Mexican Tulip-
Poppy. Leaves much dissected into narrow segments, and
bluish green. Flowers 2–3 inches wide, generally solitary or a
few in a meager cluster. **Color:** Yellow. **Height:** 12–20 inches.
**Flowering date:** July–Oct. **Varieties:** None. **Culture:** Sow seeds
in paper pots indoors, in March, in a mixture of ½ sand and ½
garden loam. When trees leaf out transfer seedlings to sandy

loam in full sun, without hurting the roots, which are brittle. Tear bottom out of paper pot and plant it down to or below the rim. Space 10–15 inches apart.

**CREAM CUPS** (*Platystemon californicus*) p. 76
A beautiful Californian wild flower, not much grown in the East, but a useful, low annual with clasping leaves and solitary, long-stalked flowers. **Color:** Cream-yellow. **Height:** 6–12 inches. **Flowering date:** July–Aug. **Varieties:** None. **Culture:** Sow seeds ¼ inch deep in sandy loam, in full sun, after warm weather has arrived. Space 6–9 inches apart. Seeds mostly carried by western dealers.

**BLOODROOT** (*Sanguinaria canadensis*) p. 76
This is probably the most popular and most easily grown of all the woodland plants of eastern North America. Early in spring the rolled leaf breaks through the ground tightly clasping the flower bud. Flowers waxy, soon wilting if picked. The root and juice are red. **Color:** White. **Height:** 6–8 inches. **Flowering date:** April–May. **Varieties:** An unnamed double-flowered form is offered by wild-flower dealers. **Culture:** Relatively easy if purchased plants or those dug from the wild (in June or July) are set in rich woodsy soil in half-shade, or under dense shade of trees (not evergreens). Space 4–7 inches apart and leave alone. It will soon cover a considerable area, for it is a thrifty perennial.

# MUSTARD OR CRESS FAMILY
## (*Cruciferae*)

IF THE Mustard Family contained only the cabbage, mustard, Brussels sprouts, cauliflower, radish, turnip, and watercress, it would have no place in a book like this. But the family includes many garden flowers that have been cultivated for centuries, among them the Wallflower, Sweet Alyssum, Ten-Weeks Stock, Candytuft, and other old favorites. It was called Cruciferae because its flowers (unless they are doubled) have only 4 petals, arranged in the form of a cross. It is a huge family (perhaps 2000 species), with the juice of its foliage often bitter, as in watercress, but never poisonous. It always has a dry pod for fruit, usually long, but broad and papery in Honesty (see p. 59). The following 14 constitute, with their relatives, the most popular garden flowers in the Mustard Family.

**SWEET ALYSSUM** (*Lobularia maritima*)                    p. 77

A low herb from the Mediterranean region, grown as an annual, although it is perennial in warm climates, and useful for carpeting the ground, or edging, with sheets of bloom. Leaves small, lance-shaped, about 1 inch long. Flowers very small, but in profuse clusters and hence numerous. **Color:** White or lilac-white. **Height:** 6–12 inches. **Flowering date:** July–Aug. **Varieties:** Violet Queen (violet), Royal Carpet (violet-purple), Carpet of Snow (pure white), Little Gem (white and lower than the type). **Culture:** Sow seeds where wanted, in mid-May, in any sandy loam, in full sun, merely raking them in. Space 5–7 inches apart. For earlier bloom sow seeds indoors (6 weeks before outdoor planting is safe). Transfer seedlings outdoors when trees leaf out. It blooms best in cool climates.

**GOLD–DUST** (*Alyssum saxatile compactum*)                p. 77

Often called Madwort or Basket-of-Gold, this valuable European perennial is one of the most popular plants in the Mustard Family. It has grayish-dusty foliage and dense, compact clusters of flowers. It is particularly useful as a ground cover, and for pavement planting, or among cracks in stone steps. **Color:** Golden yellow. **Height:** 6–8 inches. **Flowering date:** May. **Varieties:** Silver Queen, often called Citrinum (lemon-yellow). **Culture:** Set purchased plants in Oct. or early April in full sun, in any ordinary garden soil, but preferably in sandy loam. Space 6–8 inches apart. As old plants are hard to move it is safer to start new clumps from seed, sown ¼ inch deep in May. The seedlings will bloom the following year.

Related plants (not illustrated):

*Alyssum alpestre.* 2–4 inches. Flowers yellow.

*Alyssum argenteum,* often offered as *Alyssum rostratum.* 10–15 inches. Flowers deep yellow.

**CANDYTUFT** (*Iberis umbellata*)                              p. 77
Very free-flowering annual from Europe, much planted for its
succession of bloom, and chiefly used as a ground cover or edging
for borders. Its flowers are small, but crowded in profuse
clusters. **Color:** Various, see below. **Height:** 6–9 inches. **Flowering date:** June–frost, if planted in succession. **Varieties:** Cardinal
(red), Little Prince (white), Rose Cardinal (pink), and many
unnamed with pink, lilac, or violet colors. **Culture:** Sow seeds
(for continuous bloom) every 10 days from mid-April to mid-
July, in any ordinary garden soil, about ¼ inch deep, in full sun.
Space 5–7 inches apart. It prefers cool sites to hot and dry ones.
   Related plant (not illustrated):
      Perennial Candytuft (*Iberis sempervirens*). 8–10 inches.
      Flowers white.

**WALLFLOWER** (*Cheiranthus cheiri*)                          p. 77
More common in England than here, this gorgeously colored
European perennial is grown by the million in every garden in
England, especially on rock walls and for bedding. It is not
suited to regions of wet, slushy winters. **Color:** Orange-brown
or yellow. **Height:** 10–15 inches. **Flowering date:** May–June.
**Varieties:** Several, unnamed, of colors varying from yellow,
orange, nearly black, to brown. **Culture:** Start from seeds, since
the mature plant is seldom offered. Plant seeds ¼ inch deep,
in sandy loam, in July or Aug., and transfer seedlings to the cold
frame for wintering. They will not bloom until the following
year. Space 6–9 inches apart in full sun. Plants can be propagated
by rooting slips, cut from the plant after blooming, and growing
them in a mixture of ½ loam and ½ sand. Such cuttings will
bloom the next year. The plant thrives much better along the
Pacific Coast than in the East.

**SIBERIAN WALLFLOWER** (*Erysimum asperum*)              p. 92
A true perennial but best grown as a biennial, because it dies out
easily. This popular garden flower is called, for no good reason,
Siberian Wallflower, although it is native on the prairies of the
central U.S. and there called Prairie Rocket. It is more easily
grown in the East than the true Wallflower. **Color:** Orange-

yellow. **Height:** 1–3 feet. **Flowering date:** June–July. **Varieties:** Golden Bedder (yellow). **Culture:** Grow as biennial from seed sown in July–Aug., ¼ inch deep in sandy loam, in partial shade. Winter in cold frame, or where planted with a light strawy mulch. Thin to 8–10 inches apart, and plant in full sun the following spring. It is often offered under the incorrect name of *Cheiranthus allioni*.

Related plant (not illustrated):

*Erysimum murale,* often offered as *Erysimum perofski-anum*. 12–18 inches. Flowers golden yellow.

## ALPINE WALLFLOWER (*Erysimum linifolium*)     p. 92

A Spanish perennial herb with grayish foliage, not much culti-vated in this country, but its nearly prostrate bushy habit, nar-row, almost threadlike leaves and attractive flowers make it a handsome garden plant. **Color:** Lilac or mauve. **Height:** 8–12 inches. **Flowering date:** May. **Varieties:** None. **Culture:** Set purchased plants in any ordinary garden soil, in Oct. or April, in full sun and space 6–10 inches apart. It is useful in rock gardens and on rock walls planted in soil-filled crevices. Often sold as *Cheiranthus linifolius*.

## DAME'S ROCKET (*Hesperis matronalis*)     p. 77

A Eurasian perennial, usually grown as a biennial, since it tends to die out. It is often called Dame's Violet or Garden Rocket. Has a bushy habit and rather showy, night-fragrant flowers. **Color:** Lilac-purple. **Height:** 2–3 feet. **Flowering date:** July–Aug. **Varieties:** Nivea (white). **Culture:** Sow seeds ¼ inch deep in sandy loam, in July or Aug. and grow along until winter-ing them in the cold frame. Or they can be wintered in place with a light straw mulch. Set seedlings out the following spring, in partial shade, and space 12–20 inches apart, when they will bloom.

## PURPLE ROCK CRESS (*Aubretia deltoidea*)     p. 77

A protean group of short-lived perennials from southern Europe, much grown in England, but here mostly confined to *Aubretia deltoidea* and its varieties. It is a low, nearly prostrate mat-forming plant best suited to the rock garden, preferably in half-shade. **Color:** Purple. **Height:** 3–6 inches. **Flowering date:** April–May. **Varieties:** Bougainvillei (blue), Eyrei (rose-lilac), Graeca (violet), Leichtlini (pink), Purpurea (purple). **Culture:** Set purchased plants in Oct. in a fairly sandy or gritty loam, in partial shade, preferably in the rock garden, and space 4–6 inches apart. Its tendency to die out can be overcome by making cuttings in May or June set in a mixture of ½ sand and ½ loam and grown along for planting the following spring. Mulch the plants with compost or peat moss, not over ½ inch deep each spring. It does not like hot, dry places.

**TEN–WEEKS STOCK** (*Mathiola incana annua*)  p. 77
One of the most popular of all the plants of the Mustard Family, forced by the million by florists and grown in the garden for its profuse, mostly double and faintly fragrant flowers. It is not winter-hardy in this country and is grown as an annual. **Color:** Various, see varieties. **Height:** 1–2 feet, the dwarf kinds half this. **Flowering date:** July–Aug. **Varieties:** Best ordered by color because dealers' varieties are in much confusion and the named sorts are often duplicates. Color range includes red, pink, white, crimson, blue, coppery red, yellow, purple, and lavender. **Culture:** Plant seed ⅛ inch deep in pots or pans, indoors 6–8 weeks before outdoor planting is safe. Prick out seedlings when 4–6 leaves have developed and pot up in paper pots. Do not let indoor temperature get above 65°. When trees leaf out transfer seedlings outdoors into any good garden soil (not acid — if so put a teaspoonful of lime to each plant), in full sun. Space 1–2 feet apart and pinch off lateral shoots if tall terminal spikes of flowers are sought. The plant does not like hot dry places, but flowers magnificently in cool moist ones.

**NIGHT–SCENTED STOCK** (*Mathiola bicornis*)  p. 77
An extraordinarily night-fragrant annual from Eurasia, a single spray of flowers scenting a room with a haunting perfume. It is otherwise an undistinguished bushy herb with rather small, scattered flowers. **Color:** Brown-purple, opening only at sundown. **Height:** 3–9 inches. **Flowering date:** July–Aug. **Varieties:** None.

**Culture:** Sow seeds ⅛ inch deep in any ordinary garden soil, in full sun, after settled warm weather has come. Thin to 6–8 inches apart. Often called Evening-scented Stock.

**STONE CRESS** (*Aethionema grandiflorum*)                    p. 77
A Persian perennial, somewhat resembling Candytuft, but the small flowers keeping better when cut than do those of Candytuft. It is an almost unbranched plant with bluish-gray foliage and a terminal cluster of flowers that are scarcely ¼ inch wide. **Color:** Pink. **Height:** 6–9 inches. **Flowering date:** June–July. **Varieties:** None. **Culture:** Best suited to rock garden or on dry walls. Set purchased plants in Oct. or April in gritty or sandy soil, to which a teaspoonful of lime is added for each plant. Set in full sun and space 4–7 inches apart. Apt to die out in a year or two and should be regularly renewed.

Related plant (not illustrated):
> *Aethionema coridifolium.* 4–6 inches. Flowers rose or lilac-pink.

**WHITLOW GRASS** (*Draba aizoides*)                    p. 92
A tiny little perennial from the mountains of southern Europe and to be grown only in the rock garden. It grows in small tufts, and its numerous small flowers are in profuse clusters. **Color:** Yellow. **Height:** 3–4 inches. **Flowering date:** April–May. **Varieties:** None. **Culture:** Set purchased plants in Oct., in the rock garden, in a gritty or sandy soil to which a teaspoonful of lime per plant is added if the soil is acid. Space 3–5 inches apart in full sun.

Related plants (not illustrated):
> *Draba fladnizensis.* 1–3 inches. Flowers greenish white.
> *Draba sibirica.* Prostrate. Flowers yellow.

**BLADDER–POD** (*Vesicaria utriculata*)                    p. 92
A little-grown perennial herb from the mountains of central Europe, planted as much for its inflated pod as for the small flowers crowded in terminal clusters. It is a rather woody plant with numerous basal leaves, and many on the stem. **Color:** Yellow. **Height:** 7–12 inches. **Flowering date:** April–May. **Va-**

rieties: None. **Culture:** Set purchased plants in sandy or gritty soil, preferably in the rock garden, in Oct., in full sun. Space 4–7 inches apart.

**WALL CRESS** (*Arabis albida*)  p. 92
A white-foliaged perennial from the Caucasus, much grown for its ease of culture and for its white, fragrant but small flowers in loose clusters. It thrives on dry walls, in the rock garden, and in light soils in the open border. **Color:** White. **Height:** 8–12 inches, but often sprawling or prostrate. **Flowering date:** May. **Varieties:** None. **Culture:** Set purchased plants in Oct. or April in any reasonably sandy or gritty soil in the rock garden or open border or in pockets in a rock wall, in full sun. Space 5–9 inches apart and keep winter slush from its roots.

Related plants (not illustrated):
> *Arabis alpina.* 4–6 inches. Flowers white.
> *Arabis procurrens.* 7–12 inches. Flowers white.

# CAPER FAMILY
## (*Capparidaceae*)

A SMALL family of little garden interest except that it yields the caper and contains the ornamental plant below. They have alternately arranged leaves without marginal teeth, and flowers that are (falsely) irregular in contour. Fruit a long-stalked, narrow pod.

**SPIDERFLOWER** (*Cleome spinosa*)  p. 92
A tropical American annual cultivated, in spite of its peculiar odor, for its showy terminal cluster of apparently irregular flowers, which have long-stalked petals and long-protruding stamens. **Color:** White or pinkish purple. **Height:** 3–5 feet. **Flowering date:** July–Aug. **Varieties:** Pink Queen (salmon-pink). **Culture:** Sow seeds ¼ inch deep after settled warm weather, where wanted, in any ordinary garden soil, in full sun. Space 20–30 inches apart, but for the variety Pink Queen space 15–25 inches. It is sometimes offered as *Cleome gigantea*.

# MIGNONETTE FAMILY
## (*Resedaceae*)

A SMALL family of Mediterranean herbs of no interest except that among its 60–odd species is the Mignonette. They have alternately arranged leaves, and in the one below extremely fragrant flowers arranged in small clusters, followed by a small 3-horned capsule.

**MIGNONETTE** (*Reseda odorata*)                                    p. 92

One of the most fragrant of all garden flowers, the Mignonette quickly loses part of its odor when picked, unless the newer varieties are grown. The original plant is an Egyptian annual, and after it first reached Paris in the middle of the 18th century was immediately christened Little Darling, not for its flowers, which are inconspicuous, but for its odor, which is enchanting. **Color:** Greenish yellow. **Height:** 8–15 inches. **Flowering date:** July–frost if planted in succession. **Varieties:** Machet or Giant Machet (coppery red), Golden Sunset (yellow), White Pearl (white), Red Monarch or Red Goliath (red). All these varieties keep their odor better when cut than the old-fashioned typical form. **Culture:** Sow seeds broadcast ¼ inch deep, in full sun or partial shade, in any ordinary garden soil, in mid-May, and space 8–10 inches apart. For a succession of bloom sow every two weeks up to middle of July. It loses some of its fragrance in very hot weather, and does not transplant easily — often not at all.

# STONECROP OR ORPINE FAMILY
## (*Crassulaceae*)

A LARGE family (over 900 species) of fleshy-leaved or succulent plants, many of them tropical and hence grown only in the greenhouse. They are much sought after by fanciers and specialists for their curious forms, their often colored foliage, and their prevailingly yellow or reddish flowers. Over 200 species are in cultivation in this country, most of them suited only to the rock garden, the greenhouse, or semideserts of the Southwest. The 5 below, however, are of reasonably easy culture in ordinary climates and some of them are old garden favorites.

**WALL PEPPER** (*Sedum acre*)                                          p. 93
A prostrate, perennial ground cover from Europe and Asia, much grown in gardens for its cheerful bloom, often under the name of Golden Moss (it is not a moss). Leaves triangular, numerous, very small, scarcely more than $\frac{1}{8}$ inch long. Flowers in terminal, branched clusters. **Color:** Yellow. **Height:** 2–4 inches. **Flowering date:** May–June. **Varieties:** Aureum (leaves yellow). **Culture:** Set purchased plants, in Oct. or April, in full sun, in a sandy loam or even in a gritty or stony site. Space 4–7 inches apart and in a few years it makes large patches of ground-hugging verdure. It is fine for the rock garden or on rock walls.
  Related plants (not illustrated):
    *Sedum sarmentosum.* Prostrate. Flowers yellow.
    *Sedum sexangulare.* Prostrate. Flowers yellow.

**STONECROP** (*Sedum spectabile*)                                     p. 93
A strong-growing, sturdy, erect perennial from eastern Asia, much grown for its showy, late-blooming flowers, which are crowded in a terminal, dense cluster. It has a thick tuberous root, erect stem and thick bluish-gray leaves arranged in 3's or opposite each other. **Color:** Pink. **Height:** 12–20 inches. **Flowering date:** Aug.–frost. **Varieties:** Brilliant (darker pink), Atropurpureum (purple), Carneum (red). **Culture:** Set purchased plants in open sun, in April in any sandy loam, or even in a gritty stony site. Space 6–9 inches apart. Stands prolonged drought and does not like wet slushy winters, otherwise hardy everywhere.
  Related plant (not illustrated):
    *Sedum Telephium.* 12–18 inches. Flowers reddish
      purple.

**SEDUM** (*Sedum sieboldi*) p. 92

This Japanese perennial, perhaps the finest of all the sedums, has no valid common name, but is widely cultivated in spite of this failure. Foliage in 3's, grayish green or bluish green. Its profuse bloom is in a terminal dense cluster, the individual flower about ½ inch wide. **Color:** Pink. **Height:** 8–12 inches. **Flowering date:** Oct.–frost. **Varieties:** Variegatum (foliage variegated). **Culture:** Set purchased plants in full sun, in April, in sandy loam, or even in a gritty or stony site. Space 6–9 inches apart. It will stand drought, but dislikes wet or slushy winters; otherwise perfectly hardy.

Related plant (not illustrated):

*Sedum alboroseum.* 12–20 inches. Flowers greenish white.

**WORM–GRASS** (*Sedum album*) p. 93

A creeping, evergreen perennial from Eurasia and North Africa which, left to itself, forms dense mats. Leaves scarcely ½ inch long, generally alternate to each other on the stem, and fleshy. **Color:** White. **Height:** 4–6 inches. **Flowering date: July. Varieties:** Murale (purple leaves and pink flowers), Roseum (rose-pink). **Culture:** Set purchased plants in Oct. or April, in sandy loam, in full sun. Space 4–6 inches apart for quick ground cover, otherwise 6–9 inches apart.

Related plants (not illustrated):

*Sedum spurium.* 4–6 inches. Flowers pale pink.

*Sedum sarmentosum.* Prostrate. Flowers yellow.

**HOUSELEEK** (*Sempervivum tectorum*) p. 92

This Eurasian perennial is not a leek and got its Latin name of *tectorum* (house roof) from its habit of growing on thatched roofs of cottages. It has a dense, basal rosette of 50–60 small leaves, the whole rosette 3–4 inches across. From its center springs an erect stem, often clothed with other rosettes of leaves, and crowned with a 1–sided, curved cluster of flowers. **Color:** Red. **Height:** 8–12 inches. **Flowering date:** July–Aug. **Varieties:** Violaceum (violet-red). **Culture:** Set purchased plants in Oct. or April, in full sun, in any ordinary garden soil. Space 6–8 inches apart. Often called Hen-and-Chickens, and cultivated so widely it has run wild and become established in many parts of the country.

Related plant (not illustrated):

*Sempervivum arachnoideum.* 3–4 inches. Flowers red.

# SAXIFRAGE FAMILY
## (*Saxifragaceae*)

NEARLY 1000 plants belong to this family, and here would come the ubiquitous hydrangea, the mock-orange, and the currant if woody plants were admitted in this book. But the exclusion of these shrubby members of the Saxifrage Family still leaves a host of rock garden perennials, some old favorites among border plants, and a few natives found in the forests of North America and suited mostly to the wild garden. The garden importance of *Saxifraga* far outweighs any other in the family, and hence the first 3 below all belong to that group, which were named *Saxifraga* because that is Latin for break and stone, in allusion to their reputed value as a remedy for gallstones!

**ROCKFOIL** (*Saxifraga aizoon*)                              p. 93
An old and very popular perennial from northern and nearly arctic regions, with a basal rosette of many, narrow, spoon-shaped leaves. From the center springs a rather weak, lax, sticky stalk with a meager cluster of flowers; not very showy and grown as much for its rosette of leaves as for its bloom. **Color:** White, but red-spotted. **Height:** 10–12 inches. **Flowering date:** July–Aug. **Varieties:** Baldensis (leaves gray), Brevifolia (short leaves), Flavescens (flowers yellow), Lagaveana (grayish leaves, red stem), Pectinata (silver-margined leaves and white but red-spotted flowers). **Culture:** Suited to open border, but best grown on rocky walls or in the rock garden. Set purchased plants in Oct. or April, in the open but shaded from midday sun if possible, in a sandy or gritty soil to which ½ teaspoonful of lime is added per plant if the site is acid. Space 8–10 inches apart.

Related plant (not illustrated):

*Saxifraga lingulata.* 8–12 inches. Flowers white.

# ROSE FAMILY
## (*Rosaceae*)

1. **Queen-of-the-Meadow** (*Filipendula Ulmaria*)  p. 113
   Prefers moist site. Summer-blooming. Rather coarse and weedy, but useful for bold effects. Related to No. 3 but taller.

2. **Bowman's-Root** (*Gillenia trifoliata*)  p. 114
   Native woodland perennial blooming in July. Suited only to shady wild garden. Usually 2–4 feet high.

3. **Dropwort** (*Filipendula hexapetala*)  p. 113
   A spirea-like perennial, blooming in June–July. Of easy culture in any ordinary garden soil.

4. **Avens** (*Geum chiloense*)  p. 115
   Popular Chilean perennial, often double-flowered and showy. Summer-blooming, about 12–20 inches high.

5. **Goatsbeard** (*Aruncus sylvester*)  p. 114
   Spirea-like perennial, 4–6 feet high, June–flowering. Prefers partial shade; a fine border accent.

6. **New Zealand Bur** (*Acaena microphylla*)  p. 116
   Should be confined to sandy or gritty soils in the rock garden, and not easy to grow. Flowers July to frost.

7. **Japanese Burnet** (*Sanguisorba obtusa*)  p. 114
   A Japanese perennial, less grown than it should be. Summer-blooming, 18–30 inches high. Prefers moist site.

8. **Cinquefoil** (*Potentilla pyrenaica*)  p. 115
   A perennial, 12–20 inches high, flowering in June–July. Of easy culture in any ordinary porous garden soil.

9. **Cinquefoil** (*Potentilla nepalensis*)  p. 115
   A rose-colored relative of No. 8. Summer-blooming, 14–24 inches high. Prefers porous sandy loam.

# GERANIUM FAMILY (*Geraniaceae*), 1–3
# WORD SORREL FAMILY (*Oxalidaceae*), 4
# FLAX FAMILY (*Linaceae*), 5
# CITRUS FAMILY (*Rutaceae*), 6
# SPURGE FAMILY (*Euphorbiaceae*), 7–9

1. **Cranesbill or Hardy Geranium**
   (*Geranium grandiflorum*)                    **p. 118**
   An Asiatic perennial with showy, spring-blooming flowers.
   Height 8–15 inches. Profuse bloomer of easy culture.

2. **Cranesbill or Hardy Geranium**
   (*Geranium sanguineum*)                      **p. 117**
   Related to No. 1, but taller and with pale foliage. Flowers profuse in June–July. Thrives nearly everywhere.

3. **Heron's-Bill** (*Erodium chrysanthum*)     **p. 118**
   A Grecian perennial, suited only to gritty or sandy soils in the rock garden. Height 2–4 inches. Blooms June–July.

4. **Wood Sorrel** (*Oxalis adenophylla*)       **p. 119**
   Not hardy north of Washington, D.C., and difficult to grow unless in gritty or sandy soil in rock garden. Blooms in June–July.

5. **Flax** (*Linum narbonnense*)               **p. 119**
   A weak-stemmed perennial with ephemeral flowers that bloom, in succession, from July to frost. Height 12–20 inches.

6. **Gas-Plant** (*Dictamnus albus*)            **p. 120**
   An aromatic perennial, the summer bloom not showy, but its exhalation ignitable. Does better if left undisturbed for years.

7. **Castor-Oil-Plant** (*Ricinus communis*)    **p. 121**
   Gigantic annual (6–15 feet high) grown mostly as a striking foliage plant for summer bedding. Seeds poisonous.

8. **Snow-on-the-Mountain** (*Euphorbia marginata*)   **p. 121**
   Annual not over 20 inches high, grown mostly for its white-margined leaves. Flowers inconspicuous, blooming in summer.

9. **Mexican Fire-Plant** (*Euphorbia heterophylla*)   **p. 123**
   Related to florist's Poinsettia, but an outdoor annual. Height 1–3 feet. Of easy culture in any ordinary garden soil.

**SAXIFRAGA** (*Saxifraga decipiens*)                                    p. 93

Primarily a rock garden perennial from the mountains of Europe and without a common name, although grown by many rock garden enthusiasts and by some others. It grows in dense tufts, with a crowd of small wedge-shaped leaves that are cut into 3–5 segments. Flowers few, but each one about ½ inch wide. **Color:** White. **Height:** 6–12 inches. **Flowering date:** May–June. **Varieties:** Many in England, but few here, among them Crimson King (red). **Culture:** Set purchased plants in Oct., in a gritty or sandy soil to which ½ a teaspoonful of lime per plant is added if the soil is acid. Space 5–7 inches apart and choose site shaded from midday sun if possible.

   Related plant (not illustrated):

   *Saxifraga virginiensis.* 6–9 inches. Flowers white.

**LONDON PRIDE** (*Saxifraga umbrosa*)                                    p. 93

An old and popular European perennial, much grown in England, but not as much here as it should be. In Ireland often called St. Patrick's Cabbage. It has a basal rosette of thickish leaves nearly 2½ inches wide and often red on the underside, as are the flower stalks. **Color:** White. **Height:** 8–14 inches. **Flowering date:** June. **Varieties:** None. **Culture:** Set purchased plants in any ordinary garden soil, in full sun or partial shade, in Oct. or April, preferably in cooler regions as it does not thrive in hot, dry places. Space 6–9 inches apart.

**SIBERIAN TEA** (*Bergenia crassifolia*)                                    p. 93

A stout, rather coarse Siberian perennial but much prized for its very early and profuse bloom. Leaves large, thick, often 8–10 inches long, half as broad, and narrowed at the base into a winged or sheathing leafstalk. Flowers standing well above the leaves, on purplish or reddish stalks, in dense, showy clusters. **Color:** Rose-pink, lilac, or purple. **Height:** 12–18 inches. **Flowering date:** March–April. **Varieties:** None. **Culture:** Set purchased plants in Oct., in any ordinary garden soil, in full sun or partial shade, preferably in cooler regions since it dislikes hot, dry summers. Space 10–14 inches apart. Often offered as *Saxifraga crassifolia*.

Related plant (not illustrated):
> *Bergenia cordifolia.* 12–18 inches. Flowers rose-pink.

## CORAL BELLS (*Heuchera sanguinea*) p. 93

Popular with the florists for forcing and widely grown in the border for its showy bloom, this perennial from the cooler mountains of N.M., Ariz., and Mexico is one of the best garden plants in the Saxifrage Family. It has chiefly basal but long-stalked leaves and a narrow cluster of apparently bell-shaped flowers. **Color:** Typically pink, but see below. **Height:** 12–20 inches. **Flowering date:** June. **Varieties:** Perry's White (white), Gracillima Rosea (more slender, and rose-pink), Rosamundi (coral), Matin Bells (red). **Culture:** Set purchased plants in Oct. or April, in partial shade, or full sun if shade is unavailable, in any ordinary garden soil but not in a wet site. Space 8–10 inches apart and leave alone.

Related plant (not illustrated):
> *Heuchera americana.* 15–25 inches. Flowers greenish white.

## FOAM FLOWER (*Tiarella cordifolia*) p. 93

A beautiful little woodland perennial from the forests of eastern North America, suited only to the wild garden but not difficult to grow. It has basal, heart-shaped leaves, and such a profusion of small white flowers that *en masse* the forest floor seems carpeted with a white foam. **Color:** White. **Height:** 6–8 inches. **Flowering date:** May–June. **Varieties:** None. **Culture:** Set purchased plants (from a wild-flower dealer) in Oct. or April, in partial or complete shade of trees (no evergreens), in a rich, woodland soil which is definitely acid. Space 5–7 inches apart and leave it alone.

## MITREWORT (*Mitella diphylla*) p. 112

Often called Bishop's-Cap or Fairy-Cap, this close relative of the Foam Flower is a perennial from the forests of eastern North America and to be grown only in the wild garden. It has basal and stem leaves, the latter in pairs, and a delicate, small cluster of flowers that are not particularly showy. **Color:** White. **Height:** 10–18 inches. **Flowering date:** May–June. **Varieties:** None. **Cul-

Left: Mitrewort (*Mitella diphylla*), p. 111. Right: Astilbe
(*Astilbe japonica*), below.

**ture:** Set purchased plants (from a wild-flower dealer) in Oct.
or April, in deep shade, in a moist but not wet site, in rich woodland soil that is definitely acid. Space 5–9 inches apart and leave
it alone. Often called Coolwort.

**ASTILBE** (*Astilbe japonica*)                                    above
This is the plant often forced by the florists and sold under the
incorrect name of Spirea (it is not a *Spiraea*). It is a Japanese
perennial with divided or compound leaves and a spire-like terminal cluster of small but numerous flowers, the spike very handsome. Easily grown in the border. **Color:** White. **Height:** 12–30
inches. **Flowering date:** May. **Varieties:** None. **Culture:** Easy
in any ordinary garden soil. Set purchased plants in full sun,
in Oct. or April, and space 20–30 inches apart.
     Related plant (not illustrated):
          *Astilbe davidi.* 4–6 feet. Flowers pink.

# ROSE FAMILY
## (*Rosaceae*)

A HUGE family (over 2000 species) rich in ornamental shrubs and trees (flowering cherry, flowering crabapple, cotoneaster, spirea, rose, and hawthorn), but comparatively meager in garden perennials or annuals. This deficiency in garden flowers scarcely suggests the fact that the Rose Family is one of the most important horticulturally, for besides the ornamental shrubs' and trees it contains the strawberry, blackberry, raspberry, pear, peach, apple, plum, quince, and almond. The following 10 flowers and their relatives constitute most of the perennials likely to be in general cultivation. All have 4 or 5 petals (except in double-flowered varieties) and numerous stamens. All those below have dry fruits (capsules or tiny pods), quite unlike the luscious fruits so common in the Rose Family.

**DROPWORT** (*Filipendula hexapetala*)          p. 108
A stout spirea-like Eurasian perennial, often sold (and catalogued) as a *Spiraea,* with much divided, mostly basal leaves 8–15 inches long, the ultimate segments fernlike. Flowers small but numerous, and crowded in a terminal branched cluster. **Color:** White. **Height:** 15–30 inches. **Flowering date:** June–July. **Varieties:** Flore-pleno (double-flowered). **Culture:** Set purchased plants, in Oct. or April, in full sun, in any ordinary garden soil and space 1–2 feet apart. Commonly grown in the border and often forced by florists for winter use. Generally, but incorrectly, offered as *Spiraea filipendula.*

**QUEEN–OF–THE–MEADOW** (*Filipendula Ulmaria*) p. 108
Resembling the Dropwort but taller, the leaves less divided and prominently white-felty on the underside. Originally from Eurasia it has escaped from gardens here and is frequently found wild in roadside ditches. **Color:** White. **Height:** 3–5 feet. **Flowering date:** July–Aug. **Varieties:** Flore-pleno (double-flowered). **Culture:** Set purchased plants in open sun, in Oct. or April, preferably in moist site, and in almost any soil. Space 2–3 feet apart. Often sold as *Spiraea Ulmaria.*

**JAPANESE BURNET** (*Sanguisorba obtusa*)  p. 108
A Japanese relative of our native burnet (*Sanguisorba canadensis*),
but much more handsome because of its showy crimson bloom.
It has compound leaves, the leaflets toothed. Flowers in spikes
that are about 3 inches long and nod at the tip. **Color:** Crimson.
**Height:** 18–30 inches. **Flowering date:** July–Aug. **Varieties:**
None. **Culture:** Set purchased plants in Oct. or April, in full sun,
in any ordinary garden soil and in a moist but not wet site. Space
20–25 inches apart. Not common in cultivation and often offered
under the incorrect name of *Poterium obtusatum.*
    Related plant (not illustrated):
        American Burnet (*Sanguisorba canadensis*). 3–5 feet.
        Flowers white.

**GOATSBEARD** (*Aruncus sylvester*)  p. 108
An Asiatic, bold, rather striking perennial with much dissected
feathery foliage and masses of small white flowers in an open,
branched cluster. It is often mistaken for a *Spiraea,* or for *Astilbe,*
and may be offered under either name. **Color:** White. **Height:**
4–6 feet. **Flowering date:** June. **Varieties:** None. **Culture:** Set
purchased plants in Oct. or April, in partial shade, in any ordinary
garden soil. Space 2½–5 feet apart.
    Related plant (not illustrated):
        American Goatsbeard (*Aruncus dioicus*). 4–6 feet.
        Flowers white.

**BOWMAN'S–ROOT** (*Gillenia trifoliata*)  p. 108
A wandlike perennial of the forests of eastern North America,
often called Indian Physic from the emetic properties of its root.
Leaves usually 3-parted, the small flower in a terminal, branched
cluster. Suited only to the wild garden. **Color:** White. **Height:**
2–4 feet. **Flowering date:** July. **Varieties:** None. **Culture:** Set
purchased roots (from a wild-flower dealer) in rich woods soil,
not especially acid, in Oct. or April, under partial or complete
shade of trees (no evergreens). Space 18–25 inches apart, and
leave alone.
    Related plant (not illustrated):
        American Ipecac (*Gillenia stipulata*). 2–4 feet. Flowers
        white.

**CINQUEFOIL** (*Potentilla pyrenaica*) p. 108
The cinquefoils comprise a large group (over 200 species), many of them weedy, but this and the next are both rather showy perennials. *Potentilla pyrenaica* comes from the Pyrenees and is a stout, somewhat arching plant with 5 leaflets arranged finger-fashion, its flowers nearly 1 inch wide, in loose clusters. **Color:** Golden yellow. **Height:** 12–20 inches. **Flowering date:** June–July. **Varieties:** None. **Culture:** Set purchased plants in full sun, in a porous, sandy loam, in Oct. or April. Space 9–15 inches apart, and every three years take up and divide in spring or fall and replant, since it is apt to die out if crowded.
Related plants (not illustrated):
> *Potentilla grandiflora.* 6–15 inches. Flowers golden yellow.
> *Potentilla argyrophylla.* 12–18 inches. Flowers yellow.

**CINQUEFOIL** (*Potentilla nepalensis*) p. 108
A showy Himalayan perennial, with large basal leaves (nearly 12 inches long) and smaller leaves on the stem. Flowers nearly 1 inch wide, long-stalked, and in branching clusters. **Color:** Rose-red. **Height:** 14–24 inches. **Flowering date:** July–Aug. **Varieties:** Miss Willmott (salmon-pink and dwarf). **Culture:** Set purchased plants, in Oct. or April, in full sun, in a porous, sandy loam and space 10–15 inches apart. Every third or fourth year lift and divide clumps and replant in spring or fall, since it tends to die out if crowded.
Related plants (not illustrated):
> *Potentilla russelliana.* 12–20 inches. Flowers scarlet.
> *Potentilla atrosanguinea.* 12–18 inches. Flowers dark purple or red.

**AVENS** (*Geum chiloense*) p. 108
A very popular Chilean hairy perennial, much grown for its scarlet bloom. Its leaves are divided into segments, the terminal one larger than the others. Flowers nearly 1½ inches wide, the normally 5 petals much more numerous in double-flowered horticultural varieties. It has long, silky, plumed fruits. **Color:** Red or scarlet. **Height:** 12–20 inches. **Flowering date:** July–Aug. **Varieties:** Plenum (double-flowered and red), Mrs. Bradshaw

(double-flowered, orange-red), Lady Stratheden (double-flowered, yellow), Orange Queen (double-flowered, orange-scarlet). **Culture:** Set purchased plants in Oct. or April, in full sun, in a sandy loam, and space 10–15 inches apart. Lift, divide, and replant in spring or fall every third or fourth year, because it tends to die out if crowded. In severe climates provide a winter mulch of salt hay or straw. Generally offered under the incorrect name of *Geum atrosanguineum*.

Related plant (not illustrated):

> *Geum montanum*. 8–12 inches. Flowers golden yellow. Generally offered under the incorrect name of *Geum heldreichi*.

**MOUNTAIN AVENS** (*Dryas octopetala*)                        p. 122

A prostrate Eurasian perennial, grown mostly in the rock garden, and often forming dense mats. It is somewhat woody at the base and has nearly evergreen leaves that are white-felty beneath. Flowers solitary at the end of slender stalks, about 1½ inches wide. Fruit silky and plumed. **Color:** White. **Height:** 3–5 inches. **Flowering date:** June–July. **Varieties:** None. **Culture:** Set purchased plants in the rock garden, in full sun, in Oct. or April, in a sandy or gritty soil, and space 3–5 inches apart. Each spring apply a top-dressing ½ inch deep of a half-and-half mixture of gritty chips and leafmold. Not easy to grow.

Related plant (not illustrated):

> *Dryas suendermanni*. 3–5 inches. Flowers opening yellow, then white.

**NEW ZEALAND BUR** (*Acaena microphylla*)                        p. 108

A tiny New Zealand evergreen, ground-covering perennial suitable only to the rock garden. Leaves very small, greenish bronze. Flowers without petals, in small, prickly headlike clusters, the spines on the clusters nearly 1 inch long. **Color:** Crimson. **Height:** 2–4 inches. **Flowering date:** July–frost, from the colored spines. **Varieties:** None. **Culture:** Set purchased plants in full sun, in April or Oct., in the rock garden in a sandy or gritty soil where no standing water can collect in winter. Space 3–5 inches apart, and north of Philadelphia provide a winter mulch of light strawy manure or salt hay, which must be removed (not dug in) in the spring. Not easy to grow, but unique as one of the few New Zealand perennials hardy outdoors here.

Related plant (not illustrated):

> *Acaena buchanani.* 2–4 inches. Leaves bluish gray; spines of flower cluster yellow.

# GERANIUM FAMILY
## (*Geraniaceae*)

A CONFUSING family to the amateur, for it contains, among garden plants two distinct types. The first is what the florists and everyone (but the botanist) call "geranium," which is actually derived from South African plants of the genus *Pelargonium.* As this has irregular, spurred flowers it is easily distinguished from those below, and should be sought among other plants with irregular flowers (see p. 161). Those below belong to the genus *Geranium* and are commonly called Cranesbill or Wild Geranium; or to *Erodium,* which is the Heron's-bill. Both have perfectly regular, symmetrical flowers and are hardy outdoors, which the Garden Geranium (*Pelargonium*) is not, except in very mild climates.

**CRANESBILL or HARDY GERANIUM** (*Geranium sanguineum*) p. 109

The most popular of the Cranesbills for the open border, this Eurasian perennial is erect in habit, has white-hairy foliage, the leaves 5–7 parted, and rather showy flowers about ¾ inch wide. **Color:** Rose-purple. **Height:** 12–18 inches. **Flowering date:** June–July. **Varieties:** None. **Culture:** Set purchased plants in Oct. or April, in full sun or partial shade, in any ordinary garden soil, and space 8–12 inches apart. It is easy to grow and thrives nearly everywhere.

Related plants (not illustrated):

> Wild Geranium (*Geranium maculatum*). 8–12 inches. Flowers pink.
>
> *Geranium endressi.* 12–18 inches. Flowers rose-pink.

## CRANESBILL or HARDY GERANIUM

(*Geranium grandiflorum*)                                    p. 109

An Asiatic perennial, very popular for its showy bloom and its handsome 5–parted leaves. Its striking flowers are nearly 1½ inches wide, the 5 petals with purple-streaked veins. Of easy culture in the open border. **Color:** Lilac, streaked with purple. **Height:** 8–15 inches. **Flowering date:** May–June. **Varieties:** None. **Culture:** Set purchased plants in full sun or partial shade, in Oct. or April, in any ordinary garden soil, and space 7–10 inches apart. Its profusion of flowers makes it a desirable border plant.

Related plant (not illustrated):

*Geranium pratense.* 18–30 inches. Flowers purple.

## HERON'S–BILL (*Erodium chrysanthum*)                    p. 109

A Grecian tufted perennial, best suited to the rock garden, with silvery-leaved, twice-compounded foliage. Flowers about ½ inch wide, not particularly showy, followed by curious, spindle-shaped fruits that coil up when fully ripe. **Color:** Yellow. **Height:** 2–4 inches. **Flowering date:** June–July. **Varieties:** None. **Culture:** Set purchased plants in full sun in the rock garden, in Oct. or April, in a sandy or gritty soil, and keep winter slush or water from its roots. Often called Stork's-Bill.

Related plant (not illustrated):

*Erodium chamaedryoides.* 3–5 inches. Flowers white, veined with rose.

# WOOD SORREL FAMILY

(*Oxalidaceae*)

A HORTICULTURALLY unimportant family of about 350 species, the root of one of them, the fabled oca, a staple food in the Andes. Most of them are herbs, but the carambola is a tree from Malaya somewhat planted in Florida. The showy plant below is the one of chief garden interest, but some of its relatives with yellow flowers are pernicious weeds. All have clover-like leaves and 5–petaled flowers.

**WOOD SORREL** (*Oxalis adenophylla*)                              p. 109
A Chilean perennial, related to the shamrock, mostly grown in greenhouses for winter bloom, but hardy outdoors south of Washington, D.C., if cultural directions are carefully followed. It has tuberous roots and notched leaflets. Flowers few in a small cluster on a fine, slender stalk. **Color:** Pink, but veined deeper pink. **Height:** 3–5 inches. **Flowering date:** June–July. **Varieties:** None. **Culture:** Plant purchased tubers, 1–2 inches deep, in sandy or gritty soil in the rock garden, in Oct. It will die down after blooming and can "rest" outdoors south of Washington, D.C., if winter slush and water are kept from its roots. Not easy to grow.

Related plants (not illustrated):

> *Oxalis Acetosella.* 3–5 inches. Flowers white, pink-veined. Hardy outdoors.
> *Oxalis lasiandra.* 4–6 inches. Flowers rosy crimson. Not hardy outdoors.

# FLAX FAMILY
## (*Linaceae*)

A SMALL but industrially important family chiefly of herbs, one of which is the source of both linen and linseed oil. From the garden standpoint only the one below is of much interest, except for an annual relative. Both have the leaves arranged alternately, and there are no marginal teeth; flowers are 5–petaled.

**FLAX** (*Linum narbonnense*)                              p. 109
A delicate European perennial that blooms from seed the first year and persists afterward as a true perennial. It has rather weak stems, narrow leaves, and a profusion of solitary flowers that are about 1½ inches wide. The blooms last only a day but the plant continues flowering all summer. **Color:** Sky-blue with a white "eye." **Height:** 12–20 inches. **Flowering date:** July–frost. **Varieties:** None. **Culture:** Sow seeds ¼ inch deep in almost any soil but a rich one, when trees leaf out, in full sun.

Thin out so plants stand 4–6 inches apart. Do not try to transplant seedlings, since they resent it. A related annual (*Linum usitatissimum*) is the source of linen.

Related plants (not illustrated):

> Annual Flax (*Linum grandiflorum*). 12–20 inches. Flowers pink or red.
>
> Blue Flax (*Linum perenne*). Perennial, 12–20 inches. Flowers blue.
>
> Golden Flax (*Linum flavum*). Perennial, 12–20 inches. Flowers golden yellow.

# CITRUS OR RUE FAMILY
## (*Rutaceae*)

A HIGHLY aromatic family of chiefly tropical shrubs and trees, comprising the orange, lemon, grapefruit, and several other edible or ornamental trees. A mere handful of herbs are fit for temperate climates, and the Gas-Plant is the only one likely to interest the amateur. It has aromatic leaves that are arranged alternately, and 5-petaled flowers. It is often called the Rue Family from the bitter juice of one of its undershrubs.

**GAS–PLANT** (*Dictamnus albus*)                              p. 109
A peculiarly aromatic Eurasian perennial, so called because the strong odor of its foliage, and particularly of its flowers, creates a "gas" that can be ignited with a match on a windless evening. Once established should be let alone, for it does not tolerate moving. The leaves are compound, and the few flowers not especially showy. **Color:** White. **Height:** 2–3 feet. **Flowering date:** July–Aug. **Varieties:** Purpureus (purple), Rubrus (red), Caucasicus (larger and stouter form). **Culture:** Set purchased plants in a permanent location, in full sun, in April or Oct., in rich garden soil. Space 18–25 inches apart, and if left alone it will be one of the most permanent perennials in the garden. Often called Fraxinella and Dittany.

# SPURGE FAMILY
## (*Euphorbiaceae*)

An enormous family (over 4000 species) of overwhelmingly tropical plants, some, like rubber, being of great economic importance, but few of them of garden interest. Most of them have a milky (and often poisonous) juice and a complicated flower structure, best illustrated by the florist's Poinsettia. In this, as in so many of the Spurge Family the true flower is inconspicuous, while the colored bracts beneath it are often gorgeous. At the end of the species below is a single plant, the Japanese Spurge, which belongs to the closely related Box Family.

**CASTOR–OIL–PLANT** (*Ricinus communis*) p. 109
A huge annual herb (treelike in the tropics), grown here mostly as a striking foliage plant for summer bedding, and a native of tropical Africa. Leaves divided nearly to the middle, green, often 3 feet wide, the leafstalk attached to the middle of the blade. Flower cluster terminal, often 1–2 feet long, the individual flowers small. **Color:** Reddish yellow. **Height:** 6–15 feet. **Flowering date:** July–Aug. **Varieties:** Several unnamed ones, differing in having red stems, bluish-gray leaves, red leaves, or variegated leaves. As they are grown for their foliage, the color should be specified to the seedsman. **Culture:** Sow seeds 2 inches deep, after trees leaf out, in full sun, and in rich garden soil. Space 4–6 feet apart (more in rich soil). For quicker growth start seeds in pots in the house (6 weeks before outdoor planting is safe). Transfer seedlings outdoors when settled warm weather has arrived. The seeds, which yield castor oil, are poisonous if eaten.

**SNOW–ON–THE–MOUNTAIN**
(*Euphorbia marginata*) p. 109
An ever popular annual from the central U.S., often persisting in old gardens from self-sown seed. Leaves white-margined, as are the bracts beneath the inconspicuous flowers; it is for these bracts that the plant is grown. **Color:** White. **Height:** 12–20

inches. **Flowering date:** July–Aug. **Varieties:** None. **Culture:** Sow seeds ¼ inch deep in any, even poor, garden soil, in full sun, after warm weather is certain. Thin to 12–14 inches apart.

**FLOWERING SPURGE** (*Euphorbia corollata*)                below
A sand-inhabiting perennial from the southeastern part of North America, grown mostly for the white appendages among its inconspicuous flowers; suggesting Baby's-Breath. It is a stout, milky-juiced plant, useful for cutting. **Color:** White. **Height:** 18–24 inches. **Flowering date:** June–Aug. **Varieties:** None. **Culture:** Set purchased plants (from a wild-flower dealer) in sandy soil, in full sun, in Oct. or April. Be careful not to injure taproot, which makes digging out wild plants difficult. Space 15–20 inches apart and leave alone. Not easy to dig from the wild or to transplant. If started from seed germination takes 20–30 days.

Left: Mountain Avens (*Dryas octopetala*), p. 116. Center: Flowering Spurge (*Euphorbia corollata*), above. Right: Japanese Spurge (*Pachysandra terminalis*), p. 123.

**MEXICAN FIRE–PLANT** (*Euphorbia heterophylla*)   p. 109
Closely related to the florist's Poinsettia, this annual is not
quite so showy, but can be grown without a greenhouse
which the florist's Poinsettia demands. The leaves are green
toward the base of the stem and gradually pass from this to white
and finally to red near the flower cluster — hence its other name
of Fire-on-the-Mountain. **Color:** Of leaves and bracts, red and
white. **Height:** 1–3 feet. **Flowering date:** July–Aug. **Varieties:**
None. **Culture:** Sow seeds ¼ inch deep, in open sun, when warm
weather has arrived, in any ordinary garden soil. Space 12–18
inches apart. Often offered as *Poinsettia heterophylla.*

**JAPANESE SPURGE** (*Pachysandra terminalis*)      p. 122
Perhaps the finest evergreen ground cover ever to come from
Japan, this valuable perennial is grown wholly for its fine foliage,
since the flowers are negligible. Its habit of sending out under-
ground stems makes it quickly capture a site and a close, deep
green ground cover soon materializes. **Color:** Greenish white.
**Height:** 6–8 inches. **Flowering date:** May. **Varieties:** None.
**Culture:** Set purchased plants (by the dozens or scores for quick
effects) in full or partial shade, or in full sun, in Oct. or April,
in any ordinary garden soil, preferably with some humus in it.
Space 6–9 inches apart; if left alone will make a continuous
carpet in a year or two.

# MALLOW FAMILY
## (*Malvaceae*)

A LARGE family (about 1000 species), mostly tropical shrubs and
trees, but of considerable garden, and much more economic
interest, for it contains both cotton, the roselle, a tropical food
plant of some importance, and the okra. It is an easy family to
identify, for all the garden plants have the main veins of the leaf
arising at or near the base of the blade, and spreading fan-fashion
from that center. The flowers also are quite characteristic, in
that there is a central column of united stamens, very noticeable
in Hibiscus, and beneath each flower there is a row of fairly

## MALLOW FAMILY (*Malvaceae*), 1–3
## ROCKROSE FAMILY (*Cistaceae*), 4
## LOOSESTRIFE FAMILY (*Lythraceae*), 5
## ST. JOHN'S–WORT FAMILY (*Hypericaceae*), 6
## EVENING PRIMROSE FAMILY (*Onagraceae*), 7 and 9
## CACTUS FAMILY (*Cactaceae*), 8

1. **Rose Mallow** (*Hibiscus palustris*)　　　　　　p. 126
   Showy salt-marsh perennial, with many fine varieties. Easily grown. Blooms in Aug.–Sept. Height 3–6 feet.

2. **Wild Hollyhock** (*Sidalcea malvaeflora*)　　　　p. 127
   Californian perennial, but not very persistent; 12–20 inches high. Summer-blooming and showy. Needs rich soil.

3. **Hollyhock** (*Althaea rosea*)　　　　　　　　p. 126
   Often persists from self-sown seeds. Five to 9 feet high. Best varieties (among scores) are biennial in habit.

4. **Frostweed** (*Helianthemum nummularium*)　　　p. 133
   Rock garden perennial, summer-blooming, and 6–10 inches high. Not reliably hardy north of Philadelphia.

5. **Purple Loosestrife** (*Lythrum Salicaria*)　　　p. 131
   Wandlike perennial, often wild in marshes, but with several fine varieties. Height 3–4 feet. Summer-blooming.

6. **Rose-of-Sharon** (*Hypericum calycinum*)　　　p. 131
   An evergreen Eurasian perennial useful as a ground cover in shady place with sandy soil. Height 8–12 inches.

7. **Satin-Flower** (*Godetia grandiflora*)　　　　　p. 136
   Extremely showy Californian annual, 8–14 inches high. Start seedlings indoors or out. Does not thrive in hot weather.

8. **Prickly Pear** (*Opuntia compressa*)　　　　　p. 134
   A native cactus suited only to rocky or sandy sites. Summer-blooming and a ground cover in native habitat.

9. **Rocky Mountain Garland** (*Clarkia elegans*)　　p. 136
   Pacific Coast, showy annual, to be sown where wanted since transplanting seedlings is difficult. Does not thrive in hot climates.

# LOASA FAMILY (*Loasaceae*), 1
## EVENING PRIMROSE FAMILY (*Onagraceae*), 2, 3, and 5
## CARROT FAMILY (*Umbelliferae*), 4, 6, 7, and 9
## DOGWOOD FAMILY (*Cornaceae*), 8

1. **Prairie Lily** (*Mentzelia decapetala*)     **p. 132**
   Night-fragrant biennial with irritant foliage. Blooming in June–
   July. Height 9–15 inches. Sow seeds where wanted, since it
   transplants with difficulty.

2. **Sundrops** (*Oenothera fruticosa*)     **p. 135**
   Woody-stemmed native perennial, useful for dry sandy banks.
   Summer-blooming, 12–30 inches high.

3. **Evening Primrose** (*Oenothera caespitosa*)     **p. 135**
   Very showy low, native, perennial with night-fragrant, midsummer bloom. Does well in light sandy soils.

4. **Masterwort** (*Astrantia major*)     **p. 138**
   European perennial, 12–30 inches high, blooming in May–June.
   Needs moist site and partial shade.

5. **Fireweed** (*Epilobium angustifolium*)     **p. 135**
   Rampant weedy perennial to be introduced into gardens with
   caution. Height 3–4 feet. Midsummer bloom. Showy.

6. **Blue Lace-Flower** (*Trachymene caerulea*)     **p. 137**
   Delicate Australian annual, with weak stems, 18–30 inches high.
   Summer-blooming. Plant seeds in moist sandy loam. Trans-
   plants with difficulty.

7. **Goutweed** (*Aegopodium podagraria variegatum*)     **p. 138**
   A fine edging plant grown mostly for its variegated foliage,
   since flowers are rare. A perennial 8–12 inches high.

8. **Bunchberry** (*Cornus canadensis*)     **p. 139**
   Not to be attempted unless site is cool, shady, and with acid soil.
   A woodland beauty of northern regions.

9. **Sea Holly** (*Eryngium amethystinum*)     **p. 138**
   Fine European border perennial, 1–2 feet high. Plants prickly,
   the foliage bluish green. Blooms in midsummer.

conspicuous leaflike bracts, usually just beneath the flower. It contains such garden favorites as the mallows, Hollyhock, Rose-of-Sharon (a shrub), and Flowering "Maple."

**ROSE MALLOW** (*Hibiscus palustris*)                          p. 124
For many years, and by some still, this showy inhabitant of our salt marshes was called *Hibiscus Moscheutos,* and as it grows perfectly well in ordinary soil, and is very handsome, it has been the source of many horticultural forms. It has rather woody stems, is a true perennial, and has broad leaves that are white-woolly beneath. Its flowers are often 3–6 inches wide. **Color:** Typically white or pink, sometimes with a darker "eye" in the center, but see below. **Height:** 3–6 feet. **Flowering date:** Aug.–Sept. **Varieties:** Many, a reasonable selection might include Crimson Eye (white with scarlet center), Meehan's Mallow Marvels (white, pink, red, vermilion, or scarlet), White Perfection (white), Meehan's Pink (pink), Crimson Wonder (vermilion), Poinsettia (scarlet), Clown (white, pink-veined), Satan (crimson-red), Fresno (silvery pink). **Culture:** Set purchased plants, in Oct. or April, in full sun, in a rich garden soil, preferably in a moist site. Space 2–4 feet apart (depending on variety). Sometimes, incorrectly, called the Marsh Mallow.
   Related plants (not illustrated):
   *Hibiscus coccineus.* 8–10 feet. Flowers scarlet.
   *Hibiscus grandiflorus.* 3–5 feet. Flowers pink, with a
   red "eye."

**HOLLYHOCK** (*Althaea rosea*)                          p. 124
Originally a short-lived Chinese perennial, the Hollyhock, after a thousand years of cultivation, is practically always grown as a biennial or as an annual, and in both cases it is apt to persist from self-sown seeds. It is a stiffish, erect plant with large (sometimes lobed) leaves, and a stiff, terminal spike of flowers that bloom from the bottom upward. In many varieties the flowers are double, and in some the petals are fringed or crisped. **Color:** Typically white or pink, but see below. **Height:** 5–9 feet. **Flowering date:** July–Aug. **Varieties:** Many, but unstable as to names

or colors. Order by color, those available being, scarlet, maroon, white, salmon, cerise, and yellow. Order, also, as to whether single-flowered, double-flowered, or crisped types are desired. **Culture:** For annual kinds (not especially recommended), sow seed ½ inch deep in any ordinary garden soil, as soon as warm weather has arrived. They will bloom the same year. Space 2–3 feet apart. For biennial (and by far the best kinds), sow seeds ½ inch deep, outdoors in July. Transplant seedlings in Oct. to permanent site, which should be in full sun and in any ordinary garden soil. Space 2–3 feet apart. If the site is windy, Hollyhocks need staking.

**WILD HOLLYHOCK** (*Sidalcea malvaeflora*)  p. 124
A Californian perennial, often there called Checkerbloom, its lower leaves roundish, the upper ones cut into narrow segments. Flowers numerous, in many-bloomed spikes, the individual flower about 1½ inches wide, the petals blunt or notched. **Color:** Pink. **Height:** 12–20 inches. **Flowering date:** July–Aug. **Varieties:** Rosy Gem (rose-pink). **Culture:** Set purchased plants in full sun, in Oct. or April, in a good sandy loam, and space 10–15 inches apart. Although a true perennial, it is a fleeting one so dig up, divide, and replant every second or third year, enriching the ground with a forkful of manure per plant.

**TREE MALLOW** (*Lavatera trimestris splendens*)  p. 128
A widely grown annual from the Mediterranean region, with flowers often 4 inches wide, the petals blunt or notched. Its leaves are irregularly round-toothed. Flowers showy, with 3–9 leaflets beneath each bloom. **Color:** Pink. **Height:** 2–3 feet. **Flowering date:** July–frost (if later sowings are made). **Varieties:** Loveliness (pink, shaded carmine). **Culture:** Sow seeds when warm weather has arrived, ¼ inch deep in a sandy, rich loam, moist but well drained, and in full sun. For succession of bloom repeat sowing until nights get really hot. Bloom is poor and plants may die in hot places. Space 15–20 inches apart.

**POPPY MALLOW** (*Callirhoë involucrata*)  p. 128
A prairie perennial from the central U.S., not much grown as a

garden plant, its divided leaves cut almost to the center. Flowers up to 2½ inches wide, usually solitary at the leaf joints, the petals blunt and irregularly, but slightly fringed. **Color:** Red-purple. **Height:** 12–20 inches. **Flowering date:** June–Aug. **Varieties:** None. **Culture:** Set purchased plants in a sandy loam, or even in a more sandy site, in full sun, in April or Oct. Space 9–15 inches apart. It will not thrive in moist places.

Left: Tree Mallow (*Lavatera trimestris splendens*), p. 127. Center: Musk Mallow (*Malva moschata*), below. Right: Poppy Mallow (*Callirhoë involucrata*), p. 127.

**MUSK MALLOW** (*Malva moschata*)                              above
Slightly musk-scented perennial from Europe and a not uncommon escape from gardens, hence often wild in many parts of this country and Canada. Its leaves are divided almost to the center, the segments narrow. Flowers nearly 2 inches wide, mostly from the upper leaf joints. **Color:** Pink. **Height:** 12–20 inches. **Flowering date:** June–Aug. **Varieties:** Alba (white).

**Culture:** Set purchased plants in full sun in any ordinary garden soil, in April or Oct. and space 10–15 inches apart. It is of easy culture. Sometimes called Musk Rose.

**PRAIRIE MALLOW** (*Sphaeralcea coccinea*) p. 130

A not very commonly cultivated prairie perennial from the central part of North America, but well suited to poor soils and sandy places. Commonly called False Mallow, and with hoary, 5-parted leaves and terminal clusters of flowers that are about 1 inch wide. **Color:** Brick-red. **Height:** 8–12 inches. **Flowering date:** July–Aug. **Varieties:** None. **Culture:** Set purchased plants in full sun, in Oct. or April in sandy or poor soil and space 6–9 inches apart. It does not like moist or wet sites. Often known as *Malvastrum coccineum.*

**ANODA** (*Anoda hastata*) p. 130

A little-cultivated annual from central and northern South America, with lobed leaves and solitary flowers at the leaf joints, the flowers scarcely 1½ inches wide. **Color:** Blue or white. **Height:** 12–18 inches. **Flowering date:** July–Aug. **Varieties:** None. **Culture:** Sow seeds ¼ inch deep in any ordinary garden soil after settled warm weather has arrived. Space 10–15 inches apart. For earlier bloom start seeds indoors (6–8 weeks before outdoor planting is safe) and transfer seedlings outdoors when trees leaf out.

**FLOWERING "MAPLE"** (*Abutilon hybridum*) p. 130

A hybrid shrub, probably of tropical American origin, but its true parentage is unknown. It is commonly grown in green-houses, will stand no frost, but in its many decorative forms often used as a summer bedding plant. If so used it must be brought into the greenhouse over the winter. It is a small shrub with maple-like leaves, hence its misleading common name (it has nothing to do with any maple). It has attractive but few flowers. They are solitary at the leaf joints, of separate petals, but these forming a bell-shaped flower, hence its equally mis-leading name of Chinese Bellflower. **Color:** Various, see below. **Height:** 18–36 inches. **Flowering date:** July–Aug. **Varieties:**

Boule de Neige (white), Golden Fleece (yellow), Sayitzi (grown for white-edged foliage), Fireball (scarlet), Gold Ball (golden). **Culture:** Set purchased plants (to be had only from a greenhouse) in full sun or partial shade, only when settled warm weather has arrived, in any ordinary garden soil. Space 20–30 inches apart, and dig up before autumn cold kills them. If wanted as house plant over the winter (in warm room with plenty of light and frequent watering) it is better to leave the plant in its pot, burying it to the rim in summer and lifting it for indoor culture when cold weather threatens.

Left: Prairie Mallow (*Sphaeralcea coccinea*), p. 129. Center: Anoda (*Anoda hastata*), p. 129. Right: Flowering "Maple" (*Abutilon hybridum*), p. 129.

# LOOSESTRIFE FAMILY
## (*Lythraceae*)

IF THIS book covered shrubs here would come the spectacular crape myrtle and a few other trees and shrubs of warm regions such as the one that yields henna. But of over 400 species only a handful are garden plants, the Purple Loosestrife being the most showy. Leaves generally oppositely arranged, without marginal teeth. Flowers with 4–6 petals.

**PURPLE LOOSESTRIFE** (*Lythrum Salicaria*)      p. 124
Often called Purple Willow-Herb or Red Sally, this Eurasian perennial has commonly escaped from cultivation to marshes in many places in eastern North America. It is a tall, wandlike plant, woody at the base, has a 4-sided stem, opposite willow-like leaves, and showy flowers in a terminal, leafy spike. **Color:** Pinkish purple. **Height:** 3–4 feet. **Flowering date:** July–Aug. **Varieties:** Morden's Pink (showy and pink), Roseum Superbum (dark pink), Tomentosum (white-felty foliage), Dropmore Purple (bluish purple). **Culture:** Set purchased roots in Oct. or April, in full sun, in any ordinary garden soil, preferably, but not exclusively in a moist site. Space 2–3 feet apart. Although a marsh plant it will grow in ordinary soil, especially the variety Morden's Pink, which will be happy anywhere.

# ST. JOHN'S-WORT FAMILY
## (*Hypericaceae*)

RESINOUS-DOTTED foliage and chiefly yellow flowers are the main characteristics of this rather unimportant family of several hundred species. Of these only the one below is of garden interest, together with its close relatives. They have mostly stalkless leaves, arranged oppositely, and without marginal teeth.

**ROSE–OF–SHARON** (*Hypericum calycinum*)      p. 124
A low, Eurasian evergreen (or nearly so) perennial useful as a

ground cover in shady and sandy places. Flowers not numerous but nearly 2 inches wide. **Color:** Yellow. **Height:** 8–12 inches. **Flowering date:** July–Aug. **Varieties:** None. **Culture:** Set purchased plants in partially or wholly shady place (not under evergreens), in Oct. or April, preferably in a sandy soil. Space 6–9 inches apart and keep winter slush and standing water from its roots. Often called Aaron's-Beard.

Related plants (not illustrated):

Bush Broom (*Hypericum prolificum*). 4–5 feet. Flowers yellow.

*Hypericum frondosum*. 20–30 inches. Flowers yellow. (Often offered as *Hypericum aureum*.)

*Hypericum moserianum*. 12–20 inches. Flowers yellow. Not reliably hardy north of Washington, D.C.

*Hypericum repens*. Prostrate. Flowers yellow. Not reliably hardy north of Washington, D.C.

# LOASA FAMILY
## (*Loasaceae*)

NEARLY 200 species of herbs from the New World, all but the one below having stinging hairs on the foliage; the Prairie Lily having merely barbed hairs. Leaves alternately arranged, coarsely toothed. Flowers with 10 petals, night-fragrant in the one below, followed by a dry pod that opens at the top.

**PRAIRIE LILY** (*Mentzelia decapetala*)                        p. 125
A night-fragrant biennial herb from the prairies of the central U.S. and of secondary garden importance. It has much cut leaves and is clothed with barbed hairs (irritating to some, almost poisonous to others). Flowers 3–5 inches wide, opening toward evening, and deliciously fragrant. **Color:** White or yellow. **Height:** 9–15 inches. **Flowering date:** June–July. **Varieties:** None. **Culture:** Sow seeds in full sun after warm weather arrives, in a sandy loam, ¼ inch deep, and scattered where

wanted. Thin to 6–9 inches apart, since the seedlings usually die if transplanted. It will sometimes bloom from seed the first year, and often self-sown seed will perpetuate it in favorable sites.

Related plant (not illustrated):

> *Mentzelia lindleyi.* 1–4 feet, an annual. Flowers golden yellow. Often offered as *Bartonia aurea.*

# ROCKROSE FAMILY
## (*Cistaceae*)

Horticulturally an unimportant family of about 150 species of generally uninteresting and often weedy herbs, the chief exception being the one below and its relatives.

**FROSTWEED** (*Helianthemum nummularium*)          p. 124

A rock garden perennial, its foliage glistening with small frosty dots that make the plant look as if covered with hoarfrost, especially on the underside of the leaves. It is from the Mediterranean region, and is often called Sun-Rose. Its flowers last only one day, but are replaced by new ones the next. **Color:** Prevailingly yellow, but see below. **Height:** 6–10 inches. **Flowering date:** July–Aug. **Varieties:** Roseum (pink), Apricot (apricot), Ball of Gold (golden yellow), Burnt Orange (dark orange), Chocolate Queen (reddish brown), Sun Gold (golden yellow), Golden Bronze (bronze), and over 50 others. **Culture:** Set purchased plants, in Oct. or April, preferably in the rock garden, in a well-drained, gritty or sandy soil to which has been added enough lime to whiten the ground and well mixed with the soil. Keep winter slush and water away from its roots. Not reliably hardy north of Philadelphia and there needing a winter mulch of straw or evergreen boughs (no manure.) Space 5–8 inches apart. Sometimes called Sun-Rose. Often offered under the incorrect names of *Helianthemum chamaecistus* or *Helianthemum vulgare.* Not an easy plant to grow, and quite unsuited to ordinary garden conditions.

# CACTUS FAMILY
### (*Cactaceae*)

A HUGE family of over 1300 species of succulent, water-storing plants, most of them horribly spiny. They reach their greatest development from our southwestern states to the Argentine, notably the giant cactus (saguaro), which may be 40 feet high and is fantastically branched. Many smaller species are in the collections of fanciers, but the one below is the only native species in the northeastern states.

**PRICKLY PEAR** (*Opuntia compressa*)                    p. 124
Our local cactus has only 1 or 2 spines, and these may be lacking. Its joints (it has no obvious leaves) are flat, oblong, or ovalish, and 3–5 inches long. Flowers showy, solitary, borne on the edge or tip of the joints, nearly 3 inches wide. **Color:** Yellow. **Height:** Prostrate. **Flowering date:** July–Aug. **Varieties:** None. **Culture:** Will only grow well in pure sand, rocky and gritty soils, or on open prairie soils that are light. Set joints in such soil, 1–2 inches deep, in full sun, preferably in April. Space 10–15 inches apart. It is offered only by dealers in cacti and is best started from joints collected from the wild. Often known as *Opuntia vulgaris,* and recently as *Opuntia humifusa.* Wear gloves in handling it, for its barbed hairs are almost impossible to extract from the skin.

# EVENING PRIMROSE FAMILY
### (*Onagraceae*)

A MODERATE-SIZED family (470 species) of prevailingly herbaceous plants, generally with only 4 petals, and often with strikingly showy flowers. Few are in cultivation, the best known being the Fuchsia. Unlike those below, all of which have regular, symmetrical ones, the Fuchsia has irregular and unsymmetrical flowers and will be found among such flowers on p. 155. The 5 garden flowers immediately following are annual or perennial plants, all except the Fireweed are natives of North America, the latter being found throughout the North Temperate Zone. All of them have rather slender pods (capsules) following the flowers, and in the Fireweed the seeds have a tuft of silky hairs clinging to them.

**EVENING PRIMROSE** (*Oenothera caespitosa*)          p. 125
An almost stemless perennial (rarely a biennial) its leaves all basal, hairy, with wavy margins, and sometimes cleft into narrow segments. Flowers day-blooming, very showy, nearly 3 inches wide, often solitary or in a few-flowered cluster, typically cross-like. **Color:** White or pink. **Height:** 4–8 inches. **Flowering date:** July–Aug. **Varieties:** None. **Culture:** Set purchased roots in full sun, in Oct. or April, in a light, somewhat sandy loam. Space 5–9 inches apart and avoid wet or heavy clay soil.
   Related plants (not illustrated):
      *Oenothera missouriensis.* 8–12 inches. Flowers yellow.
      *Oenothera speciosa.* 1–2 feet. Flowers white, changing
         to pink.

**SUNDROPS** (*Oenothera fruticosa*)                    p. 125
A native American perennial, with rather woody, reddish stems, its leaves lance-shaped to oblong, generally short-stalked. Flowers nearly 2 inches wide, day-blooming, the 4 petals broad. It is particularly suited for dry, sandy banks and is common in such places throughout the eastern U.S. **Color:** Yellow. **Height:** 12–30 inches. **Flowering date:** July–Aug. **Varieties:** Youngi (strong, bushy form, with more profuse bloom), Major (profuse bloomer). **Culture:** Set purchased plants in full sun, in Oct. or April, in relatively sandy soil, and space 15–20 inches apart. Avoid wet or heavy clay soils.
   Related plant (not illustrated):
      *Oenothera glauca.* 1–2½ feet. Flowers yellow, foliage
         bluish green.

**FIREWEED** (*Epilobium angustifolium*)               p. 125
A rampant weedy perennial found throughout the North Temperate Zone, very common after forest fires, and worth cultivating only because of its showy flowers, followed by its silky-seeded

fruit, and its ease of culture. Not to be introduced into the garden unless care is used to control it, since its propensity to become a nuisance is notorious. **Color:** Rose-purple. **Height:** 3–4 feet. **Flowering date:** July–Aug. **Varieties:** None. **Culture:** Almost impossible to kill. Start purchased plants in spring or fall, in any soil, and in full sun. Space 1–2 feet apart and watch, to prevent their capturing too much ground. It has many common names, among them Giant Willow-Herb, French Willow, Blooming Sally, Rose Bay, and, in Calif., Buckweed.

**ROCKY MOUNTAIN GARLAND** (*Clarkia elegans*)   p. 124
An extremely showy annual from the Pacific Coast much prized for cutting, as a single spray, if cut while still in bud, will bloom for several days. It is a reddish-stemmed plant, stiff and erect with ovalish leaves. Flowers with 4 petals, but much doubled in most horticultural forms. **Color:** Prevailingly rose-purple, but see below. **Height:** 18–30 inches. **Flowering date:** July–Aug. **Varieties:** Vesuvius (rose-red), Salmon King (salmon), Queen Mary (carmine), Scarlet Queen (orange-scarlet), White Queen (white). All the varieties are double-flowered. **Culture:** Sow seeds in sandy loam, in partial shade, or full sun (only in cool regions), as soon as warm weather arrives. Scatter the seeds ¼ inch deep where wanted and thin to 6–8 inches, since they bloom better when reasonably crowded. It is difficult (or impossible) to transplant seedlings. The plant will fail to bloom or be killed outright in regions with hot summers.

**SATIN–FLOWER** (*Godetia grandiflora*)                    p. 124
A showy Californian annual, good for cutting, and a nearly unbranched plant. Leaves oblongish, but tapering at both ends. Flowers in a short spike, the individual flower 3–5 inches wide, dark-eyed in the center. Fruit a 4–sided pod. **Color:** Prevailingly red, but see below. **Height:** 8–14 inches. **Flowering date:** July–Aug. **Varieties:** Several, but without names or dubious ones, and best ordered by color (salmon-orange, rose, carmine, blue, white, lavender, etc.). Some are double-flowered. **Culture:** Sow seeds in partial shade, or in full sun (only in cool regions), in sandy loam, as soon as warm weather arrives. Scatter seeds where

wanted, ¼ inch deep, and thin to 5–8 inches apart; bloom is more profuse if the plants are reasonably crowded. In very hot weather the bloom is reduced and the plant may die. For earlier bloom sow seeds indoors (6–8 weeks before outdoor planting is safe). Plant seeds in paper pots or Lily cups and when trees leaf out transfer pots outdoors, cutting large holes in the pots, and plunge them to the rim. Satin-Flower does not transplant easily.

Related plant (not illustrated):

Farewell-to-Spring (*Godetia amoena*). 12–30 inches. Flowers lilac-crimson, red or white, and some double-flowered.

# CARROT FAMILY
## (*Umbelliferae*)

THE LATIN name of this family epitomizes its chief characteristic, for Umbelliferae means umbel-bearing. And all the huge family (over 2000 species) have their flowers arranged in an umbel, which means that all the individual flower stalks in a cluster arise at the same point. Common examples are the weedy Queen Anne's-Lace of our roadsides, and the huge inflorescence of the Cow Parsnip, found in swamps. The family is important, containing the carrot, parsnip, celery, dill, caraway, fennel, and parsley, but relatively unimportant so far as garden flowers are concerned. All have minute flowers (often wrongly called "rays") arranged in a simple umbel, or the umbels themselves gathered in a much branched cluster.

**BLUE LACE–FLOWER** (*Trachymene caerulea*)          p. 125
An Australian annual, common in florists' windows but easily grown in the garden, and fine for its long-lasting flowers. It is a rather weak-stemmed plant with twice- or thrice-compounded leaves, the ultimate segments of which are narrow. Flowers minute, arranged in a flat-topped umbel, suggesting a blue edition of our Queen Anne's-Lace. **Color:** Lavender-blue. **Height:** 18–30 inches. **Flowering date:** July–Aug. **Varieties:** A white

variety is sometimes offered as *Didiscus*. **Culture:** Sow seeds
outdoors, ¼ inch deep, in a sandy loam, preferably somewhat
moist, after all danger of frost. Scatter seeds where wanted and
thin to 6–9 inches apart; bloom is more profuse if plants are
reasonably crowded. It will stop blooming or die in hot climates.
For earlier bloom, sow seeds indoors (6–8 weeks before outdoor
planting is safe). Use paper pots or Lily cups and after slitting
them well plunge to the rim outdoors when warm weather arrives. It transplants with difficulty.

**MASTERWORT** (*Astrantia major*)                       p. 125
A European perennial with aromatic roots, the deeply cleft
leaves with deep marginal teeth. Flowers small, in a large umbel,
from beneath which are purplish leaflets (bracts), nearly as
showy as the flower cluster. **Color:** Pink or white. **Height:** 12–
30 inches. **Flowering date:** May–June. **Varieties:** None. **Culture:**
Set purchased plants, in Oct. or April, in partial shade, in a moist
site, the soil being of less importance than moisture. Space 15–20
inches apart. Called Masterwort from the ancient use of its roots
as an alterative. Called also Black Sanicle.

**GOUTWEED** (*Aegopodium podagraria variegatum*)      p. 125
An old, weedy medicinal herb of Europe, perennial, and once
reputed to be a specific for gout. Today it is cultivated only in
the variegated-leaved form, which makes a fine edging plant.
The flowers are negligible. Leaves with clasping stems, the leaflets prominently white-margined. **Color:** White. **Height:** 8–12
inches. **Flowering date:** June. **Varieties:** None. **Culture:** Very
simple, since it thrives anywhere. Set purchased plants (in
quantity if used as a ground cover) in any ordinary garden
soil, in Oct. or April, in full sun or partial shade. Space 6–8
inches apart if for edging or ground cover, 10–12 inches apart
if for isolated plants.

**SEA HOLLY** (*Eryngium amethystinum*)                 p. 125
The Sea Hollies are the only really showy garden plants of the
Carrot Family. This one is a stout European perennial, with
beautiful bluish-green foliage, the deeply cut leaves with spiny

margins. Flowers small, but crowded in a dense, ball-like cluster which is about ½ inch in diameter, and beneath which are bluish-green leaflets (bracts). **Color:** Bluish purple. **Height:** 1–2 feet. **Flowering date:** July–Aug. **Varieties:** None. **Culture:** Set purchased plants in April or Oct., in any ordinary garden soil, preferably in a moist site, and add a pinch of lime for each plant if the soil is acid. Space 2–3 feet apart as the plants are bushy and prickly.

# DOGWOOD OR CORNEL FAMILY
## (*Cornaceae*)

A SMALL family (less than 100 species) of showy shrubs and trees, containing the flowering dogwood and its close relative, the plant below, which is one of the only herbs in the family.

**BUNCHBERRY** (*Cornus canadensis*)      p. 125

A forest plant of the far North, or on high mountains, and suited only to the wild garden in cool regions. It is low, somewhat woody and has a basal rosette of bluntish, nearly evergreen leaves, from the center of which spring the inconspicuous, greenish flowers, which would pass notice if they were not surrounded by 4 conspicuous, pointed bracts — the whole about 1 inch wide. Berries scarlet. **Color:** Flowers greenish, bracts greenish white. **Height:** 4–6 inches. **Flowering date:** May. **Varieties:** None. **Culture:** Not to be attempted without deep shade, a highly acid soil (sphagnum moss is fine), a cool site, and preferably a fairly high elevation. Set purchased plants (only to be had from dealers in native material), in good, acid woods soil or sphagnum moss, in Oct. Space 5–7 inches apart and do not disturb or cultivate. If water is needed at planting time use only rain water. Subsequent rainfall should suffice. Not suited to the coastal plain or to ordinary garden soil. Often called Dwarf Cornel.

## PEA FAMILY (*Leguminosae*), 1–6
## VIOLET FAMILY (*Violaceae*), 7–9

**1. Sweet Pea** (*Lathyrus odoratus*)      p. 143
    Related to No. 5, but an annual needing cool sites and much
    care to produce its fragrant showy bloom. Not for careless
    growers in hot regions.

**2. Annual Lupine** (*Lupinus* hybrids)      p. 144
    An annual relative of the next, but not so showy. Sow seeds
    where wanted since transplanting is difficult.

**3. Perennial Lupine** (*Lupinus* hybrids)      p. 144
    Extraordinary showy perennials, but not suited to regions of
    great summer heat. Some of the finest varieties are 3½ feet
    high, with an immense spike.

**4. Blue False Indigo** (*Baptisia australis*)      p. 145
    A stiffish perennial, 3–4 feet high, showy, and summer-blooming.
    Not reliably hardy north of New York City.

**5. Everlasting Pea** (*Lathyrus latifolius*)      p. 143
    A rampant perennial relative of the Sweet Pea, sprawling and
    fine for covering banks. Midsummer bloom.

**6. Aaron's-Rod** (*Thermopsis caroliniana*)      p. 147
    Stiffish perennial, 3–5 feet high, good for sandy or gritty soils.
    Bloom in June–July. Not reliably hardy north of New York City.

**7. Pansy** (*Viola tricolor hortensis*)      p. 149
    So popular for bedding that few realize the exacting care needed
    to produce flowering plants from this biennial. Over 50 horti-
    cultural varieties.

**8. Tufted Pansy** (*Viola cornuta*)      p. 150
    A tufted perennial relative of the Pansy and much easier to grow.
    Height 12–20 inches. Blooms June–July.

**9. Sweet Violet** (*Viola odorata;* Royal Robe)      p. 150
    Semihardy varieties of the florist's violet, but not of easy culture
    in hot, dry places. Early spring bloom.

# BUTTERCUP FAMILY (*Ranunculaceae*), 1–3
# BLEEDING–HEART FAMILY (*Fumariaceae*), 4–6
# GERANIUM FAMILY (*Geraniaceae*), 7
# NASTURTIUM FAMILY (*Tropaeolaceae*), 8
# JEWELWEED FAMILY (*Balsaminaceae*), 9

1. **Monkshood** (*Aconitum fischeri*)        **p. 153**
   An Asiatic perennial, 4–5 feet high, easier to grow than the related larkspurs. Blooms Sept.–Oct.

2. **Larkspur** (*Delphinium* hybrids)        **p. 152**
   Magnificent but short-lived perennials partial to coolness and moisture. Height 3–8 feet. Summer-blooming.

3. **Columbine** (*Aquilegia chrysantha*)        **p. 152**
   Rocky Mountain perennial, 2–4 feet high, flowering in June–July. Easily grown in any ordinary garden soil.

4. **Corydalis** (*Corydalis cheilanthifolia*)        **p. 155**
   A weak-stemmed perennial with fugitive flowers in June–July. Needs partial shade, rich soil, little wind and no great heat.

5. **Bleeding-Heart** (*Dicentra spectabilis*)        **p. 154**
   Easily grown showy perennial, 12–24 inches high, blooming in May–June. Dissected leaves weak.

6. **Climbing Fumitory** (*Adlumia fungosa*)        **p. 154**
   A fragile, weak-stemmed native biennial, suited only to shady, windless sites in the wild garden.

7. **Garden Geranium** (*Pelargonium* hybrids)        **p. 161**
   South African perennial common everywhere and easily handled by the amateur if directions are carefully followed.

8. **Nasturtium** (*Tropaeolum* hybrids)        **p. 159**
   Popular Peruvian annual, both in dwarf and climbing varieties. Plant seed in poor soil for best bloom.

9. **Garden Balsam** (*Impatiens balsamina*)        **p. 160**
   A long-season annual to be started in the house; 6–8 weeks before outdoor planting is safe. Height 24–30 inches. Summer-blooming.

# *Flowers Irregular*

HERE belongs a considerable group of garden plants, some of them old favorites like the Sweet Pea and its relatives, the Nasturtium, the Garden Geranium, all the violets, the Larkspur and its relatives, and several others. In all of them their flowers are irregular, unsymmetrical, spurred, or lopsided — quite different from those already treated (see pp. 65–136), in which the parts of the flower are perfectly regular and symmetrical.

Flowers with irregular corollas are familiar enough in the Sweet Pea or Violet, because the spur of the latter and the "wings" in a Sweet Pea make both flowers incapable of division without uncovering the fact that all the petals of both of them are not alike; as they are, for instance, in a Buttercup. Botanists use the somewhat horrible term "zygomorphic" for such flowers. All it means is that the next 25 plants have a lack of perfect symmetry to their flowers and are hence "irregular."

They may, for ease of identification be divided thus:

*Flowers pea-like; the Pea Family. See below.*

*Flowers violet-like (except in the pansy); the Violet Family. See p. 149.*

*Flowers otherwise irregular. See p. 152.*

## PEA FAMILY
### (*Leguminosae*)

A GIGANTIC family (over 10,000 species) of shrubs, trees, vines, and herbs found all over the world, and including many timber trees, vetch, clover, peas and beans, the wisteria, and a variety of tropical gums, oils, and resins. So far as garden plants are concerned its importance is considerably less, although it contains the Sweet Pea and the lupines. In all of them the flower has an upstanding petal (the standard), 2 lateral ones (the wings) and 2 lower and more or less united ones which form the keel. All those below have compound leaves, the leaflets arranged feather-fashion in most, but fanlike in the lupines. The fruit of all is a pod, of which the common garden pea is a familiar example — actually a legume, hence the name Leguminosae.

**SWEET PEA** (*Lathyrus odoratus*) p. 140
A Sicilian annual with weak stems now found in many varieties, some of which have lost the beautiful fragrance of the originals. Stems vine-like and needing brushwood or chicken wire for support. Leaves with its leaflets tipped by a softly spiny prickle. Flowers usually 1–3 in a cluster, rarely as many as 4, all long-stalked. The individual flowers may be, in some horticultural forms, at least 2 inches wide. **Color:** All, except yellow. **Height:** 4–6 feet. **Flowering date:** June-July. **Varieties:** At least 50–60. Among them are: Spencers, which flower rather early and do not stand the heat (in all colors but yellow); Cuthbertsons, reputedly able to stand summer heat; so-called Giants (taller than the type); Early Flowering; Multiflora (reputedly with 5–6 flowers in a cluster). For fragrance choose Ambition (lavender-lilac), Cheers (pink), Fragrance (cream), Kames (white), Light Blue (blue), and Myra (salmon). **Culture:** Prepare bed weeks before sowing seed by double-digging and incorporating a wheelbarrow load of well-rotted manure to each 10 feet of row. Allow soil to settle. In a trench 2 inches deep, in late Feb. or early March, place treated seeds 3–4 inches apart and cover. Treat seeds before planting as follows: all seeds of a light color should be soaked in water 24 hours before planting; all seeds of a dark color should be similarly soaked and those that do not swell should be nicked with a file on the side away from the "eye." Germination is slow and speed is essential, if blooms are not to wither and the plants die in summer heat. Successful culture is most likely in coastal regions of New England and the Pacific Northwest, and most difficult or all but impossible in regions of great summer heat. Cheesecloth shading will sometimes help where summers are too hot. Provide brush or chicken wire support both sides of each row at time of planting.

**EVERLASTING PEA** (*Lathyrus latifolius*) p. 140
A rampant, sprawling European perennial, much resembling

the Sweet Pea and often called the Perennial Pea. It is showy, but can become a nuisance from its propensity to spread and clamber over other plants, shrubs, fences and walls. Flowers several, in a long-stalked cluster. **Color:** Prevailingly red or pink. **Height:** If erect 6–9 feet, without support sprawling or prostrate. **Flowering date:** June–Aug. **Varieties:** Albus (white), Pink Beauty (pink), White Pearl (white), Rosea (rose-pink). **Culture:** Difficult to kill and standing all kinds of soils and exposure. Plant purchased roots in spring or fall. Watch out or it will become an extremely showy pest.

Related plants (not illustrated):
> Beach Pea, on Atlantic seashore (*Lathyrus maritimus*).
> Sprawling. Flowers violet-purple.
> Beach Pea, on the Pacific seashore (*Lathyrus littoralis*).
> Sprawling. Flowers purple and white.

**ANNUAL LUPINE** (*Lupinus* hybrids)                              p. 140
Resembling the Perennial Lupines, but lower and not so showy. All of the many horticultural varieties are thought to be based upon *Lupinus hartwegi,* a Mexican annual. **Color:** Practically all. **Height:** 12–20 inches. **Flowering date:** July–Aug. **Varieties:** Many unnamed ones, in all colors. **Culture:** Sow seed ¼ inch deep, in late March or early April, in a well-drained sandy loam, in full sun or partial shade. Sow where wanted, since they resent transplanting, and space 8–12 inches apart by thinning out. They do not thrive in places with too high summer temperatures. If in cool regions a succession of sowings will provide bloom until frost.

**PERENNIAL LUPINE** (*Lupinus* hybrids)                          **p. 140**
A stout, very showy perennial, originally derived from *Lupinus polyphyllus* of western North America, but now in many forms and colors, especially among the Russell Lupines, developed by George Russell of Yorkshire. These are the finest lupines in cultivation. They have stiffish stems, leaves with 5–7 leaflets arranged finger-fashion. Flowers in a dense, terminal spike, very showy. **Color:** Yellow, white, blue, or pink. **Height:** 2–3½ feet. **Flowering date:** June–July. **Varieties:** Several unnamed, but the

Russell hybrids, which are by far the best, come in various colors, and should be specified by the desired color. **Culture:** Set purchased plants in a well-drained sandy loam, in full sun or partial shade, in April or Oct., and put where wanted as they resent transplanting. Space 2–3 feet apart. In regions of great summer heat they may stop blooming or be killed outright. Not suited to the hot coastal plain south of Del. but thriving along cool coasts of New England and the Pacific; also in cool places in the mountains. If raised from seeds (a slow procedure) nick the seeds with a file and follow directions for planting annual lupines.

Related plants (not illustrated):

Quaker Bonnets (*Lupinus perennis*). 1–2 feet. Flowers blue to white.

Texas Bluebonnet (*Lupinus subcarnosus*). 8–12 inches. Flowers blue, with a white or yellow spot. Often offered as *Lupinus texensis*.

**GENISTA** (*Genista sagittalis*)                              p. 146

A low, practically prostrate shrubby plant from Eurasia, mostly suited to the rock garden and not much cultivated. Unlike most of the Pea Family, it has only a single leaflet (often mistaken for a leaf), which is only about 1 inch long and narrow. Stems winged. Flowers pea-like, in a small terminal cluster, followed by silky pods. **Color:** Yellow. **Height:** 8–10 inches. **Flowering date:** June. **Varieties:** None. **Culture:** Set purchased plants in a well-drained sandy soil, in the rock garden, in April or Oct., preferably on a south-facing warm slope, and do not move, since they resent transplanting. Not reliably hardy north of New York City, except along the coast to Boston. Unsuited to high, cool places.

Related plant (not illustrated):

Woadwaxen (*Genista tinctoria*). 2–3 feet. Flowers yellow.

**BLUE FALSE INDIGO** (*Baptisia australis*)          p. 140

A native perennial found wild from Pa. to Texas, and often cultivated for its moderately showy bloom; often called Rattle-

bush. It is a stiffish plant with wedge-shaped leaflets that are
1–2½ inches long, and terminal clusters (2–3 inches long) of
small, pea-like flowers. **Color:** Blue. **Height:** 3–4 feet. **Flowering
date:** July–Aug. **Varieties:** None. **Culture:** Set purchased plants,
in Oct. or April, in sandy loam in full sun, and space 2–3 feet
apart. It does not like to be moved and is not reliably hardy
north of New York City. Best suited to open, relatively sandy
sites in the wild garden.

Related plant (not illustrated):

Yellow False Indigo (*Baptisia tinctoria*). 18–30 inches.
Flowers yellow.

**CROWN VETCH** (*Coronilla varia*)                          below
A pretty little European creeper, useful as a perennial ground
cover or for edging a border. It is a sprawling, weak, vine-like
plant with 12 to 25 oblong leaflets arranged feather-fashion, and

Left: Genista (*Genista sagittalis*), p. 145. Center: Goat's-Rue (*Galega
officinalis*), p. 147. Right: Crown Vetch (*Coronilla varia*), above.

small very numerous flowers in dense, long-stalked clusters. **Color:** Pink. **Height:** 9–12 inches. **Flowering date:** July–Sept. **Varieties:** None. **Culture:** Set purchased plants, in full sun, in Oct. or April, in any ordinary garden soil (it must be well drained), and space 8–12 inches apart.

### GOAT'S–RUE (*Galega officinalis*) p. 146

A vetchlike Eurasian perennial, with erect stems, the 6–8 pairs of leaflets arranged feather-fashion. Flowers pea-like, small, but in dense clusters which are both terminal and from among the leaves. **Color:** Purplish blue. **Height:** 2–3 feet. **Flowering date:** July–Aug. **Varieties:** Carnea (rose-pink), Albino (white), Hartland (lilac), Sunset (rose pink). **Culture:** Set purchased plants in Oct. or April, in any ordinary garden soil, in full sun, and space 15–18 inches apart. Not well known or much grown in this country.

### AARON'S–ROD (*Thermopsis caroliniana*) p. 140

A stout, stiffish native perennial, found wild from N.C. to Ga. and often cultivated for its lupine-like flowers. Leaflets oblong, silky on the underside. Flowers pea-like, in a stiff cluster that may be 8–12 inches long, followed by a hoary pod 2 inches long. **Color:** Yellow. **Height:** 3–5 feet. **Flowering date:** June–July. **Varieties:** None. **Culture:** Set purchased plants in full sun, in April or Oct., in a sandy loam, or even in a definitely sandy or gritty soil. Space 2–3 feet apart. It stands great heat and considerable drought, but is not reliably hardy north of New York City.

### BUSH CLOVER (*Lespedeza thunbergi*) p. 148

A shrubby plant, often dying to the ground each winter, hence herblike, but actually an Asiatic shrub with 3 leaflets and long, drooping clusters of small, pea-like flowers. **Color:** Pink or rose-purple. **Height:** 3–7 feet. **Flowering date:** Sept.–Oct. **Varieties:** None. **Culture:** Set purchased plants in April, in full sun, in a sandy loam or even in sandy or gritty soil, preferably on a south-facing slope. It stands heat and dryness better than most garden plants, but is not reliably hardy north of Philadelphia, unless cut back to the ground after blooming and covered with a winter mulch of strawy manure.

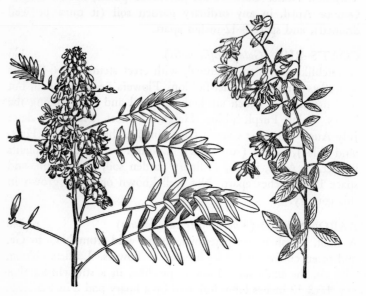

Left: Wild Senna (*Cassia marilandica*), below. Right: Bush Clover (*Lespedeza thunbergi*), p. 147.

**WILD SENNA** (*Cassia marilandica*)                                    above
A native perennial found wild from Pa. southward and westward, sparingly cultivated only in open places in the wild garden, but suited also to the partly shaded border. It has 12–18 leaflets, arranged feather-fashion, and showy flowers that are not pea-like, and only slightly unsymmetrical, borne in clusters among the leaves, or terminal. **Color:** Yellow. **Height:** 3–6 feet. **Flowering date:** July–Aug. **Varieties:** None. **Culture:** Set purchased plants (to be had from dealers in wild flowers), in April or Oct., in partial shade, in a reasonably moist, rich loam, and space 2–3 feet apart. While primarily a wild garden plant, it will grow in the garden border if there is partial shade and a fairly moist site.

# VIOLET FAMILY

## (*Violaceae*)

THE most obvious character of flowers in the Violet Family is the spurred lower petal, familiar to everyone in the florist's Sweet Violet, and in the native violets of our woodlands. This typically unsymmetrical feature of the flowers in this family, however, has a notable exception in the Pansy, where the flower lacks the spur or has only a small one, and is almost, but not quite perfectly symmetrical. Many (over 40) native violets must be omitted here, except for the Confederate Violet, and the Sweet Violet. These two plus the Pansy and the Tufted Pansy, or Horned Violet, are all that can be included here, but anyone can dig from the wild many beautiful native violets, useful mostly in the wild garden. All plants in the family have a dry capsule for fruit, usually with many seeds. There are nearly 300 species in the Violet Family, widely distributed over the Temperate Zone. Only the Sweet Violet of the florists (*Viola odorata*) and some of its hardy varieties are really fragrant.

**PANSY** (*Viola tricolor hortensis*)                              **p. 140**
Some of the simpler types of the pansy are often called Hearts-ease, and the ancestry of both is a bit complicated. All pansies are probably derived by hybridization, using the European *Viola tricolor* as one of the original parents. As now developed the Pansy is an annual or best treated as a biennial plant with rather sprawling habit, mostly basal, heart-shaped leaves, with flattish, velvety flowers that are nearly regular. **Color:** Basically blue, white, and yellow, but variously colored in its many varieties. **Height:** 6–8 inches. **Flowering date:** June–July (forced plants two months earlier). **Varieties:** Over 50, in all colors, but the names are in some confusion. Best ordered by color. **Culture:** As a biennial, sow seeds in late July, ¼ inch deep in a soil mixture of ½ rich loam and ½ sand, thoroughly mixed. Choose a cool, moist, half-shady place, and carry the seedlings over the winter in a cold frame or cool greenhouse or well mulched with straw or light salt hay (no manure), outdoors. As soon as pos-

sible the following spring transplant seedlings to permanent site which should be cool and moist, and have a rich, well-manured soil. Space 6–8 inches apart. The plant in some varieties tends to become a poorly persistent perennial, but for certainty of flowers it is essential to plant fresh seed each year. Without a cold frame or greenhouse (kept at 45°–60°) the Pansy is not easy to propagate for the amateur. Purchased plants, ready to put out, are the easiest solution. Summer heat usually kills it.

### TUFTED PANSY or HORNED VIOLET
  (*Viola cornuta*)                                                 p. 140
These are the plants, now found in many varieties that are commonly called Violas by most gardeners, originally developed from *Viola cornuta,* a tufted perennial from Spain and the Pyrenees. It has branching stems, and ovalish, rather crinkled, alternate leaves. Flowers with a slender, rather long, sharp spur. **Color:** Typically violet or white, but various in its many varieties. **Height:** 12–20 inches. **Flowering date:** June–July. **Varieties:** Over 70, of which a good selection of pansy-like sorts might include Arkwright Ruby (red with darker marking), Yellow Queen (yellow), Avalanche (white), Blue Butterfly (blue). Among smaller-flowered, more definitely violet-like sorts are Jersey Gem (blue), Apricot Gem (apricot), Mauve Queen (mauve), Lutea Splendens (yellow), and White Perfection (white). **Culture:** Much easier than the Pansy, because it stands summer heat better and is a true perennial. Set purchased plants in Sept. or April in partially shaded place, in rich garden soil, preferably in a moist site, and space 8–12 inches apart. It does not like great summer heat or too much slush or wet sites in winter. Frequent cutting of flowers may prolong bloom most of the summer.

### SWEET VIOLET (*Viola odorata*)                        p. 140
This is the Sweet Violet of the florists, and is not hardy over most of the U.S., except for the semihardy varieties noted below. All are fragrant, but not so much so as the true Sweet Violet of the florists, which must be wintered in a greenhouse or hotbed. The semihardy varieties are tufted perennials, originally from Eurasia

and North Africa, with basal broadly heart-shaped, stalked leaves, and producing runners. Flowers with an obvious but short spur, very fragrant. **Color:** Typically deep violet or white, but see below. **Height:** 5–7 inches. **Flowering date:** April–June, and some in the fall. **Varieties:** Only semihardy kinds — Rosina (pink), Royal Robe (violet-blue), White Czar (white), Governor Herrick (blue), Princess of Wales (violet). **Culture:** Even the semihardy varieties will not stand winter temperatures of 10°–15° above zero, nor will they thrive in places of great summer heat. Set purchased plants (if in a favorable climate), in Oct. in a rich garden soil to which a 5-inch layer of manure has been spaded in. Select a site reasonably moist, partly shaded, protected from north winds, but not too exposed to summer sun. Space 6–8 inches apart. If grown in regions of bitter winters, lift the plants and put in a cold frame from Nov. to March, well protected at night with straw mats. A precarious plant outdoors except in the most favorable places, of which the Pacific Northwest is one.

**CONFEDERATE VIOLET** (*Viola priceana*)      p. 158
The most showy and easily grown of all our native violets, and wild from Ky. and Ga. westward. It has stout rootstocks, long-stalked, heart-shaped leaves, and very handsome flowers that stand above the mass of foliage. **Color:** Whitish blue, strongly veined with deeper blue. **Height:** 6–8 inches. **Flowering date:** April–May. **Varieties:** None. **Culture:** Set purchased plants in any ordinary garden soil, in Oct., in partial shade or full sun. Space 8–10 inches apart, and self-sown seeds will in a year or two make a compact mat of foliage. Offered by some dealers as *Viola papilionacea priceana,* and by others as *Viola papilionacea alba.* It frequently escapes from cultivation from Md. to N.C., and digging up these semi-wild plants is easy. Hardy up to New York City.

# BUTTERCUP FAMILY
## (*Ranunculaceae*)

As NOTED on p. 81, most of the plants in this family have perfectly symmetrical flowers, but a few do not and they are among the most showy relatives of the buttercups. All those below have spurred, 1-sided, or otherwise irregular flowers that are not symmetrical, as the illustrations plainly show.

**COLUMBINE** (*Aquilegia chrysantha*)                    p. 141
A showy Rocky Mountain perennial much grown for its handsome clusters of long-spurred flowers. It is a stiffish, branched plant, with much divided leaves and flowers that may be 2–3 inches wide, the 5 long spurs straight, neither knobbed nor hooked at the tip, as in so many related columbines. **Color:** Yellow. **Height:** 2–4 feet. **Flowering date:** June–July. **Varieties:** Alba (white). **Culture:** Set purchased plants in full sun or partial shade, in April or Oct., in a reasonably rich sandy loam. Space 15–20 inches apart, and replant every second or third year as it tends to be a short-lived perennial.
   Related plants (not illustrated):
      *Aquilegia caerulea.* 2–3 feet. Flowers blue.
      *Aquilegia flabellata.* 12–18 inches. Flowers lilac.
      *Aquilegia vulgaris.* 15–25 inches. Flowers blue.
      *Aquilegia canadensis.* 15–20 inches. Flowers red and
         yellow. Only for the woodland garden.

**LARKSPUR** (*Delphinium* hybrids)                    p. 141
Gorgeous, garden, short-lived perennials, of highly uncertain parentage, but probably derived from an Asiatic group of species which have been much hybridized. All of them have a poisonous juice. Plants stiff and erect, the leaves divided or dissected finger-fashion. Flowers highly irregular, one of the segments produced into a long spur, two others prolonged into shorter spurs. The flowers are borne in a dense, spire-like, terminal, sometimes branched cluster, which in some choice varieties may be 6–8 feet high, but usually less in unfavorable climates or under

poor cultivation. **Color:** Various, see below. **Height:** 3–8 feet. **Flowering date:** July–Aug. **Varieties:** There are 3 main divisions — Pacific Hybrids, including forms with lavender, blue, white, and violet flowers; Wrexham types, originating in England and in all colors but yellow; Pudor types, which have pyramidal flower clusters instead of spire-like clusters, and the plants not so high. **Culture:** Set purchased plants in full sun or partial shade in a well-manured, rich garden soil, in April or Oct. Space 2–3 feet apart and stake all tall varieties in windy places. It is a cool-season plant and thrives best along the northern New England coast, Pacific Northwest, on cool mountains, but not so well, or not at all, in hot seasons or places. Because of its propensity to die out, many gardeners raise fresh crops from seed, sown in Aug., carried through the first winter in a cold frame and set out the following spring.

Related plant (not illustrated):

Annual Larkspur (*Delphinium ajacis*). 12–24 inches. Flowers in many colors; often called Rocket Larkspur.

## MONKSHOOD (*Aconitum fischeri*) p. 141

An Asiatic perennial, its juice poisonous (a close relative yields aconite), with divided leaves, the segments of which are arranged finger-fashion. Flowers very showy, highly irregular and unsymmetrical, the corolla simulating a monk's hood, two of the petals also spurred. **Color:** Blue, rarely white. **Height:** 4–5 feet. **Flowering date:** Sept.–Oct. **Varieties:** None. **Culture:** Set purchased plants in April, in partial shade, in a well-manured, rich garden soil. Space 2–3 feet apart and stake in all windy places, because stems are rather weak. It is more tolerant of heat and dryness than the closely related Larkspurs. Warn all children of its dangerously poisonous juice (harmless unless eaten).

Related plants (not illustrated):

*Aconitum anthora.* 1–2 feet. Flowers yellow.

*Aconitum napellus.* 4–5 feet. Flowers blue. The source of aconite.

*Aconitum autumnale.* 4–5 feet. Flowers blue, white, or lilac.

# BLEEDING-HEART FAMILY
## (*Fumariaceae*)

A SMALL family of rather weak-stemmed plants, with a watery juice and generally glistening foliage. Flowers highly irregular and unsymmetrical, one or two of the petals projected into a conspicuous spur, as in the Bleeding–Heart and Dutchman's–Breeches. Fruit a dry pod. Only the 3 below are of garden interest.

**BLEEDING–HEART** (*Dicentra spectabilis*)                    p. 141
An old garden favorite, native of Japan, and a leafy-stemmed perennial of the easiest culture. Leaves much dissected, weak, and the showy flower cluster, arching, 1-sided and unbranched. **Color:** Pink or red. **Height:** 12–24 inches. **Flowering date:** May–June. **Varieties:** None. **Culture:** Set purchased plants in full sun or partial shade, in any ordinary garden soil, preferably in Oct., and space 12–15 inches apart.

Related plants (not illustrated):

Wild Bleeding–Heart (*Dicentra eximea*). 8–10 inches. Flowers pink.

Dutchman's–Breeches (*Dicentra Cucullaria*). 4–7 inches. Flowers cream-yellow. Only for the most windless place in the wild garden, in deep shade.

**CLIMBING FUMITORY** (*Adlumia fungosa*)                    p. 141
A weak, sprawling, or climbing biennial plant of the deep woods of eastern North America which might almost have been included with the vines, since it sprawls over shrubs and may climb if its stems can find something to clamber over. Leaves cut-lobed and very fragile. Flowers irregular, prominently spurred, hanging in a loose cluster, not over ¾ inch long. **Color:** White or purplish white. **Height:** Often 3–8 feet long when sprawling. **Flowering date:** June–Aug. **Varieties:** None. **Culture:** Sow seeds (only to be had from dealer in wild flowers) about ¼ inch deep in a fine sandy soil well supplied with humus, but not too acid, in May. The site must be shady and as free of wind as possible. Once established, self-sown seed should ensure per-

petuation. It is fit only for a sheltered nook in the woodland garden, preferably away from the heat and dryness of low elevations.

**CORYDALIS** (*Corydalis cheilanthifolia*) p. 141
A weak-stemmed Chinese perennial with such finely divided leaves as to suggest a fern frond, each leaf nearly 8 inches long. Flowers in a lax cluster, about ½ inch long, spurred as in the Bleeding–Heart, rather fugitive, and useless for cutting. **Color:** Cream-yellow. **Height:** 9–20 inches. **Flowering date:** June–July. **Varieties:** None. **Culture:** Set purchased plants in partial shade, in rich soil well supplied with humus, in Oct. or April, and space 10–15 inches apart. It will not thrive in places with great summer heat and drought.

Related plants (not illustrated):
*Corydalis lutea.* 6–8 inches. Flowers yellow.
*Corydalis sempervirens.* 10–20 inches. Flowers pale pink.

# EVENING PRIMROSE FAMILY
## (*Onagraceae*)

As NOTED at p. 134, most of the plants of this family have perfectly regular flowers, but Fuchsia does not, as one petal is often lacking and the flower is pendulous. It is the only semi-hardy species of a group of nearly 80 shrubs, chiefly tropical.

**FUCHSIA** (*Fuchsia magellanica riccartoni*) p. 158
Of all the many species of Fuchsia this is the only one that is even partially hardy up to New York City, and then only with a winter mulch. It is a variety developed in Scotland of a Chilean shrub that reaches 6–9 feet in Calif. and lines the roadsides of southwestern Ireland. It is here useful chiefly as a summer bedding plant. Leaves opposite or in 3's, ovalish, wavy, and toothed on the margin. Flower always drooping, very showy, and nearly regular, and beneath it a row of colored and handsome sepals. **Color:** Blue and red. **Height:** 12–30 inches. **Flowering date:** July–Sept. **Varieties:** None. **Culture:** Set purchased plants in partial shade in rich garden soil only after settled warm weather

# HEATH FAMILY (*Ericaceae*), 1–6
# GALAX FAMILY (*Diapensiaceae*), 7
# PRIMROSE FAMILY (*Primulaceae*), 8 and 9

**1. Spike Heath** (*Bruckenthalia spiculifolia*)    **p. 168**
A low, European, evergreen sub-shrub, 8–10 inches high. Difficult to grow and not hardy north of New York City.

**2. Trailing Arbutus** (*Epigaea repens*)    **p. 165**
Prostrate, very fragrant evergreen so difficult to grow that few attempt it. See text for directions.

**3. Bearberry** (*Arctostaphylos uva-ursi*)    **p. 165**
The finest native evergreen ground cover, very difficult to transplant from the wild. See text for directions.

**4. Irish Heath** (*Daboecia cantabrica*)    **p. 167**
Evergreen sub-shrub, 8–12 inches high, its bloom from July to Oct. Rather difficult to grow and not reliably hardy north of New York City.

**5. Heather** (*Calluna vulgaris*)    **p. 166**
Low evergreen sub-shrub, blooming Aug.–Oct. Needs acid, sandy soil, and in warm regions a mulch of pine needles.

**6. Spring Heath** (*Erica carnea*)    **p. 167**
A nearly prostrate, evergreen sub-shrub with bloom in April–May. Needs sandy, acid site.

**7. Shortia** (*Shortia galacifolia*)    **p. 168**
A native evergreen perennial suited only to shady wild gardens. Height 3–8 inches. Blooms in June, its flowers waxlike.

**8. English Primrose** (*Primula vulgaris*)    **p. 170**
The primrose of history, but more easily grown in England than here. It needs partial shade, rich soil, coolness, and moisture.

**9. Polyanthus** (*Primula polyantha*)    **p. 169**
Related to No. 8, but easier to grow. May-blooming, and 8–12 inches high. It prefers partial shade and a cool, moist site.

## PRIMROSE FAMILY (*Primulaceae*), 1 and 3
## PLUMBAGO FAMILY (*Plumbaginaceae*), 2
## DOGBANE FAMILY (*Apocynaceae*), 4, 5, and 9
## GENTIAN FAMILY (*Gentianaceae*), 6 and 8
## MILKWEED FAMILY (*Asclepiadaceae*), 7

**1. Rock Jasmine** (*Androsace sarmentosa*)     **p. 175**
Silvery-white prostrate perennial, May-flowering and best confined to sandy or gritty soil in the rock garden.

**2. Leadwort** (*Ceratostigma plumbaginoides*)     **p. 176**
Late-blooming, nearly prostrate perennial, thriving in any ordinary garden soil, neither wet nor slushy in winter.

**3. Shooting Star** (*Dodecatheon Meadia*)     **p. 175**
A native woodland perennial, 8–12 inches high, flowering in May–June. Needs partial shade and good woods soil.

**4. Madagascar Periwinkle** (*Vinca rosea*)     **p. 179**
Long-season annual, fine for summer bedding. Sow seeds indoors, 8–10 weeks before outdoor planting is safe.

**5. Amsonia** (*Amsonia Tabernaemontana*)     **p. 179**
A little-grown native perennial, 2–3 feet high, flowering in May–June. Easy to grow if site is moist, but not wet.

**6. Buckbean** (*Menyanthes trifoliata*)     **p. 178**
Suited only to cool, acid sites that are wet or at least moist. June-flowering and not for hot regions.

**7. Butterfly-Weed** (*Asclepias tuberosa*)     **p. 180**
Only native milkweed worth growing. Thrives in dry sandy sites. Aug.-flowering and 12–20 inches high.

**8. Closed Gentian** (*Gentiana andrewsi*)     **p. 177**
The easiest of all the native gentians to grow, needing reasonable moisture, partial shade, and humusy soil.

**9. Periwinkle** (*Vinca minor*)     **p. 178**
Splendid ground-covering perennial for shady places, the foliage evergreen. Plant prostrate, June-flowering.

Left: Confederate Violet (*Viola priceana*), p. 151. Center: Fuchsia (*Fuchsia magellanica riccartoni*), p. 155. Right: Hardy Begonia (*Begonia evansiana*), p. 160.

has arrived, and only in protected sites from Washington, D.C., to New York City, its northern limit of safe culture outdoors. From Richmond, Va., southward often winter-hardy without protection. Elsewhere, cut to the ground after blooming, and cover with a thick mulch of straw, salt hay, or strawy manure. If used as a summer bedding plant, plunge the pot to the rim and lift in the fall for growing in the house over the winter.

## TROPAEOLUM FAMILY
### (*Tropaeolaceae*)

A SMALL but important family of weak-stemmed plants mostly from the Andes, the leaf blade usually attached to its stalk from the center of the blade (peltate). Flowers highly irregular, generally spurred, followed by an often pungent seed.

**NASTURTIUM** (*Tropaeolum* hybrids)                    p. 141

This ever popular Peruvian annual comes in two forms — a
dwarf bushy sort and a tall climbing strain that needs wire or
trellis support. This twining Nasturtium, now largely supplanted
by the lower kinds, could almost be included among the annual
vines (for others see pp. 1–8). Nasturtiums have very irregular, spurred flowers, fragrant in varieties so specified, and are
fine for cutting. Leaves roundish in outline, the leafstalk
attached to the middle of the leaf blade. The young flower buds
and unripe seeds are beloved by children for their pungent
flavor. Scarcely any annual blooms so rapidly from seed. **Color:**
Typically orange-yellow, but in some forms red, pink, or even
white. **Height:** Tall kinds 6–8 feet, dwarf types 15–30 inches.
**Flowering date:** June–frost. **Varieties:** Golden Gleam (late-
flowering tall and yellow), Golden Globe (golden-yellow dwarf
and double-flowered), Scarlet Gleam (red, fragrant, and tall),
Indian Chief (scarlet and tall), Garnet Gem (garnet-red and
dwarf), Salmon Gleam (salmon, fragrant, and dwarf). **Culture:**
Sow seeds in any poor soil (rich soils produce more foliage than
flowers) ½ inch deep, when trees leaf out. Space dwarf types
12–20 inches apart and tall kinds 2–3 feet apart. Tall sorts need
wires or a trellis, or they will sprawl. Nasturtiums, coming originally from the high Andes, prefer cool regions to hot ones, but
will stand no frost.

  Related plant (not illustrated):
    Canary-Bird Flower (*Tropaeolum peregrinum*). 3–8
    feet, climbing. Flowers yellow.


# JEWELWEED OR BALSAM FAMILY
## (*Balsaminaceae*)

Nearly 500 species of weak-stemmed, watery-juiced, showy-
flowered plants comprise the Jewelweed Family, which is often
called the Balsam Family. Flowers highly irregular, nearly
always spurred. Fruit an elastically explosive capsule that dis-
charges its seed when ripe.

**GARDEN BALSAM** (*Impatiens balsamina*)                    p. 141
Related to our common Jewelweed, the Garden Balsam is an
annual from subtropical India and China with erect, rather stiff
but brittle stems. Flowers unsymmetrical, spurred, borne close
to the stem, at the leaf joints. **Color:** Various, according to
variety, some salmon-pink, old rose, scarlet, yellow, purple, or
white. **Height:** 24–30 inches. **Flowering date:** July–Aug. **Varieties:** Several but poorly defined and with uncertain names;
best ordered by color. **Culture:** Sow seeds ¼ inch deep in a
mixture of ½ garden loam and ½ sand, thoroughly mixed, in
pots or pans, indoors (6–8 weeks before outdoor planting is safe).
Transfer seedlings outdoors when warm weather arrives, into
rich garden soil, in full sun, and not in a dry site. Space 15–20
inches apart. Some of its forms are often but incorrectly called
Lady's–Slipper — from the shape of the flower. The plant will
stand no frost.
    Related plant (not illustrated):
        *Impatiens sultani*. 1–2 feet. Flowers scarlet, pink,
    salmon, purple, or white.

# BEGONIA FAMILY
## (*Begoniaceae*)

A LARGE family (over 400 species) of tropical herbs, often with
colored and handsomely veined leaves that are always somewhat
oblique or lopsided. Flowers irregular, very showy in some
tropical kinds and often in large clusters, but in the one below
only slightly irregular.

**HARDY BEGONIA** (*Begonia evansiana*)                    p. 158
Of the 400 species of tropical begonias, all are of greenhouse
culture except this hardy one and a group of Tuberous Begonias,
which must be lifted in the fall. The Hardy Begonia came
originally from eastern Asia and is not reliably hardy north of
New York City, and even there needs a protected site and a
winter mulch. Leaves thick and fleshy, lobed, the lobes with
marginal teeth, red on the underside. Flowers irregular but only

slightly so, large, and somewhat fleshy. **Color:** Pink. **Height:** 12–20 inches. **Flowering date:** July–Sept. **Varieties:** None. **Culture:** Set purchased tubers in rich garden soil in a moist but not wet site, in partial shade, and preferably out of strong winds, in April. Space 10–15 inches apart. From Washington, D.C., southward it is generally winter-hardy, but from Washington to New York City it must have a protected site and a winter mulch of strawy manure. Not hardy northward.

Related plants (not illustrated):

> Tuberous Begonias. A magnificent group of tuberous-rooted plants, nowhere hardy in cool regions, and their bulblike tubers must be planted each spring and lifted in the fall. Flowers often double, waxy, of almost all colors, and nearly camellia-like.

# GERANIUM FAMILY
## (*Geraniaceae*)

Most of the garden flowers in this family have regular flowers and are noted at pp. 117–118. But first in importance in the family is the plant below, common in every florist shop and the most popular window-box plant.

**GARDEN GERANIUM** (*Pelargonium* hybrids)          p. 141
An immense group of tender, South African perennial herbs or low shrubs, some vine-like, from among which, by hybridization, has been developed the Garden Geranium and its many relatives. All have strong-smelling foliage, the leaves in the common geranium more or less kidney- or heart-shaped. Flowers irregular and unsymmetrical (often nearly regular in much doubled forms), arranged in a long-stalked close cluster (umbel). **Color:** Pink, red, scarlet, or white. **Height:** 12–20 inches, if properly grown, but often straggling and 2–3 feet if left alone. **Flowering date:** May–frost. **Varieties:** Over 650, most of them ill-defined; best ordered by color. **Culture:** Start with purchased pot plants in May, and bed out in full sun, in any good garden soil. Space 10–15 inches apart. Before the first frost dig up the

plants, plant them in a pot, and grow in the house in a cool, relatively moist room (kitchen is best). During summer outdoors and winter in the house, pinch off shoots that may make the plant a straggler. Another, and easier method of wintering these tender geraniums is to lift the plants in fall, shake off nearly all soil from the roots, and hang them upside down in a cool cellar (no furnace heat). In mid-May, cut back the withered stems to 6–8 inches and plant outdoors, repeating the initial procedure. They will sprout new leaves and shoots and bloom in a short time. All Garden Geraniums root easily in moist sand if a slip 4–6 inches long, with most leaves removed, is inserted 1–2 inches deep, covered with a bell jar and kept moist. For related hardy plants belonging to the genus *Geranium,* usually called Cranesbill or Wild Geranium, see p. 117.

Related plants (not illustrated):

>All tender, except in frostless regions.

>Rose Geranium (*Pelargonium graveolens*). 2–3 feet. Flowers rose-pink. Foliage fragrant.

>Nutmeg Geranium (*Pelargonium odoratissimum*). 12–18 inches. Flowers white, nutmeg-scented.

>Ivy Geranium (*Pelargonium peltatum*). 1–4 feet, trailing. Flowers white to rose.

# Flowers Cuplike, Bell- or Funnel-Shaped,

## or Otherwise Tubular

ALL of the garden flowers already described on pp. 64–162 have **separate** petals, **not united** into any sort of a tube, nor are they cuplike, or bell-shaped, or in the form of a funnel, or cornucopia-like. But from here to the end of the book the flowers (with a few exceptions, noted where they occur) never have separate petals, since these are always joined into some sort of a united corolla. Familiar examples are the Primrose, Phlox, Snapdragon, Foxglove, all the Daisy Family, and many others. Botanists call this large group the Gamopetalae, i.e., with a union or fusion of petals.

The distinction marks a fundamental dividing point in the plant world and provides us with a simple method of arranging the balance of the plants in the book into definite families. This has little or no garden significance, but is essential to a proper understanding of why related families come close together while others, more distantly related, are grouped in other parts of the book.

There are over 170 different plants in this large group of families all having a united corolla, and it is obvious that some scheme of separating them is imperative for easy identification. Some have a regular, symmetrical corolla, like the Bellflower, while others have an unsymmetrical, irregular corolla like the Snapdragon or Lobelia. And the largest single group have specialized flowers of the Daisy Family and are easily recognized by everyone.

Reducing these complexities to a simple scheme provides us with the following:

*The Daisy Family. See p. 241.*

*Flowers not as in the Daisy Family.*

　*Flowers irregular, unsymmetrical, often 2-lipped. See p. 202.*

　*Flowers regular and symmetrical. See immediately below.*

# *Flowers Regular and Symmetrical; Never 2-Lipped, or Lopsided or Otherwise Irregular*

HERE belong a considerable number of old garden favorites, all of which have regular and symmetrical flowers. These never look like the Snapdragon or Foxglove, for instance, but are perfectly cup-shaped, tubular, or more or less funnel-shaped — never 2-lipped like the Lobelia. It comprises several families of plants, especially the Heath, Primrose, Gentian, and Phlox Families, as well as some others of less importance. The sequence of them from here to p. 202 will help the seeker to find what he seeks, because it brings related families close together. That it is the sequence usually followed by the experts in plant classification does not detract from its usefulness to the gardener who wants to know something of the relationship and affinities of garden flowers.

## HEATH FAMILY
### (*Ericaceae*)

IF THIS book included shrubs and trees here would come the azaleas, mountain laurel, rhododendrons, rhodora, and several others. Those below, all somewhat woody, are herblike shrubs or shrubby herbs and considered by everyone as garden flowers. All of them are difficult to grow, and without special preparation of the soil next to impossible. All of them require a highly acid soil, and are consequently unfit to grow in ordinary garden soil. In all except the Trailing Arbutus the flowers are small, urn- or cup-shaped, while in the Trailing Arbutus they appear (falsely because of the short tube) to be of 5 separate petals. All have alternate or much crowded leaves and a dry pod with almost microscopic seeds, in some; berry-like in others.

**TRAILING ARBUTUS** (*Epigaea repens*)      p. 156
Perhaps the most fragrant plant of eastern North America, and often called Mayflower, Ground Laurel, and Winter Pink. It is a prostrate, woody herb with alternate, leathery often brown-mottled, evergreen leaves that are ovalish, about 2–3 inches long, and minutely hairy on the margins. Flowers about ½ inch long, apparently of 5 separate petals but actually with a short tube crowned by its 5 pointed lobes. **Color:** Pink or whitish. **Height:** Prostrate. **Flowering date:** April. **Varieties:** None. **Culture:** Difficult. It is essential to buy potted plants from a dealer in wild flowers in Oct. or Nov. Knock out of the pot (or if in a paper pot simply tear it partly off the ball of soil) and plant in partial or deep shade (evergreens are fine, especially pines), in a highly acid, somewhat sandy or gritty soil. If this is not naturally available, do not attempt to grow Trailing Arbutus without a mixture of prepared soil. This must include ½ sand and ½ chopped peat. Remove all old soil for depth of 18 inches and fill the hole with the mixture and allow to settle for a few weeks before planting. Water only with rain water. After planting provide a permanent mulch of pine needles, or if these are not available use spruce or fir needles. Oak leaves make a third and less satisfactory mulch. Never cultivate the soil; if weeds come, hand-pull them. It is next to useless to attempt transplanting Trailing Arbutus from the woods to your wild garden. Nor should the amateur attempt the tedious and difficult procedure of growing it from seeds or cuttings. Even with all these precautions Trailing Arbutus may fail. It should never be attempted in a limestone region.

**BEARBERRY** (*Arctostaphylos uva–ursi*)      p. 156
One of the finest evergreen, prostrate ground covers in our native

flora, but difficult to grow. It is a long-trailing woody plant, its leaves about 1 inch long, bright green in summer, bronzy in winter. Flowers urn-shaped, scarcely ⅛ inch long, followed by a dull red, insipid berry about pea size. **Color:** White, rarely pink. **Height:** Prostrate and forming dense mats. **Flowering date:** June. **Varieties:** None. **Culture:** Difficult. Start with potted plants from a dealer in wild flowers, in Nov. or Dec., and plant only in a prepared bed. Unless this is naturally very sandy and acid, dig out all old soil 18 inches deep. Put in a layer of coal ashes 5 inches deep. Fill the rest of the excavation with a mixture of 5 parts sand and 2 parts of chopped peat, which must be acid peat, thoroughly mixed. Allow to settle a few weeks before planting and water only with rain water. Knock out plants from the pot (if in paper pots tear off enough to preserve the ball) and plant in the prepared bed. It must be in full sun. Provide a mulch of pine needles and do not disturb or cultivate the soil. Hand-pull weeds, if any. The plant has many names, Kinnikinnick, Hog Cranberry, Mealberry, and Barren Myrtle among them. Its ubiquitous occurrence along dunes and even railway banks on Cape Cod and Long Island should deceive no one as to its difficult culture. It is practically useless to attempt transplanting it from the wild, except by digging frozen clumps in midwinter and plunging them in the prepared bed outlined above.

**HEATHER** (*Calluna vulgaris*)                                    p. 156

A European undershrub, covering the highland moors of Scotland and a universal garden favorite wherever it can be grown. It is a stiffish erect plant, growing naturally in masses and best planted so. Leaves evergreen, very tiny (scarcely ⅒ inch long) so densely crowded as to completely clothe the twigs. Flowers small, in dense, terminal clusters, urn-shaped, followed by a tiny, dried pod. **Color:** Various, see below; purple in the wild plant. **Height:** 8–15 inches. **Flowering date:** Aug.–Oct. **Varieties:** Many, a good selection might include: Alba (white), Alba Spicata (taller, white), Aurea (pink, foliage golden), Cuprea (purple, winter foliage bronze), Rubra (red), Tenella (lavender), Carnea (flesh color), Alporti (crimson, taller). **Culture:** Start only with potted plants in early April and unless the soil is naturally sandy and acid, or gritty and acid, prepare a mixture of 6 parts sand and 3 parts chopped, acid peat, thoroughly mixed. Excavate all old soil and fill in at least 1 foot deep with prepared mixture. Water only with rain water. Set plants 4–6 inches apart, in full sun and for effective display by the dozen or score. In a few years they will make a dense mat, especially in dry sandy places. Also called Ling.

## IRISH HEATH (*Daboecia cantabrica*) p. 156

A low European evergreen sub-shrub, not very common in American gardens. It has alternate leaves that are about ½ inch long, rather numerous, and a terminal cluster of small, bell-shaped flowers that are nearly ½ inch long. Fruit a dry pod. **Color:** Purple or white. **Height:** 8–12 inches. **Flowering date:** July–Oct. **Varieties:** Alba (white). **Culture:** Start only with potted plants set out in April, in full sun, in a sandy or gritty soil that is acid. If it is not acid add enough chopped acid peat to make it so. Water only with rain water. Often offered as *Menziesia polifolia,* and called by some St. Dabeoc's Heath. Not reliably hardy north of Philadelphia, except in sheltered places and with a winter mulch of straw or salt hay. Not hardy north of New York City.

## SPRING HEATH (*Erica carnea*) p. 156

A low, sometimes prostrate, evergreen sub-shrub from the Mediterranean, with densely crowded small leaves. Flowers scarcely ¼ inch long, urn-shaped, borne in a terminal 1-sided cluster. **Color:** Red. **Height:** 8–12 inches, often prostrate. **Flowering date:** April–May. **Varieties:** Carmine (scarlet), Rosy Pink (pink), Snow Queen (white), Ruby Glow (red), Springwood White (white). **Culture:** Start only with potted plants in Oct., and plant in a prepared bed of 5 parts sand and 2 parts of chopped acid peat thoroughly mixed, and at least 1 foot deep. Space 6–8 inches apart, and plant by the dozen or score. Water only with rain water.

Related plants (not illustrated):
> Cross-leaved Heath (*Erica tetralix*). 1–2 feet. Flowers
> rose-red.
> Fringed Heath (*Erica ciliaris*). 8–12 inches. Flowers
> rose-red.
> Cornish Heath (*Erica vagans*). 8–12 inches. Flowers
> pinkish purple.

**SPIKE HEATH** (*Bruckenthalia spiculifolia*)               p. 156
A European sub-shrub with tiny evergreen leaves (about ⅛ inch
long) so numerous as to clothe the twigs. Flowers scarcely ¼
inch long, crowded in a dense spike that is hardly more than ¾
inch long. Fruit a dry pod. It is not widely grown in American
gardens. **Color:** Pink. **Height:** 8–10 inches. **Flowering date:**
July. **Varieties:** None. **Culture:** Start only with potted plants in
Oct. or April, planted in a sandy loam that is acid or can be made
so by the addition of chopped acid peat. Plant in dozens or
scores for effective show, in full sun, and water only with rain
water. Space 4–6 inches apart. Not reliably hardy north of Philadelphia unless in a protected place and with a winter mulch of
straw or salt hay. Not hardy north of New York City.

# GALAX FAMILY
## (*Diapensiaceae*)

A SMALL family, separated from the heaths only by technical characters, and comprising besides the florist's galax a few low herbs
somewhat difficult of cultivation. Flowers solitary, of apparently
5 separate petals (united at the base), followed by a dry, small
capsule.

**SHORTIA** (*Shortia galacifolia*)                          p. 156
A native evergreen herb from the mountains of N.C. with roundish basal leaves, the margins wavy. Flowers solitary, on leafless
stalks, the flower of 5 separate petals, waxlike and bell-shaped.
The plant was lost to science and cultivation before its redis-
covery in 1878. It has no other valid common name but Shortia,

although the manufactured one of Oconee Bells has some currency. **Color:** White. **Height:** 3–8 inches. **Flowering date:** June. **Varieties:** None. **Culture:** Set purchased plants, to be had only from dealers in wild flowers, in deep shade, in Oct. or April, in an acid woods soil. Mulch with oak leaves or pine needles and leave alone. Water only with rain water, and space 5–7 inches apart. Suited only to the most shady part of the wild garden.

# PRIMROSE FAMILY
## (*Primulaceae*)

A FAMILY of chiefly herbs, found mostly in the North Temperate Zone, including the Primrose, Cowslip, Oxlip, Loosestrife, and, if greenhouse plants were included here, the Cyclamen. Among native plants is the Shooting Star, suited to the wild garden. In some, like the primroses the leaves are in a basal rosette, but in others borne on the stem. Flowers funnel-shaped or tubular. Fruit a dry pod.

**POLYANTHUS** (*Primula polyantha*) p. 156
The most easily grown of all primroses and a perennial of hybrid origin, derived from crossing the English Primrose, the Oxlip, and the Cowslip. It has leaves with a winged leafstalk and almost stalkless flowers in a dense cluster, rarely solitary. **Color:** Various, see below at varieties. **Height:** 8–12 inches. **Flowering date:** May. **Varieties:** Numerous, a good selection including Blue Boy (blue), Copper (bronzy), Deep Gold (orange-yellow), Alba (white), Winter White (white), Rose Ash (pink), Marine Blues (blue), Orange Glow (orange), Indian Red (red), Velvet Maroon (maroon). **Culture:** While a true perennial in favorable sites, often grown as a biennial because some plants are not worth saving after blooming, and such must be renewed each year by sowing seed. For permanent perennial effects set purchased plants in Oct. or March, in partial shade if possible, otherwise under filtered sunlight in a rich, cool, moist soil (not wet) and space 8–10 inches apart. They do not thrive in summer heat and drought.

**ENGLISH PRIMROSE** (*Primula vulgaris*)                    p. 156
*The* primrose of history and the poets and a perennial from
northern Europe. Leaves all basal, wrinkled, and the margins
crinkled. Flowers few or solitary almost stalkless, nearly 1½
inches wide. **Color:** Prevailing yellow, but see below. **Height:**
4–6 inches. **Flowering date:** April–May. **Varieties:** Alba (white),
Bronzy Tones (bronze), Indigo Blue (blue), Rose Gold (pinkish
gold), Double Yellow (yellow and double-flowered), Double
Lavender (lavender and double-flowered), Rubra (red). **Culture:**
Set purchased plants in deep or partial shade, in Oct., in a soil of
1 part rich loam, 1 part leafmold and ½ part of sand, thoroughly
mixed. If there is natural woods soil the mixture is unnecessary.
The site must be cool and moist, or it can be wet at times in
summer. They do not like summer heat, drought, or slush at
their roots in winter. Keep a mulch of leafmold continuously.

**COWSLIP** (*Primula veris*)                                p. 171
A Eurasian perennial with basal, wrinkled leaves and fragrant
flowers about ¼–¾ inches wide, borne in a dense, close, nearly
stalkless cluster (umbel), the whole plant somewhat hairy. The
corolla has scale-like folds near its mouth. **Color:** Prevailingly
yellow with a dark eye, but see below. **Height:** 5–8 inches.
**Flowering date:** May. **Varieties:** Munstead Red (red), Munstead
Cream (cream-yellow), Gold Lace (golden yellow), Munstead-
Blue (blue), Rubra (red). **Culture:** Set purchased plants in Oct.
or March, in full or partial shade, in rich woods soil, or if lacking, in a mixture of 1 part rich loam, ½ part cow manure, 2 parts
leafmold and 1 part sand. Choose a moist or even wet (in summer) site and space 4–6 inches apart. They will not stand great
summer heat or dryness, nor slush at their roots in winter. Keep
a continuous mulch of leafmold.
    Related plants (not illustrated):
        Auricula (*Primula Auricula*). 6–8 inches. Flowers in all
        colors, each with a darker eye.

**OXLIP** (*Primula elatior*)                                p. 171
Scarcely different from the Cowslip, but without the scale-like
folds at the mouth of the flower. It is a perennial from Europe

to Iran, somewhat hairy, and more commonly grown in England than here. **Color:** Yellow, but see below. **Height:** 5–8 inches. **Flowering date:** April–May. **Varieties:** Alba (white), Purpurea (purple), Atrocoerulea (dark blue), Rubra (red). **Culture:** Same as for the Cowslip, immediately above.

Related plants (not illustrated):

*Primula beesiana.* 1–2 feet. Flowers rose-red, with yellow eye.

*Primula cortusoides.* 8–12 inches. Flowers rose-colored.

*Primula denticulata.* 10–15 inches. Flowers lilac.

*Primula japonica.* 1–2 feet. Flowers purple, pink, or white.

*Primula juliae.* 1–3 inches. Flowers red.

*Primula marginata.* 2–5 inches. Flowers purple-red.

*Primula pulverulenta.* 15–30 inches. Flowers purple, with orange eye.

Left: Oxlip (*Primula elatior*), p. 170.
Right: Cowslip (*Primula veris*), p. 170.

## PHLOX FAMILY (*Polemoniaceae*), 1–6
## WATERLEAF FAMILY (*Hydrophyllaceae*), 7–8
## BORAGE FAMILY (*Boraginaceae*), 9

1. **Blue Gilia** (*Gilia capitata*)     **p. 184**
   A fine Pacific Coast annual, splendid for cutting. Flowering from July to frost, and 18–24 inches high.

2. **Jacob's-Ladder** (*Polemonium caeruleum*)     **p. 184**
   Eurasian perennial, 18–30 inches high and flowering in May–June. Easily grown, preferably in moist sites.

3. **Annual Phlox** (*Phlox drummondi*)     **p. 181**
   An enormously diverse and confused group of annual phloxes, easily grown summer-bloomers.

4. **Wild Sweet William** (*Phlox maculata*)     **p. 183**
   Native perennial, 12–30 inches high, blooming in June–July. Needs partial shade and reasonable moisture.

5. **Ground Pink** (*Phlox subulata*)     **p. 183**
   A prostrate perennial, useful as a ground cover in dry, sandy places, where it carpets the site with bloom in April–May.

6. **Perennial Phlox** (*Phlox paniculata*)     **p. 182**
   Summer-blooming perennial in many varieties. Easy to grow in any ordinary garden soil. Height 18–30 inches.

7. **California Bluebell** (*Phacelia campanularia*)     **p. 186**
   A desert annual from Calif. 4–6 inches high, summer-flowering and easily grown, in full sunshine.

8. **Baby Blue-Eyes** (*Nemophila menziesi*)     **p. 186**
   A low, Californian annual, summer-blooming, and of easy culture. Not over 6 inches high.

9. **Alkanet** (*Anchusa azurea*)     **p. 187**
   Hairy European perennial, 2–3 feet high, mostly June-flowering. Of easy culture anywhere.

# BORAGE FAMILY
## (*Boraginaceae*)

1. **Brunnera** (*Brunnera macrophylla*)     **p. 193**
A perennial, 12–18 inches high, spring-blooming. Useful in the blue garden.

2. **Lungwort** (*Pulmonaria angustifolia*)     **p. 193**
A perennial, 6–12 inches high, flowering in April or May.

3. **Borage** (*Borago officinalis*)     **p. 194**
An aromatic annual, 1–2 feet high. Summer-blooming and relished by bees.

4. **Chinese Forget-Me-Not** (*Cynoglossum amabile*)     **p. 190**
A summer-blooming biennial, 18–24 inches high, grown as an annual.

5. **Virginia Cowslip** (*Mertensia virginica*)     **p. 193**
A native spring-blooming perennial, 1–2 feet high, useful in shady, moist places.

6. **Forget-Me-Not** (*Myosotis scorpioides*)     **p. 187**
A prostrate perennial, mostly spring-blooming, useful as ground cover among taller plants.

7. **Annual Forget-Me-Not** (*Myosotis sylvatica*)     **p. 190**
A low annual, blooming from May to Aug. Not over 9 inches high.

8. **Heliotrope** (*Heliotropium arborescens*)     **p. 191**
A perennial, 2–4 feet high, generally grown as a long-season annual. Flowers from July to frost.

9. **Lithodora** (*Lithodora diffusa*)     **p. 192**
An evergreen prostrate undershrub, useful in the rock garden.

**LOOSESTRIFE** (*Lysimachia clethroides*)                    below
A somewhat weedy Asiatic perennial useful chiefly for moist or
even wet places, otherwise of little garden importance. It is a
somewhat hairy, erect plant with the long narrow leaves arranged alternately, and with a terminal, spire-like cluster of flowers that are about ½ inch wide. Fruit a dry pod. **Color:** White.

Left: Loosestrife (*Lysimachia clethroides*),
above. Upper Right: Anagallis (*Anagallis
linifolia*), p. 175. Lower Right: Douglasia
(*Douglasia vitaliana*), p. 176.

**Height:** 2–3 feet. **Flowering date:** Aug.–Sept. **Varieties:** None.
**Culture:** Set purchased plants in Oct. or April, in full sun or
partial shade, in almost any soil that is moist or wet. Space 15–20
inches apart.

   Related plants (not illustrated):
       Creeping Charlie (*Lysimachia nummularia*). Prostrate.
       Flowers yellow.
   *Lysimachia punctata.* 2–3 feet. Flowers yellow.

**ANAGALLIS** (*Anagallis linifolia*)                          p. 174

A close relative of the Scarlet Pimpernel (*Anagallis arvensis*)
which is often a prostrate, weedy pest in the eastern states. Unlike the pimpernel our plant is erect, with narrowly lance-shaped
leaves, and solitary flowers at the leaf joints. Flowers about ¾
inch wide, not particularly showy, and the plant of secondary
garden importance. **Color:** Blue, but reddish toward the base.
**Height:** 10–18 inches. **Flowering date:** June. **Varieties:** Collina
(rose-purple). **Culture:** Set purchased plants in Oct. or April,
in full sun, in any ordinary garden soil and space 5–9 inches apart.
Sometimes offered as *Anagallis grandiflora.*

**SHOOTING STAR** (*Dodecatheon Meadia*)                     p. 157

A delightful native perennial, found wild from Pa. to Texas and
a wild-garden favorite, or often grown in the rock garden. It
has a basal rosette of oblongish leaves with winged stalks. Flowers apparently upside down, pointed, almost cyclamen-like, only
a few in a lax, terminal, long-stalked cluster. **Color:** Pink, but
white at the base, and the stamens a blend of reddish yellow and
purple. **Height:** 8–12 inches. **Flowering date:** May–June. **Varieties:** None. **Culture:** Set purchased plants (from a dealer in wild
flowers) in partial shade, in fine woodland soil that is moist but
not wet. Plant in Oct. or April, preferably under shrubs or small
trees with not too dense a shade. Space 6–8 inches apart and do
not disturb. Sometimes called Prairie Pointer and not difficut to
grow if the right site is chosen.

　　Related plants (not illustrated):

　　　　All rather difficult to grow.

　　　　Sierra Shooting Star (*Dodecatheon jeffreyi*). 9–12
　　　　　　inches. Flowers reddish purple.

　　　　Mosquito Bills (*Dodecatheon hendersoni*). 8–10 inches.
　　　　　　Flowers purple.

**ROCK JASMINE** (*Androsace sarmentosa*)                     p. 157

A silvery white Himalayan prostrate perennial, useful only in
the rock garden. It has creeping runners, which at intervals are
dotted with basal rosettes of silvery white young leaves that turn
greener later in the season. Flowers about ¼ inch wide in a pro-

fuse, terminal cluster that may stand 6 inches above the foliage. **Color:** Rose-pink. **Height:** Prostrate. **Flowering date:** May. **Varieties:** Chumbyi (leaves decidedly woolly). **Culture:** Set purchased plants (from dealer in rock garden plants) in Oct. or late March in full sun or filtered light, in the rock garden, in a sandy or gritty soil, preferably on a north-facing slope, since it does not like heat or dryness. The site should be moist but not wet, and the plants must be watered to go through droughts. Not easy to grow and not for the open border.

Related plants (not illustrated):

> *Androsace lactiflora,* an annual. 8–12 inches. Flowers white.
>
> *Androsace lanuginosa.* Prostrate. Flowers rose-pink.

**DOUGLASIA** (*Douglasia vitaliana*)                              p. 174

A close relative of the Rock Jasmine (preceding), much resembling it, and a native of the Alps and Pyrenees. It is suited only to the rock garden. Plant perennial, prostrate, its hairy leaves in rosettes. Flowers almost stalkless, usually solitary. **Color:** Yellow. **Height:** Prostrate. **Flowering date:** June. **Varieties:** None. **Culture:** Same as for the Rock Jasmine (see above).

# PLUMBAGO FAMILY
### (*Plumbaginaceae*)

A MEDIUM-SIZED family (300 species) of widely distributed herbs, some of them tropical, but containing the Thrift, the Prickly Thrift, and the Sea Lavender (see pp. 59–63 among the everlastings), and the one below. They have leaves alternately arranged and flowers with 5 segments to the corolla.

**LEADWORT** (*Ceratostigma plumbaginoides*)                p. 157

A Chinese semi-woody perennial, almost prostrate, and valued for its very late-blooming flowers. Leaves nearly 3 inches long, oblongish, decidedly hairy on the margins. Flowers in a dense, terminal cluster, each flower about ½ inch wide and beneath it a row of leaflets (bracts) that are also hairy on the margin.

**Color:** Deep cobalt-blue. **Height:** Half prostrate, rarely up to 8–10 inches. **Flowering date:** Sept.–Frost. **Varieties:** None. **Culture:** Set purchased plants in March or April, in any ordinary garden soil in full sun, preferably in a warm site. It does not thrive in wet places, nor with winter slush at its roots. Often sold under its old but incorrect name of *Plumbago Larpentae*.

# GENTIAN FAMILY
### (*Gentianaceae*)

THE gentians are prolific in alpine meadows in the Rockies and Sierras, and still more so in the Alps. Most of them, in spite of their beauty, are possible garden plants only for the experts with an alpine garden. Of the native sorts the beautiful Fringed Gentian (*Gentiana crinita*) should never be picked, and its cultivation is possible only by those who can give it the exacting conditions it demands. (See Norman Taylor's *Wild Flower Gardening,* New York, 1955, pp. 116–18.) The Closed Gentian is much easier to grow. The family contains over 700 species, widely distributed. All except the Buckbean have leaves that are generally arranged opposite each other. Flowers tubular, beautifully fringed in some, often pure blue (which is rare among plants). Fruit a dry pod, the seeds usually microscopic.

**CLOSED GENTIAN** (*Gentiana andrewsi*)　　　　p. 157
Often called the Bottle Gentian, from the shape of its flower, which either never opens or is forced open only by bees. It is the commonest gentian of eastern North America and the easiest to grow. It has opposite, oblongish, pointed leaves, without marginal teeth, short-stalked. From the upper pairs of leaves and at the summit are the close, almost stalkless clusters of flowers, which are each about 1½ inches long. **Color:** White at base, blue at tip. **Height:** 10–18 inches. **Flowering date:** Aug.–Oct. **Varieties:** None. **Culture:** Set purchased plants in March or April, in half-shade, in a moist or even wet site in soil that is rich in humus, but not too acid. Space 6–9 inches apart. It is a true perennial and will persist if let alone. The related Fringed Gentian of our

meadows is a shy biennial and practically impossible to capture from the wild.

Related plants (not illustrated):

Only easily grown perennials. All alpine species omitted.
*Gentiana asclepiadea.* 12–18 inches. Flowers blue.
*Gentiana septemfida.* 9–15 inches. Flowers blue.
*Gentiana sino-ornata.* 6–8 inches. Flowers whitish yellow.

**BUCKBEAN** (*Menyanthes trifoliata*)                          p. 157
A bog perennial found in the cooler parts of the North Temperate Zone and best suited only to a highly acid bog. It has compound leaves with 3 leaflets that have no marginal teeth, and a long leafstalk, sheathed at the base. Flowers 10–20 in a cluster, each flower funnel-shaped and about ½ inch long. Fruit a dry pod about ¾ inch long. **Color:** White, rarely pinkish. **Height:** Sprawling, not over 8 inches. **Flowering date:** June. **Varieties:** None. **Culture:** Set purchased plants in sphagnum moss or peat in a cool, acid bog, in April or Oct. Space 8–12 inches apart and leave alone. Not suited to ordinary garden soils, and best grown in cool regions.

# DOGBANE FAMILY
## (*Apocynaceae*)

A LARGE family (over 1100 species) of generally trees, shrubs, woody vines, and herbs, most of them tropical, but the few below comprise such old garden favorites as the Periwinkle. Most of them have a milky juice, dangerously poisonous in some, notably the Oleander. Flowers more or less bell-shaped, followed by a dry, podlike fruit. There are no marginal teeth on the leaves of any of those below.

**PERIWINKLE** (*Vinca minor*)                          p. 157
A European trailing evergreen vine, often mistakenly called Myrtle (it is not a true myrtle) or Running Myrtle, and a most useful ground cover for shady places. It has lance-shaped, shin-

ing, evergreen leaves, arranged opposite each other on the tough, wiry stems. Flowers solitary at the leaf joints, slightly twisted. **Color:** Blue. **Height:** Prostrate. **Flowering date:** June. **Varieties:** None. **Culture:** Set purchased plants in Oct. or late Sept. in any ordinary garden soil, in partial or deep shade (it will also tolerate open sun), and space 12 inches apart. In a season or two it will form a dense evergreen mat.

Related plant (not illustrated):

> *Vinca major variegata.* Prostrate. Flowers blue, leaves variegated. Not frost-hardy, but a favorite vine for summer window boxes.

## MADAGASCAR PERIWINKLE (*Vinca rosea*)      p. 157

An erect showy, Madagascan annual, not hardy northward but easily grown as a summer bedding plant, since it blooms from seed in a single season if the directions below are followed. In the tropics it is a perennial. Leaves lance-shaped, prominently veined. Flowers with a distinct darker "eye," slightly twisted. **Color:** Pink or white. **Height:** 10–20 inches. **Flowering date:** July–frost. **Varieties:** Purity (white without the central eye), Willie Winkle (rose-pink). **Culture:** For certainty of bloom (especially north of Philadelphia), sow seeds ¼ inch deep indoors (8–10 weeks before outdoor planting is safe). Transfer outdoors when settled warm weather arrives, spacing them 8–12 inches apart, in partial shade or full sun, in any ordinary garden soil. They do better in warm regions than cool ones.

## AMSONIA (*Amsonia Tabernaemontana*)      p. 157

A native perennial, neither very common from N.J. to Texas, where it grows wild, nor much cultivated in gardens, although it has handsome flower clusters. Leaves arranged alternately on the stem. Flowers about ¼ inch long, arranged in a loose, rather lax terminal cluster. Fruit a pointed pod nearly 3 inches long. **Color:** Blue. **Height:** 2–3 feet. **Flowering date:** May–June. **Varieties:** None. **Culture:** Set purchased plants in Oct. or April, in full sun, in any ordinary garden soil, preferably in a moist, but not wet site. Space 1–2 feet apart. Very easily grown.

# MILKWEED FAMILY
## (*Asclepiadaceae*)

A VERY large family (over 2000 species) many of them shrubs, vines or trees, mostly tropical, and with a handful of herbs from temperate regions, most familiar as our common milkweeds. Leaves without marginal teeth, generally alternately arranged. Flowers with the outer segments recurved, the inner ones united to form a central "crown." The one below is the only species of milkweed that does not have a milky juice.

**BUTTERFLY–WEED** (*Asclepias tuberosa*)          p. 157
The only one of our native milkweeds worth growing in the garden, and suited only to hot dry, sandy sites. Butterfly-Weed, often called Pleurisy Root, is an extremely showy native perennial, found wild from New England to Texas, and is a rather sprawling, rough-hairy plant; also called Orange Milkweed. Leaves oblongish, thick, and coarse. Flowers in a handsome, flat-topped cluster, each flower scarcely ¼ inch wide. **Color:** Orange. **Height:** 12–20 inches. **Flowering date:** Aug. **Varieties:** None. **Culture:** Set purchased plants (from dealer in wild flowers) in full sun, in Oct. or April, preferably on a warm slope, in sandy loam or in practically pure sand. Take care that its brittle deep root is not injured; which makes it difficult to dig from the wild. Space 1–2 feet apart, and more if it is inclined to sprawl.

# MORNING-GLORY FAMILY
## (*Convolvulaceae*)

A LARGE family (over 1000 species) of woody or herbaceous vines and many tropical shrubs and trees. In the section on vines (see pp. 1–8) the plants that climb have already been noted, but the one below is not vine-like, although its flowers resemble the more showy morning-glories. All have leaves alternately arranged, without marginal teeth but sometimes wavy-margined.

Flower typically cornucopia-shaped, its apex 5-lobed. Fruit a round pod, splitting by 4 valves.

**BUSH MORNING–GLORY** (*Convolvulus tricolor*)     p. 185
An annual, low herb from southern Europe, often weedy but somewhat grown for its miniature bloom. Its flowers resemble the tall climbing morning-glories (see vines at p. 3) but are much smaller and the plant scarcely grows more than 12 inches high. **Color:** Blue. **Height:** 8–12 inches. **Flowering date:** July–Aug. **Varieties:** None. **Culture:** Sow seeds in full sun, ¼ inch deep, in sandy or poorish soil, after warm weather arrives. Thin to 8–10 inches apart. It does not thrive in humid, hot regions.
     Related plant (not illustrated):
          Bindweed (*Convolvulus mauritanicus*). Prostrate.
          Flowers violet-blue. Not frost-hardy.

# PHLOX FAMILY
## (*Polemoniaceae*)

Wʜɪʟᴇ not very large, the Phlox Family (only about 270 species) contains some of the most widely grown garden favorites, among them the Annual and Perennial Phlox, Wild Sweet William, the Ground Pink, Jacob's-Ladder, and the gilias, all except one from the U.S. The Jacob's-Ladder has divided or compound leaves; all the phloxes have simple, undivided leaves that are arranged opposite each other; while in the gilias below the leaves are divided into unequal or needle-like segments. Flowers typically bell-shaped, or in the phloxes with a very short tube and the lobes of the corolla (always 5, except in double-flowered forms) spreading so that the flower appears (falsely) to have 5 separate petals. Fruit a dry pod. Not one of the family has a poisonous or medicinal juice.

**ANNUAL PHLOX** (*Phlox drummondi*)                    p. 172
One of the most widely cultivated of all annuals, and a native of Texas, often called Texan Pride or Drummond's Phlox. It has been so long cultivated that its varieties and color range are legion. It is an erect plant with lance-shaped leaves that are 2–3

inches long. Flowers in a close, terminal cluster (umbel-like), about 1 inch broad, but so profuse as to make the cluster showy. **Color:** Basically white or pink, but see below. **Height:** 12–20 inches. **Flowering date:** July–Aug. **Varieties:** Innumerable and unreliable as to name. They come in all colors but yellow. Various seedsmen advertize many "novelties," including so-called Bush Phloxes, some with reputed larger flowers than the type, and other so-called Tetra Phloxes (short for tetraploids treated with colchicine). **Culture:** Sow seeds in any ordinary garden soil, ¼ inch deep, in full sun, where wanted, as soon as trees leaf out. Thin to 6–8 inches apart, for they resent transplanting. For earlier bloom sow seeds indoors 6–8 weeks before outdoor planting is safe, and transfer seedlings outdoors when trees leaf out. Seedlings must be handled very carefully; the plant does not like to be moved.

**PERENNIAL PHLOX** (*Phlox paniculata*)                          p. 172
This is the commonest garden phlox; a perennial originating in the southern U.S. but hardy everywhere and now found in over 200 named varieties, some of which are certainly duplicates of well-known sorts, and others hardly differ from better-known varieties. Leaves broadly lance-shaped, 3½–5 inches long, rather thin and veiny. Flowers nearly 1 inch wide, in a close, showy, pyramidal cluster. **Color:** All but yellow and blue. **Height:** 18–30 inches. **Flowering date:** June–Sept. **Varieties:** Of the scores of valid sorts a fair selection might include Africa (carmine, with red "eye"), Antonin Mercier (lilac, with white eye), B. Compte (purple), Blue Boy (bluish, no true blues in *Phlox paniculata*), Border Queen (low and pink), Charles Curtis (red), Enchantress (salmon-pink, with dark eye), Fiancée (white), George Stripp (salmon-pink, with lighter eye), Harvest Fire (salmon-orange), Lilian (light pink), Mary Louise (white), Rhinelander (salmon-pink, with red eye), Widar (reddish violet, with white eye). **Culture:** Set purchased plants, in Oct. or April, in full sun or partial shade, in any reasonably rich garden loam. Space 10–15 inches apart. Often offered under the incorrect name of *Phlox decussata*.

Related plants (not illustrated):
> *Phlox arendsi.* 15–24 inches. Flowers lavender or white (in variety Miss Lingard).
> *Phlox amoena.* 8–12 inches. Flowers purplish red.
> *Phlox ovata.* 1–2 feet. Flowers purple.
> *Phlox stolonifera.* 8–12 inches. Flowers violet-purple.

## WILD SWEET WILLIAM (*Phlox maculata*)      p. 172

An erect perennial from the lowlands of the eastern U.S., its stem distinctly purple-spotted (hence its name of *maculata,* i.e., spotted). Leaves lance-shaped, 3–5 inches long. Flowers about ½ inch wide, in a loose, few-flowered cluster. **Color:** Purplish pink. **Height:** 12–30 inches. **Flowering date:** June–July. **Varieties:** None. **Culture:** Set purchased plants (from a dealer in wild flowers) in a low, moist but not wet place, in partial shade, in Oct. or April. Soil may be rich garden loam or non-acid woods soil. Space 10–15 inches apart.

Related plant (not illustrated):
> Blue Phlox (*Phlox divaricata*). 12–18 inches. Flowers lavender or lilac (not blue).

## GROUND PINK (*Phlox subulata*)      p. 172

Quite different from any other phlox in its prostrate habit and its many, tiny, needle-like leaves. It is a perennial and found wild from N.Y. to N.C. and westward, often growing in large patches naturally, and a fine ground cover in the garden. It has nothing to do with the true pinks in spite of its name. Flowers in profuse clusters, each one about ¾ inch wide, its lobes deeply notched. **Color:** Pink or magenta, but see below. **Height:** Prostrate. **Flowering date:** April–May. **Varieties:** Alba (white), Alexander's Rose Gem (rose-pink), Alexander's Pink (pink). **Culture:** Set purchased plants in Oct. in full sun, in a sandy or gritty loam, or even in pure sand. Space 6–8 inches apart and leave alone. It will soon form an exclusive mat of ground-hugging color.

Related plant (not illustrated):
> *Phlox stolonifera.* Creeping, but 8–10 inches high. Flowers purple or violet.

**JACOB'S–LADDER** (*Polemonium caeruleum*)                    p. 172
An erect, Eurasian perennial, often called Greek Valerian and
Charity. Leaves much compounded, its leaflets opposite each
other, narrow and lance-shaped, so arranged as to give a ladder-
like appearance. Flowers broadly bell-shaped, in a loose, branching cluster, about 1 inch wide and drooping. **Color:** Blue. **Height:**
18–30 inches. **Flowering date:** May–June. **Varieties:** Alba (white).
**Culture:** Set purchased plants in Oct. or April in full sun, in
any ordinary garden soil and space 1–2 feet apart. They do better
in reasonably moist sites than dry ones.
    Related plants (not illustrated):
        *Polemonium reptans.* 8–12 inches. Flowers light blue.
        *Polemonium richardsoni.* 5–9 inches. Flowers blue to
            purple.

**BLUE GILIA** (*Gilia capitata*)                              p. 172
A very popular Pacific Coast annual sometimes known as Thim-
ble-Flower. It is an erect plant with finely divided or dissected
leaves, the segments very narrow. Flowers small, crowded in a
dense, clover-like head, and one of the most prized for cut
flowers. **Color:** Blue. **Height:** 18–24 inches. **Flowering date:**
July–frost. **Varieties:** None. **Culture:** Sow seeds ¼ inch deep,
in full sun, in almost any ordinary garden soil, as soon as warm
weather arrives. Space 10–15 inches apart.
    Related plant (not illustrated):
        Bird's-Eyes (*Gilia tricolor*). 18–24 inches. Flowers lilac,
            the tube yellowish, but purple-streaked.

**TREE CYPRESS** (*Gilia rubra*)                              p. 185
Called also Standing Cypress, Texas Plume, and Trailing Fire,
and often offered under the incorrect name of *Gilia coronopiflora.*
It is a perennial (or perhaps a biennial in some regions) native
in the southeastern U.S., but can be made to flower in one season
by following directions below. It is an erect plant with dissected
leaves, the segments of which are thread-thick. Flowers very
showy in a long, narrow cluster. **Color:** Scarlet outside, yellow
and red-dotted inside. **Height:** 3–5 feet. **Flowering date:** June–
July. **Varieties:** None. **Culture:** Sow seeds indoors (6–8 weeks

before outdoor planting is safe), ¼ inch deep in ½ garden soil and ½ sand, thoroughly mixed. When trees leaf out transfer seedlings outdoors in full sun, in any ordinary garden soil, and space 2–3 feet apart. In the South it may persist as a biennial or perennial.

**Left:** Tree Cypress (*Gilia rubra*), p. 184. **Right:**
**Bush** Morning-Glory (*Convolvulus tricolor*), p. 181.


# WATERLEAF FAMILY
### (*Hydrophyllaceae*)

A SMALL family (about 225 species) nearly all herbs, and almost but not quite confined to North America. Like the Borage Family, which follows, its most notable feature is that the flowers are arranged in 1-sided clusters, although each flower is perfectly regular and symmetrical. Leaves opposite each other on the stem (except in the lower leaves of the Baby Blue-Eyes), often lobed or deeply cut. Fruit a dry pod. The Waterleaf of our woodlands (*Hydrophyllum*), for which the family is named, is apparently little known in cultivation and hence omitted here.

**BABY BLUE–EYES** (*Nemophila menziesi*)                    p. 172
A low, Californian, hairy annual widely grown for its attractive blue flowers, and used chiefly for edging or in the rock garden. Leaves cut into 7–9 segments. Flowers bell-shaped, growing in a somewhat 1-sided cluster at the tips of the branches. **Color:** Blue. **Height:** 4–6 inches. **Flowering date:** July–Aug. **Varieties:** Unnamed white, and blue and white forms are offered. **Culture:** Sow seeds where wanted, ¼ inch deep, in full sun, in any ordinary garden soil, after danger of frost is over. Space 3–6 inches apart.
   Related plant (not illustrated) :
      *Nemophila insignis.* 4–6 inches. Flowers similar to
      Baby Blue-Eyes, from which it may not be different.

**CALIFORNIA BLUEBELL** (*Phacelia campanularia*)    p. 172
A velvety-leaved Californian annual, much grown for its showy bloom. Leaves alternately arranged, ovalish and wrinkled. Flowers bell-shaped, in a decidedly 1-sided cluster, which uncoils as the flowers open (scorpioid, i.e., like a scorpion's tail). **Color:** Blue with white lines. **Height:** 5–8 inches. **Flowering date:** July–Aug. **Varieties:** None. **Culture:** Sow seeds ¼ inch deep in any ordinary garden soil, as soon as warm weather arrives, in full sun. Space 4–6 inches apart, by thinning out seedlings, since the plant does not thrive after transplanting.


# BORAGE FAMILY
### (*Boraginaceae*)

A LARGE family (over 1500 species) of chiefly herbaceous plants, but with a few trees and shrubs in the tropics. It comprises a fair number of garden plants, some of them — like the Forget-Me-Not, Heliotrope, Borage, and the Virginia Cowslip — old garden favorites. They have the leaves arranged alternately on the stem, and they are usually hairy or even bristly. The small flowers are regular and symmetrical, but often arranged in a 1-sided cluster, most noticeable in the forget-me-nots, Alkanet, and Heliotrope, where the flower cluster uncoils as it blooms, hence scorpioid (like the coiled tail of a scorpion). Fruit a tiny nut.

**ALKANET** (*Anchusa azurea*)                                    p. 172
A very popular European perennial, often called Bugloss, grown for its profusion of flowers that are borne in a decidedly 1-sided cluster. Leaves coarsely hairy, oblongish, 3–5 inches long. Flowers trumpet-shaped, the cluster leafy. **Color:** Prevailingly blue. **Height:** 2–3 feet. **Flowering date:** June, and sometimes in Sept. **Varieties:** Dropmore (light, sky-blue; also in a dwarf form), Opal (light blue), Perry's (dark blue). **Culture:** Relatively easy in any ordinary garden soil. Set purchased plants in full sun, in Oct. or April, and space 2–3 feet apart. Often sold under the incorrect name of *Anchusa italica*. For the plant often offered as *Anchusa myosotidiflora* see *Brunnera,* below.

Related plants (not illustrated):

> *Anchusa barrelieri.* 18–30 inches. Flowers blue, but the tube white with a yellow throat.
>
> *Anchusa capensis.* A biennial, 12–18 inches. Flowers red in bud, ultimately blue. Grown as an annual, and the variety "Blue Bird" is offered by seedsmen, often under the name of Cape Forget-Me-Not.

**FORGET–ME–NOT** (*Myosotis scorpioides*)               p. 173
A Eurasian, spring-blooming perennial, rather sprawling or even prostrate. Leaves oblongish, without marginal teeth, about 1 inch long. Flowers salver-shaped, always with a central "eye" differently colored from the rest of the corolla, borne in a usually coiled, 1-sided cluster. **Color:** Prevailingly blue. **Height:** Essentially prostrate. **Flowering date:** April–June. **Varieties:** Pink Beauty (pink), Semperflorens (blooming all summer). **Culture:** Set purchased plants in Oct., in partial shade, in rich garden loam, only in a moist or even wet place. Space 6–8 inches apart. Often sold under incorrect name of *Myosotis palustris.*

Related plant (not illustrated):

> *Myosotis arvensis.* Nearly prostrate. Flowers blue or white.

## MADDER FAMILY (*Rubiaceae*), 1 and 2
## HONEYSUCKLE FAMILY (*Caprifoliaceae*), 3
## VALERIAN FAMILY (*Valerianaceae*), 5 and 6
## BELLFLOWER FAMILY (*Campanulaceae*), 4 and 7–9

1. **Bluets** (*Houstonia caerulea*)      **p. 194**
   A delicate native perennial, 3–6 inches high, June-flowering and suited to moist sites in the wild garden.

2. **Partridge-Berry** (*Mitchella repens*)      **p. 195**
   A prostrate, evergreen perennial with bloom in June–July, sometimes confused with the next, but it has a red berry.

3. **Twinflower** (*Linnaea borealis*)      **p. 196**
   Prostrate, evergreen perennial of northern regions. Not suited to coastal plain. Fruit yellow.

4. **Canterbury Bells** (*Campanula Medium*)      **p. 197**
   Striking biennial from southern Europe, 2–3 feet high, flowering in May–June. Seeds must be planted a season before bloom is wanted.

5. **Garden Heliotrope** (*Valeriana officinalis*)      **p. 196**
   Fragrant Eurasian perennial, 2–5 feet high, flowering in June–July. Easily grown anywhere.

6. **Red Valerian** (*Centranthus ruber*)      **p. 197**
   Very fragrant Eurasian perennial, 1–3 feet high, and flowering from July to frost. Easily grown anywhere.

7. **Peach Bells** (*Campanula persicifolia*)      **p. 198**
   Mulch plants in gritty or sandy soil of this Eurasian perennial, 2–3 feet high. Flowers in May–July.

8. **Bellflower** (*Campanula carpatica*)      **p. 199**
   A rock garden perennial, suited only to gritty or sandy soils. Summer-flowering and under 1 foot high.

9. **Bellflower** (*Campanula portenschlagiana*)      **p. 198**
   Not over 6 inches high and flowering in June–July. Suited to the rock garden, and, with care, to other sites.

# VERBENA FAMILY (*Verbenaceae*), 1 and 2
## MINT FAMILY (*Labiatae*), 3–9

1. **Lantana** (*Lantana Camara*)  **p. 206**
   Tropical shrub used as summer bedding plant, not over 30 inches as grown here. Summer-flowering.

2. **Garden Verbena** (*Verbena hortensis*)  **p. 203**
   Fragrant perennial now in many varieties, mostly grown as an annual. Blooms July to frost, mostly 12 inches or less high.

3. **Blue Sage** (*Salvia pitcheri*)  **p. 211**
   A hairy, native perennial, 4–5 feet high, blooming in Aug.–Sept. Easily grown in any ordinary garden soil.

4. **Lavender** (*Lavandula spica*)  **p. 208**
   Odorous, woody perennial, best grown in poor soil if fragrance is object of culture. Summer-flowering, 1–2 feet high.

5. **Bugle** (*Ajuga reptans*)  **p. 212**
   Horticultural forms of this weedy, prostrate perennial are useful ground covers. Blooms in May–June. Difficult to keep from rampant spreading.

6. **Garden Sage** (*Salvia officinalis*)  **p. 210**
   Aromatic woody perennial grown mostly for seasoning. Summer-blooming, 1–2 feet high.

7. **Rosemary** (*Rosmarinus officinalis*)  **p. 207**
   Fragrant undershrub with highly aromatic flowers and foliage. Not reliably hardy north of New York City.

8. **Nepeta** (*Nepeta mussini*)  **p. 213**
   An aromatic perennial, easily grown anywhere. Flowers in May–July; not over 15 inches high.

9. **Scarlet Sage** (*Salvia splendens*)  **p. 210**
   A long-season annual as grown here; perhaps too common but useful for midsummer color. Not frost-hardy.

**ANNUAL FORGET–ME–NOT** (*Myosotis sylvatica*)   p. 173
A Eurasian biennial often catalogued under the incorrect name
of *Myosotis alpestris*. It is a charming, essentially prostrate
ground cover, under tulips or spring-blooming perennials. It has
tiny, oblongish leaves, without marginal teeth, and small, salver-
shaped flowers, with a differently colored "eye," arranged in a
1-sided, coiled cluster. **Color:** Prevailingly blue, but see below.
**Height:** 3–8 inches. **Flowering date:** May–Aug. **Varieties:** Rose
(pink), Blue Eyes (bright blue), White (white), Royal Blue
(indigo). **Culture:** Sometimes flowering from seed in a single
season, but best treated as a biennial. Sow seeds, in July, ¼ inch
deep, in any good garden loam and transplant seedlings in Sept.
or Oct. to cold frame (in the North) or nursery bed south of
Philadelphia. Early in spring transfer seedlings to wanted place,
which should be in full sun or partial shade, in rich garden loam,
and space 5–7 inches apart. Discard plants after they bloom or,
if possible, leave them alone; they will often persist from self-
sown seed.

**CREEPING FORGET–ME–NOT** (*Omphalodes verna*) p. 192
Often known as Navelwort, this European perennial is a close
relative of the traditional Forget-Me-Not, but not so much grown.
It has trailing stems but erect flowering tips. Leaves ovalish, the
lower ones long-stalked, pointed, the stem leaves short-stalked.
Flowers starlike, not over ½ inch wide, in loose, 1-sided clusters.
**Color:** Blue. **Height:** 5–8 inches. **Flowering date:** June. **Va-
rieties:** Alba (white). **Culture:** Set purchased plants in April or
Oct., in partial shade, in any ordinary garden soil that is not
acid (neutral or slightly alkaline). Space 5–8 inches apart.

**CHINESE FORGET–ME–NOT**
(*Cynoglossum amabile*)                                          p. 173
An eastern Asiatic biennial, but grown as an annual since it
blooms from seed in a single season. It is a somewhat weedy
plant with rough foliage, the leaves oblong, 2–3 inches long.
Flowers funnel-shaped, in 1-sided clusters. **Color:** Blue or white.
**Height:** 18–24 inches. **Flowering date:** July–Oct. **Varieties:** Fir-
mament (indigo), Snow Bird (white), Blue Bird (blue), White

Cloud (white). **Culture:** Sow seeds ⅛ inch deep, either broad-cast or in rows 18 inches apart, in any ordinary garden soil, in full sun. Thin out to 10–18 inches apart.

Related plants (not illustrated):

> *Cynoglossum grande.* A perennial 2–3 feet. Flowers blue or purple with white "eye."
>
> *Cynoglossum nervosum.* 2–3 feet. Flowers blue. A Himalayan perennial.

**HELIOTROPE** (*Heliotropium arborescens*) p. 173

A Peruvian perennial, but usually grown as an annual that needs heat and a long growing season. It should not be confused (but often is) with the Garden Heliotrope, for which see p. 196. Leaves alternately arranged, hairy and oblongish, not dissected as in the Garden Heliotrope. Flowers rather small, deliciously vanilla-scented, borne in forked, 1-sided very showy clusters. **Color:** Purple or violet. **Height:** 2–4 feet. **Flowering date:** July–frost. **Varieties:** Royal Fragrance (especially fragrant), Mme. Bruant (violet-blue with white "eye"). **Culture:** Sow seeds ⅛ inch deep in pots or boxes indoors in Feb. and grow seedlings indoors until early June or late May. Transfer seedlings outdoors into rich garden soil, in full sun or partial shade, and space 1–2 feet apart. For winter pot-plant indoors, take cuttings in Sept. from outdoor plants, planting them in a mixture of ½ soil and ½ sand. Carry them through the winter indoors (night tempera-ture of 50°–55°) and plant them outdoors the following May 15–June 1. Often sold under incorrect name of *Heliotropium peruvianum,* and sometimes, but rather inappropriately, called Cherry Pie.

**YELLOW PUCCOON** (*Lithospermum incisum*) p. 192

A North American perennial from dry prairies and other open places, not particularly showy, but grown for its orange-yellow flowers, the lobes of which are distinctly toothed on the margin. It is a diffusely branched plant with very narrow, alternate leaves and a terminal cluster of funnel-shaped flowers that are not arranged in an obviously 1-sided cluster. **Color:** Orange-

Left: Yellow Puccoon (*Lithospermum incisum*),
p. 191. Right: Creeping Forget-Me-Not (*Omphalodes verna*), p. 190.

yellow. **Height:** 1–2 feet. **Flowering date:** April–June. **Varieties:**
None. **Culture:** Set purchased plants (from middle–western and
Pacific Coast dealers) in sandy or gritty loam in full sun, in Oct.,
and space 8–10 inches apart. Not much grown, but it will stand
more heat and dryness than better plants. Often offered as *Lithospermum angustifolium,* and frequently called Gromwell.

**LITHODORA** (*Lithodora diffusa*)                    p. 173
Commonly, but incorrectly, offered as *Lithospermum prostratum,*
this woody perennial from southern Europe, with evergreen foliage, provides masses of blue bloom in midsummer in the rock
garden. Leaves narrowly lance-shaped, alternate, without marginal teeth. Flowers small, arranged in slightly 1-sided very profuse clusters. **Color:** Blue. **Height:** Prostrate. **Flowering date:**
July–Aug. **Varieties:** Heavenly Blue (intense blue, and the preferred sort). **Culture:** Set purchased plants in the rock garden,
in partial shade in sandy or gritty loam, in April or Oct. Space
5–7 inches apart and leave alone. Not reliably hardy north of

New York City, and a winter mulch of straw or strawy manure is useful anywhere.

Related plant (not illustrated):

*Lithodora fruticosa.* Prostrate, shrubby. Flowers blue.

**BRUNNERA** (*Brunnera macrophylla*) p. 173

This showy perennial from the Caucasus and Siberia is usually listed under the incorrect name of *Anchusa myosotidiflora,* perhaps because it is somewhat like the Alkanet and has flowers resembling a forget-me-not. But it has large, basal, heart-shaped leaves and an erect, rather hairy stem. Flowers about ⅙ inch wide, borne in a profuse, naked, scarcely 1-sided, showy cluster. **Color:** Blue. **Height:** 12–18 inches. **Flowering date:** May–June. **Varieties:** None. **Culture:** Set purchased plants in Oct. or April, in partial shade, in rich, rather moist garden loam. Space 10–15 inches apart, or more if soil is rich.

**VIRGINIA COWSLIP** (*Mertensia virginica*) p. 173

A beautiful perennial native to moist or even swampy woods of the eastern U.S., often and more appropriately called Virginia Bluebells or even Lungwort, a name properly confined to the next species. It has bluish-green, mostly basal, elliptic leaves, 3–7 inches long, their stalks somewhat winged. Flowers funnel-shaped about 1 inch long, drooping, in a terminal cluster only slightly 1-sided. **Color:** Blue, but often fading to pinkish. **Height:** 10–20 inches. **Flowering date:** May–June. **Varieties:** None. **Culture:** Set purchased plants (they survive digging from the wild with difficulty) in partial or deep shade, in a moist or even wet place in the wild garden, in woods soil that is not acid. Space 8–12 inches apart. It is sometimes successful in ordinary garden soil if the site is partly shady and reasonably moist.

**LUNGWORT** (*Pulmonaria angustifolia*) p. 173

A low, European perennial, once thought to be a remedy for lung affections, but now grown for its handsome, coiled, 1-sided clusters of early bloom. Leaves hairy, mostly basal, lance-shaped, tapering into a winged stalk and often mottled. Flowers small in a naked, coiled, 1-sided cluster. **Color:** Blue. **Height:** 8–12 inches. **Flowering date:** April–May. **Varieties:** Azurea (light blue). **Culture:** Set purchased plants in any ordinary garden

soil, in Oct., in partial shade and a reasonably moist site. Space
6–10 inches apart.
   Related plants (not illustrated):
      *Pulmonaria officinalis.* 6–12 inches. Flowers purplish red.
      *Pulmonaria saccharata.* 10–18 inches. Flowers white or
         reddish purple; sometimes called Bethlehem Sage.

**BORAGE** (*Borago officinalis*)                                    p. 173
A coarse, stiff-hairy annual from southern Europe and northern
Africa, its aromatic foliage liked by some to mix in salads. Its
leaves are oblongish, 3–5 inches long, narrowed at the base into
a winged stalk. Flowers wheel-shaped, about ¾ inch wide, in
a loose, leafy, somewhat 1-sided cluster; much sought by bees.
**Color:** Blue. **Height:** 12–20 inches. **Flowering date:** June–Aug.
**Varieties:** None. **Culture:** Sow seeds ¼ inch deep, in ordinary
garden soil, after warm weather has arrived, in full sun, where
wanted. Space (or thin out) to 10–15 inches apart. They do not
transplant easily.

# MADDER FAMILY
## (*Rubiaceae*)

I**F** **THIS** book contained trees and shrubs it would give more of
an idea of the importance of the Madder Family, for here would
come the button-bush and the trees that yield coffee, quinine, and
ipecac. But among its 4500 species, mostly tropical, there is a
dearth of garden plants. The leaf arrangement is prevailingly
opposite, and they generally have no marginal teeth. Flowers
perfectly regular, sometimes salver-shaped, borne in pairs or quite
solitary in those below. Only two plants of the Madder Family
are included here.

**BLUETS** (*Houstonia caerulea*)                                    p. 188
This delightful little meadow plant of eastern North America
is often known as Quaker Ladies and Innocence. It carpets cool,
moist meadows and can be grown in the wild garden only in
places that approach such conditions. It has tiny, basal leaves and

a single flower usually not over ½ inch wide, on a thread-thin stalk. **Color:** Pale blue or white, with a yellow "eye." **Height:** 3–6 inches. **Flowering date:** June. **Varieties:** None. **Culture:** Set purchased plants (from dealer in wild flowers), in Oct. in full sun, in the wild garden only if there is a moist or wettish site. Plant in masses and in a few years it will carpet the ground. Not suited to hot or dry regions.

Related plant (not illustrated):

Star Violet (*Houstonia serpyllifolia*). Prostrate. Flowers deep blue.

**PARTRIDGE–BERRY** (*Mitchella repens*)  p. 188

A prostrate, creeping, somewhat woody plant of eastern North America, mostly in dry or moist woods and sometimes confused with the Twinflower because both bear their flowers in pairs. The Partridge-Berry has thin trailing stems, not much over 15 inches long, which root at the joints and hence soon make new plants. Leaves evergreen, almost round, about ¾ inch wide. Flowers funnel-shaped, borne in pairs at the end of a short stalk. There are only 4 lobes to the corolla (5 in the Twinflower). Fruit a scarlet berry. **Color:** White. **Height:** Prostrate. **Flowering date:** June–July. **Varieties:** None. **Culture:** Set purchased plants (from wild–flower dealer) in good woodland soil, in the wild garden, in Oct. or April, in partial or complete shade (no evergreens). Soil only faintly or not at all acid. Space 10–15 inches apart and leave alone to make its natural mat. Suited to warm dry regions. Very popular as winter terrarium plant, for its neat, evergreen leaves and scarlet berries make a fine show. Not suited to indoor culture otherwise.

# HONEYSUCKLE FAMILY
## (*Caprifoliaceae*)

A SMALL (350 species) family of highly important garden plants all of them showy shrubs, vines and trees such as *Weigela*, honeysuckle, *Viburnum,* and the elderberry, but with only the one below included here since all the rest are woody plants. Leaves oppositely arranged. Flowers regular (in the one below) and more or less tubular. Fruit small, dry, and 1-seeded.

**TWINFLOWER** (*Linnaea borealis*) p. 188
This creeping denizen of the North was found by Linnaeus in Lapland and named for him. It is found throughout the cooler regions of the North Temperate (and even arctic) Zone and some call our American plant *Linnaea americana*. It somewhat resembles the Partridge-Berry, but has 5 lobes to its corolla (4 in the Partridge-Berry), and yellow fruit. Leaves evergreen, opposite each other, broadly oval, about ¾ inches wide. Flowers in pairs on a thread-thin stem that is much above the foliage. **Color:** Rose-pink to white. **Height:** Prostrate. **Flowering date:** June–July. **Varieties:** None. **Culture:** Set purchased plants (from wild-flower dealer) in an acid woods soil, in the wild garden, only if you are in a cool region. Plant in April or Oct., in partial or complete shade (evergreens help acidity), and leave alone. Not suited to warm, dry regions.

# VALERIAN FAMILY
## (*Valerianaceae*)

A COMPARATIVELY unimportant and relatively small family included here only because it contains the Garden Heliotrope and the Red Valerian, both commonly cultivated. Leaves arranged oppositely. Flowers more or less tubular (slightly spurred in the Red Valerian), followed by a small seedlike fruit.

**GARDEN HELIOTROPE** (*Valeriana officinalis*) p. 188
A spicily fragrant Eurasian perennial, sometimes confused with the true Heliotrope (which see at p. 191), and with unpleasantly scented roots. Leaves finely dissected, almost fernlike. Flowers in dense, headlike, long-stalked clusters, the corolla about ½ inch long. **Color:** White, pink, or lavender. **Height:** 2–5 feet. **Flowering date:** June–July. **Varieties:** None. **Culture:** Set purchased plants in full sun in any ordinary garden soil, in April or Oct., preferably in a moist spot. Space 2–2½ feet apart, and replant every 3–4 years, since it tends to die out.

**RED VALERIAN** (*Centranthus ruber*)                    p. 188

A Eurasian perennial, and an old garden favorite, with very fragrant flowers in dense, terminal clusters. From its prevailingly scarlet flowers it is called by some Scarlet Lightning; also Jupiter's-Beard. It is a bushy plant with ovalish, stalkless, undivided leaves. Flowers tubular, about ½ inch long, faintly spurred at the base. **Color:** Scarlet or crimson. **Height:** 1–3 feet. **Flowering date:** June–frost. **Varieties:** Albus (white). **Culture:** Set purchased plants in Oct. or April, in full sun, in any ordinary garden soil, and space 12–18 inches apart. Often sold under the incorrect name of *Valeriana coccinea.*

# BELLFLOWER FAMILY
## (*Campanulaceae*)

Showy and prevailingly blue-flowered, the Bellflower Family contains many old garden favorites. Most of the 1000 species are herbs from temperate regions, but a few tropical kinds are shrubs and trees. As the technical name of the family suggests (*Campanula* is Latin for a little bell) the flowers are almost exactly bell-shaped, perfectly regular, and have 5 pointed or blunt lobes to the corolla. Fruit a dry-splitting pod with numerous seeds. Over 50 species are in cultivation, of which the following are the best known.

**CANTERBURY BELLS** (*Campanula Medium*)              p. 188

A much planted biennial from southern Europe with oblong hairy leaves, coarsely toothed on the margin, and 6–9 inches long. Flowers about 1 inch wide, solitary, or in loose clusters. Two distinct types of flower are common: one has the bell-like flower included within a similarly colored envelope (hose-in-hose type), while another has the bell-like flower set on a similarly colored "saucer" (cup-and-saucer type, sometimes offered as *Campanula calycanthema*). **Color:** Prevailingly blue, but see below. **Height:** 2–3 feet. **Flowering date:** May–June. **Varieties:** Alba (white), Rosea (pink); also lavender and purple (but unnamed). **Culture:** Sow seeds in July, ¼ inch deep, in any good garden soil, in half-shade. Transplant seedlings to cold frame or nursery in Sept., and carry through winter with a light, airy mulch of straw or salt hay. Transplant seedlings where wanted early in May, into good garden soil in full sun, spacing them 15–20 inches apart. They do not like winter rain and slush.

Related plants (not illustrated):

Coventry Bells (*Campanula Trachelium*). 2–3 feet. Flowers bluish purple.

*Campanula glomerata.* 12–20 inches. Flowers blue or white.

**PEACH BELLS** (*Campanula persicifolia*)                p. 188

A European perennial with finely toothed, narrow leaves that are 6–8 inches long. Flowers nearly 1½ inches wide in very showy terminal clusters, and now in several varieties, some very popular as pot plants. **Color:** Prevailingly blue, but see below. **Height:** 2–3 feet. **Flowering date:** May–July. **Varieties:** Blue Gardenia (blue), Snowdrift (white), Coerulea (blue), Telham Beauty (blue), White Pearl (white). **Culture:** Set purchased plants in Oct. or April, in full sun or half-shade, in a sandy or gritty loam (no clay), and space 15–20 inches apart. Each winter mulch with light, strawy manure, and in the spring dig it in.

Related plants (not illustrated):

Chimney Bellflower (*Campanula pyramidalis*). 3–5 feet. Flowers pale blue.

*Campanula lactiflora.* 2–4 feet. Flowers pale blue or white (in a variety).

**BELLFLOWER** (*Campanula portenschlagiana*)          p. 188

A low, beautiful, Dalmatian perennial, often grown in the rock garden but suited to other sites with proper attention given to details. Leaves nearly round or kidney-shaped, about 1 inch wide. Flowers few, but handsome, about ¾ inch long. **Color:** Purplish blue. **Height:** 6–8 inches. **Flowering date:** June–July. **Varieties:** None. **Culture:** Set purchased plants in Oct. or April in partial shade or full sun, in a gritty or sandy loam (no clay or wet soggy soil), and space 5–10 inches apart. Suited particularly to the porous, drained soils of the rock garden. Mulch with strawy manure over the winter, in spring digging it in. Often sold as *Campanula muralis.*

Related plants (not illustrated):

*Campanula cochlearifolia.* 4–7 inches. Flowers blue or white.

*Campanula poscharskyana.* 4–6 inches. Flowers blue.

## BELLFLOWER (*Campanula carpatica*) p. 188

A rock garden perennial from eastern Europe, with large, handsome flowers, mostly solitary, hardly ever in clusters. Leaves ovalish, toothed, not over 1 inch long. Flowers erect, nearly 2 inches wide, very showy. **Color:** Prevailingly blue, but see below. **Height:** 8–12 inches. **Flowering date:** July–Aug. **Varieties:** Alba (white), Cullinmore (an improved strain, with longer flowering period; blue). **Culture:** Set purchased plants in gritty or sandy loam (no soggy clay!) either in the rock garden or in partial shade or full sun in the open border, in Oct. or April. Provide a winter mulch of strawy manure to be dug in in the spring. Space 6–9 inches apart.

Related plants (not illustrated):

Blue-Bells-of-Scotland (*Campanula rotundifolia*). **6–9** inches. Flowers blue.

*Campanula Elatines.* Prostrate. Flowers sky blue.

*Campanula garganica.* Practically prostrate. Flowers blue.

## BALLOON–FLOWER (*Platycodon grandiflorum*) p. 200

A showy perennial from eastern Asia (sometimes, but incorrectly, called Chinese Bellflower) cultivated for its handsome, broadly bell-shaped or saucer-shaped flowers that may be 2–3 inches wide. It is closely related to the true Bellflower, differing only in technical characters. It is a weak-stemmed, brittle plant which must be staked to keep it erect, or allowed to sprawl over walls, etc. **Color:** Blue. **Height:** 18–30 inches. **Flowering date:** July–Aug. **Varieties:** Album (white), Mariesi (dwarf, or lower than the typical sort), Mariesi Album (white and dwarf), Japonicum (flower starlike). **Culture:** Set purchased plants in sandy, well-

drained soil (its roots rot easily in moist places), in full sun,
in Oct. or April. Space 12–18 inches apart and leave alone, since
they do not take kindly to transplanting. Handle with care;
plants break off with ordinary weeding, etc.

Left: Shepherd's Scabious (*Jasione perennis*), below. Right:
Balloon-Flower (*Platycodon grandiflorum*), p. 199.

**SHEPHERD'S–SCABIOUS** (*Jasione perennis*)                    above
A not much cultivated perennial from southern Europe, differing
from most of the plants in the Bellflower Family by having its
small flowers in compact long-stalked heads that may be 1–2
inches wide. The flowers are cut into narrow segments and the
tight head suggests a plant of the Daisy Family. **Color:** Blue.
**Height:** 8–12 inches. **Flowering date:** July–Aug. **Varieties:** None.
**Culture:** Set purchased plants in full sun in Oct. or April, in
well-drained garden loam that is somewhat sandy. Space 8–12
inches apart and leave alone, since it resents moving.

**LADYBELL** (*Adenophora potanini*)                    below

An infrequently planted Chinese perennial, the stem hairy, and grown for its handsome flowers borne in a terminal cluster. It is closely related to the true bellflowers and differs only in technical characters. The flowers are about ¾ inch long, broadly bell-shaped, followed by a small dry pod. **Color:** Blue. **Height:** 2–3 feet. **Flowering date:** June–July. **Varieties:** None. **Culture:** Set purchased plants in Oct. or April, in full sun, in moist, rich garden loam, and space 1–2 feet apart. It does not transplant easily, and is best left alone.

**HORNED RAMPION** (*Phyteuma scheuchzeri*)          below

A rock garden perennial from the mountains of southern Europe grown mostly only by rock garden enthusiasts. It is an erect plant with oblongish or narrower leaves and a dense head of flowers, about 1 inch in diameter. Below the head is a cluster

Left: Horned Rampion (*Phyteuma scheuchzeri*), above. Upper Right: Ladybell (*Adenophora potanini*), above. Lower Right: Thyme (*Thymus vulgaris*), p. 208.

of tiny long leaflets (bracts). **Color:** Violet-blue. **Height:** 10–15 inches. **Flowering date:** June. **Varieties:** None. **Culture:** Set purchased plants in a sunny site in the rock garden, in Oct. or April, in a gritty or sandy soil with perfect drainage. Space 8–12 inches apart and leave alone, since they resent transplanting. Often called merely Rampion.

Related plants (not illustrated):

*Phyteuma hemisphaericum.* 4–6 inches. Flowers blue (rarely white).

*Phyteuma orbiculare.* 1–2 feet. Flowers purple.

# *Flowers Irregular, Unsymmetrical, Lopsided or 2-Lipped*

ALL the plants with a united corolla, such as those between pp. 163 and 202 have flowers that are perfectly cup-shaped, funnel-shaped, cornucopia-shaped, or otherwise regular and symmetrical, common examples being Phlox, primroses, all plants of the Heath Family, Alkanet, and many others.

But from here to p. 240 most of the flowers are decidedly irregular, unsymmetrical, lopsided, and most of them are 2-lipped. In the latter case there is an upper lip, usually 3-lobed, and an under lip, mostly 2-lobed. Good examples of a 2-lipped flower are the Snapdragon, Lobelia, and Foxglove. In these, the unsymmetrical nature of the corolla is perfectly obvious (as compared to phlox, for instance), but in some families that have 2-lipped flowers they are small enough to require close scrutiny to divulge their 2-lipped character. All such flowers are called by the experts zygomorphic, a term that needs no further use here.

This irregularity in the symmetry of the corolla is so nearly universal in all plants between pp. 203 and 240 that it will come as a shock to find that Nature, as in so many other things, has a streak of inconsistency which results in a few of the plants below having nearly or quite regular flowers. All such are noted where they occur. They are included here because they belong to families that are overwhelmingly characterized by unsymmetrical flowers in spite of these few exceptions.

There are over 50 plants in this group that have unsymmetrical, 2-lipped, or otherwise irregular flowers. Among them such old garden favorites as Snapdragon, Lobelia, Foxglove, Pentstemon, Speedwell, Red Turtlehead, Garden Verbena (only weakly 2-lipped), Butterfly-Flower, all the Mint Family, and many others not so well known.

For convenience of arrangement and ease of identification all plants in this group are divided into well-defined families and these are arranged below in the most helpful sequence. Four of them are of outstanding garden importance, the Verbena, Mint, Potato, and Figwort Families, while a small group at the end are scattered in 4 less-known families.

# VERBENA FAMILY
## (*Verbenaceae*)

A MEDIUM-SIZED family (perhaps 750 species) mostly tropical or subtropical shrubs and trees, but containing some handsome shrubs (blue spirea), and only two garden flowers of any importance. Both have leaves arranged opposite each other. Flowers only weakly 2-lipped and often appearing (superficially) as nearly symmetrical.

**GARDEN VERBENA** (*Verbena hortensis*)                    p. 189
A fragrant garden perennial of hybrid origin (its parents almost certainly South American) grown mostly as an annual, since it blooms from seed the first year, if started early, indoors. It is a rather weak or sprawling plant, except in dwarf varieties, with oppositely arranged lance-shaped, blunt-toothed leaves. Flowers small usually with a differently colored "eye," in compact terminal clusters, very showy. **Color:** Various, see below. **Height:** 8–12 inches in regular form, compact and 5–8 inches in dwarf types. **Flowering date:** July–frost. **Varieties:** TALL TYPES: Miss Willmott (pink), Etna (red), Spectrum Red (red), Lavender Glory (lavender), Salmon King (salmon), Vivid (scarlet), White

# MINT FAMILY
## (*Labiatae*)

1. **Sweet Marjoram** (*Majorana hortensis*)     **p. 209**
An aromatic plant grown for seasoning and for its summer-blooming flowers.

2. **Pot Marjoram** (*Origanum vulgare*)     **p. 209**
An aromatic perennial, 15–30 inches high. Summer-blooming.

3. **Horehound** (*Marrubium vulgare*)     **p. 210**
A weedy perennial beloved for the fragrant oil used in horehound drops. It is 15–25 inches high and summer-blooming.

4. **Skullcap** (*Scutellaria baicalensis coelestina*)     **p. 215**
An Asiatic perennial, worthy of wider cultivation, 8–15 inches high. Summer-blooming.

5. **Dragonhead** (*Dracocephalum nutans*)     **p. 214**
A Siberian perennial, 8–12 inches high. It does not flower until Aug.

6. **Betony** (*Stachys grandiflora*)     **p. 212**
An Asiatic perennial, 2–3 feet high. Blooms in June or July.

7. **Creeping Mint** (*Mentha requieni*)     **p. 212**
A prostrate perennial, useful only in gritty soil in the rock garden. Blooms in June–July.

8. **Russian Sage** (*Perovskia atriplicifolia*)     **p. 215**
A sage-scented Siberian perennial, 3–5 feet high, blooming in Aug. and Sept.

9. **Germander** (*Teucrium chamaedrys*)     **p. 215**
A little-grown woody perennial, 6–8 inches high. Autumn-blooming.

# MINT FAMILY (*Labiatae*), 1–3
# POTATO FAMILY (*Solanaceae*), 4–9

1. **Bee-Balm** (*Monarda didyma;* Salmon Queen)                    **p. 214**
   Aromatic, almost weedy perennial, 1–2 feet high, and summer-blooming. Many varieties are better than the typical wild plant.

2. **False Dragonhead** (*Dracocephalum virginianum*)               **p. 213**
   A stately native perennial, 3–5 feet high, blooming July–Sept. Best grown in partial shade. Flowers often reddish.

3. **Coleus** (*Coleus blumei*)                                     **p. 216**
   Grown only for colored foliage. Not frost-hardy and to be used only as summer bedding plant.

4. **Browallia** (*Browallia speciosa*)                             **p. 222**
   A tropical annual, 12–18 inches high, blooming from July to Sept. Start seeds indoors; 8–10 weeks before outdoor planting is safe.

5. **Angel's-Trumpet** (*Datura Metel*)                             **p. 222**
   Poisonous annual from India, with immense flowers. Blooms July–Sept. Height 3–5 feet.

6. **Petunia** (*Petunia* hybrids)                                  **p. 217**
   Protean group of popular bedding plants doing best along the seashore. Long-season annuals to be started in the house.

7. **Winter Cherry** (*Physalis alkekengi*)                         **p. 223**
   Eurasian perennial grown more for its fruits than for flowers. Height 1–2 feet.

8. **Nicotiana** (*Nicotiana alata grandiflora*)                    **p. 218**
   A beautifully night-fragrant perennial, 3–4 feet high, usually grown as an annual. Flowers closed in sunshine.

9. **Butterfly-Flower** (*Schizanthus wisetonensis*)               **p. 219**
   Brittle, showy, hybrid annual, 2–4 feet high. Sow seeds indoors; 8–10 weeks before outdoor planting is safe.

Beauty (white), Royale (blue, with yellow eye), Sutton's Blue (blue). Dwarf types: Sparkle (red with white eye), Crystal (white), also unnamed varieties with salmon, pink, red, scarlet, blue, and white flowers, but no yellows. **Culture:** Sow seeds indoors in March, ⅛ inch deep, in pans or boxes in a mixture of ¼ sand and ¾ good garden soil, thoroughly mixed. Transfer seedlings outdoors only after settled warm weather has arrived, in full sun, in any good garden soil. Space 8–10 inches apart and pinch out a few leaves of the tall types to promote bloom. The dwarf types need no pinching. If wanted for next year, dig up the tuberous root before frost, pot up, and carry through the winter indoors.

Related plants (not illustrated):

*Verbena rigida.* 12–20 inches. Flowers purplish blue; usually offered under incorrect name of *Verbena venosa.*

Vervain (*Verbena canadensis*). 12–20 inches. Flowers purple.

Vervain (*Verbena hastata*). 2–3 feet. Flowers blue.

The Lemon Verbena (*Lippia citriodora*) is omitted here because it is a subtropical shrub. For the Sand Verbena see p. 66.

## LANTANA (*Lantana Camara*) p. 189

A tropical American, rather weak-stemmed shrub, which should be excluded here except that it is widely used as a summer bedding plant. It will stand no frost, and is sometimes (not very appropriately) called Red or Yellow Sage. Leaves ovalish or heart-shaped, roughish, 3–6 inches long. Flowers small, in a flat-topped cluster, the individual flower not noticeably 2-lipped and only slightly unsymmetrical. **Color:** Yellow at first, then orange or red, often with the 3 colors simultaneously. **Height:** Naturally 3–5 feet, as bedding plant 18–30 inches. **Flowering date:** July–frost. **Varieties:** At least a dozen, but uncertainly named and not available everywhere; including white, yellow, pink, orange, and cream kinds. **Culture:** Hardy outdoors throughout the year from S.C. south and along the Gulf Coast to Calif., northward to coastal Ore. and Wash. Elsewhere set purchased pot plants in full sun, only after warm weather arrives, in a rather poor soil (rich soil promotes luxuriant leaves but few flowers). Space 12–18 inches apart. If wanted for indoor winter culture, dig up before frost and pot up in same soil, keeping indoor temperature 55°–65° (no dry heat).

# MINT FAMILY
### (*Labiatae*)

An enormous group (over 3000 species) containing many aromatic plants such as Mint, Rosemary, Balm, Horehound, Lavender, Sage, Savory, and Thyme, but only a handful of garden flowers, the most noteworthy being *Salvia* and a few others. Some of these aromatic plants are cultivated also for their flowers, and these are noted below. The Mint Family is one of the easiest to identify, for practically all of them have a square or angled stem, with their leaves arranged opposite each other. Flowers are often small, always with an upper and lower lip (very noticeable in *Salvia*), and usually crowded in close clusters either at the leaf joints, or terminal. They are thus, of course, highly irregular and unsymmetrical flowers.

In such a large group as the Mint Family, the distinctions between the different kinds are technically difficult and it will hence be convenient to group them as follows:

*Plants grown mostly for their flowers; aromatic but not as seasoning herbs. See p. 210.*

*Plants grown mostly for the aromatic oil in their foliage; "herbs" in the sense of the herb gardeners.*

## Aromatic Herbs of the Mint Family

This book cannot include all plants in the Mint Family used as fragrant or seasoning herbs. Those that are both fragrant and have attractive flowers include only the 7 immediately below.

**ROSEMARY** (*Rosmarinus officinalis*)                    p. 189
A perennial, evergreen, undershrub from the Mediterranean

region with highly aromatic flowers and foliage. Leaves small, lance-shaped, about 1 inch long and ashy-colored. Flowers small, crowded in clusters at the leaf joints, 2-lipped, the upper lip 2-lobed, the lower lip 3-lobed. **Color:** Pale blue. **Height:** 3–5 feet. **Flowering date:** July–Aug. **Varieties:** None. **Culture:** Set purchased plants in full sun, in any rather poor or indifferent garden soil that is well drained, in Oct. or April. Space 2–3 feet apart and protect from north winds if possible. It is not reliably hardy much north of New York City. An old English garden saying has it that "Where rosemary grows best the mistress is master." In the South it is often clipped as a low, fragrant hedge. To maintain most odor, apply no fertilizer.

## LAVENDER (*Lavandula spica*)                                    p. 189
A highly odorous woody perennial from the Mediterranean region grown both for its aromatic foliage and handsome fragrant flowers. Leaves white-felty, the margins rolled, about 1½ inches long and lance-shaped, without marginal teeth. Flowers about ½ inch long, 2-lipped, and crowded in clusters at the leaf joints. **Color:** Lavender-blue. **Height:** 1–2 feet. **Flowering date:** July–Aug. **Varieties:** Alba (white), Rosea (pink). **Culture:** Set purchased plants in April or Oct., in full sun, in any poor or indifferent garden soil. Space 10–15 inches apart and see that the site is well drained. Often, with the related plant below, known as French Lavender. Frequently offered under the incorrect names of *Lavandula vera* or *Lavandula officinalis*. Do not fertilize if fragrance is the chief object.
   Related plant (not illustrated):
      *Lavandula stoechas.* 2–3 feet. Flowers dark purple. Not
      hardy in the North.

## THYME (*Thymus vulgaris*)                                    p. 201
A low, somewhat woody perennial from the Mediterranean region, mostly grown for seasoning, but also having attractive small flowers. Leaves nearly stalkless, ovalish, the margins rolled. Flowers 2-lipped, scarcely ¼ inch long, usually crowded in interrupted clusters, often at the leaf joints. **Color:** Lilac-purple. **Height:** 6–8 inches. **Flowering date:** June. **Varieties:** Several,

but poorly defined and not significantly differing from the type. **Culture:** Set purchased plants in Oct. or April, in full sun, in any rather poor or indifferent garden soil that is well drained. Space 5–7 inches apart and renew plants every third or fourth year, for it tends to die out.

Related plant (not illustrated):

Mother-of-Thyme or Creeping Thyme (*Thymus serpyllum*). Prostrate. Flowers purplish. Found in many varieties.

**SWEET MARJORAM** (*Majorana hortensis*)                          p. 204
A Mediterranean perennial grown mostly for its aromatic and spicy foliage. While a perennial in warm regions it is grown here as an annual, needing a long growing season. It should be distinguished from the Pot Marjoram (see below), which is a true perennial and grown as such. Sweet Marjoram has stalked leaves, elliptic in outline and only ½ inch long. Flowers small, crowded in dense, white-hairy clusters, which are grouped in spikes. **Color:** Purplish or white. **Height:** 1–2 feet. **Flowering date:** July–Aug. **Varieties:** None. **Culture:** Sow seeds ⅛ inch deep in boxes or pots, indoors in March, in a mixture of ½ garden loam and ½ sand, thoroughly mixed. Set seedlings outdoors when trees leaf out, in full sun, in any ordinary garden soil. Space 10–18 inches apart, or grow in rows, for seasoning. Often and confusingly offered under the incorrect name of *Origanum majoranum.*

**POT MARJORAM** (*Origanum vulgare*)                          p. 204
Often called Wild Marjoram and sometimes Winter-Sweet, this European perennial has become naturalized in North America as a weedy escape from gardens. It is an erect aromatic plant with oval leaves about 1 inch long. Flowers fragrant, small, crowded in dense clusters that are borne on forked terminal branchlets. **Color:** Purplish pink. **Height:** 15–30 inches. **Flowering date:** July–Aug. **Varieties:** None. **Culture:** Set purchased plants in Oct. or April, in full sun, in any ordinary garden soil. Space 12–15 inches apart. Easy to grow and may become weedy. Not to be confused with the Sweet Marjoram (see above).

**HOREHOUND** (*Marrubium vulgare*)                              p. 204
A coarse, weedy Eurasian perennial with highly aromatic foliage
(used fresh to make horehound drops); and often a rampant
weed as an established escape along our roadsides. Leaves white-
woolly, ovalish, ¾–1½ inches long. Flowers small, crowded in
dense almost stalkless clusters at the leaf joints. **Color:** Whitish
or dirty white. **Height:** 15–25 inches. **Flowering date:** July–Aug.
**Varieties:** None. **Culture:** Easy, and difficult to keep it within
bounds. Set purchased plants (or ones collected from thickets)
in any soil in full sun, in Oct. or April. Space 1–2 feet apart.
Watch out for its tendency to become a garden nuisance!

**GARDEN SAGE** (*Salvia officinalis*)                          p. 189
A highly aromatic, woody perennial from the Mediterranean
region, grown for centuries for seasoning, but also for its attractive flower clusters. Leaves 2–3 inches long, wrinkled, broadly
lance-shaped, covered with short white hairs. Flowers in many-
flowered clusters, these mostly terminal and interrupted. **Color:**
Purplish blue or white. **Height:** 1–2 feet. **Flowering date:** July–
Aug. **Varieties:** None. **Culture:** Set purchased plants in Oct. or
April, in full sun, in any ordinary garden loam that is well
drained (no clay). Space 1–2 feet apart.


## PLANTS OF THE MINT FAMILY WITH
## SHOWY FLOWERS


**SCARLET SAGE** (*Salvia splendens*)                          p. 189
An extraordinarily showy, even gaudy, Brazilian shrub not
winter-hardy except in frostless regions, but grown by the millions
as a summer bedding plant, since it blooms easily from seed in a
single long growing season. As a shrub in warm regions it may
be 6–8 feet high, but much less as an annual. Leaves stalked,
light green, ovalish, 2½–3½ inches long, the margins toothed.
Flowers conspicuously 2-lipped, borne in terminal, extremely
showy clusters. **Color:** Scarlet. **Height:** As an annual 15–30
inches. **Flowering date:** July–frost. **Varieties:** Blaze (or Globe)

of Fire, also called America (only 16 inches high), Clara Redman, also called Bonfire (plant more bushy than the type), Zurich (only 12 inches tall and bushy), St. John's Fire (earlier flowering; only 10 inches tall). It is doubtful if any of these varieties are persistently different from typical *Salvia splendens*. **Culture:** Start seeds indoors in boxes or pots in late Feb. or early March in a mixture of ¾ good garden loam and ¼ sand thoroughly mixed, planting them ⅛ inch deep. Set seedlings (which are sold by all florists) outdoors when settled warm weather has arrived, in full sun, in any ordinary garden soil. Space 15–30 inches apart (less for dwarf varieties). Often called Red Sage or Red Salvia. One garden expert has called it "the first resort of the inexperienced gardener," but used with caution ( on account of its violent color) it adds a dramatic touch to any bed or border. It will stand no frost, but can be grown all winter in the house from cuttings made in the autumn and potted up in a mixture of ¾ their own soil and ¼ sand, thoroughly mixed.

Related plants, annuals or treated as such (not illustrated):
*Salvia farinacea.* 2–3 feet. Flowers violet-blue.
*Salvia patens.* 18–30 inches. Flowers gentian-blue.

## BLUE SAGE (*Salvia pitcheri*) p. 189

This perennial from the prairies of central U.S. is often offered under the incorrect name of *Salvia azurea grandiflora*. It is an erect, bushy plant, the foliage covered with short grayish hairs. Leaves lance-shaped and slightly toothed. Flowers about 1 inch long, conspicuously 2-lipped, the lower lip much larger than the upper. They are borne in many-flowered, usually spike-like, terminal or lateral clusters. **Color:** Blue. **Height:** 4–5 feet. **Flowering date:** Aug.–Sept. **Varieties:** None. **Culture:** Set purchased plants in Oct. or April, in full sun, in any rich garden loam, preferably in a moist but well-drained site. Space 18–24 inches apart and provide winter mulch of salt hay or strawy manure in severe winters. It tends to die out if not divided and replanted every third or fourth year.

Related plants, perennials (not illustrated):
Clary (*Salvia sclarea*). 2–3 feet. Flowers bluish white.

A variety, *turkestanica,* is blush-pink, and offered as Vatican.

*Salvia pratensis.* 2–3 feet. Flowers bluish purple.

*Salvia viscosa.* 2–3½ feet. Flowers pink or red.

*Salvia nemorosa.* 2–3 feet. Flowers purplish violet.

*Salvia greggi.* 2–3 feet. Flowers red or purplish red.

**BETONY** (*Stachys grandiflora*)                                    p. 204

Sometimes (but incorrectly) offered as *Betonica grandiflora,* this perennial from Asia Minor is a stout plant with roughish, crinkled leaves that are oval in outline, and sharply toothed on the margin. Flowers conspicuously 2-lipped, about 1 inch long, crowded into dense, 20–30-flowered, showy clusters. **Color:** Violet. **Height:** 18–30 inches. **Flowering date:** June–July. **Varieties:** Superba (mauve purple or white). **Culture:** Set purchased plants in April or Oct., in full sun, in good rich garden loam, in a moist but well-drained site. Space 20–25 inches apart, and replant (by dividing the clumps) every third or fourth year, for it tends to die out.

Related plants (not illustrated):

> Lamb's-Ears (*Stachys lanata*). 12–18 inches. Flowers purple.
>
> *Stachys officinalis.* 2–3 feet. Flowers purple.

**CREEPING MINT** (*Mentha requieni*)                                    p. 204

This prostrate relative of the Mint and Peppermint (omitted here because they are culinary herbs) is a Corsican perennial and the only one of the true mints worth cultivating for its bloom. It is a peppermint-scented vine-like plant with thread-thin stems hugging the ground, and very small, round leaves. Flowers small, but in crowded, rather attractive clusters at the leaf joints. **Color:** Purple or mauve. **Height:** Prostrate. **Flowering date:** June–July. **Varieties:** None. **Culture:** Only in the rock garden. Set purchased plants in Oct. or April, in half-shade, in a gritty or sandy soil, preferably in a moist, well-drained site. Space 8–10 inches apart, and it will soon make a ground-covering mat.

**BUGLE** (*Ajuga reptans*)                                    p. 189

This prostrate European perennial is widely established as a weed throughout North America, but in some of its horticultural varieties is a valuable ground cover. Leaves ovalish to oblong, 1–2 inches long, tapering into a stalk. Flowers small, in a leafy, terminal cluster, the corolla 2-lipped. **Color:** Prevailingly blue, but see below. **Height:** Prostrate. **Flowering date:** May–June. **Varieties:** Alba (white), Atropurpurea (bronze foliage, blue flowers), Metallica Crispa (foliage crisped and metallic), Rubra (red), Variegata (white-blotched foliage). **Culture:** Almost too easy, and the plant can become a rampant nuisance. Set purchased plants (which root freely at any joint) in any soil, sun or shade, autumn or spring, and see that they do not get out of bounds!

Related plant (not illustrated):

*Ajuga genevensis.* 6–10 inches. Flowers blue.

**NEPETA** (*Nepeta mussini*) p. 189

An upright aromatic, bushy perennial from the Caucasus to Persia, widely grown for its showy clusters of bloom. Foliage covered with rough, white hairs, making the whole plant ashy gray. Flowers spotted, about ½ inch long, 2-lipped, in long, loose, mostly terminal clusters. **Color:** Pale blue, with darker spots. **Height:** 9–15 inches. **Flowering date:** May–July. **Varieties:** Blue Beauty (longer flowering period), Souvenir de André Chaudron (same as, or little different from Blue Beauty), Six Hills Giant (lavender). **Culture:** Set purchased plants in full sun, in April or Oct., in any ordinary garden soil, but see that they are well drained. Space 10–15 inches apart and replant (by dividing the clump) every third or fourth year. The related common, weedy catnip (*Nepeta cataria*) is wild over much of North America; introduced from Europe.

Related plant (not illustrated):

*Nepeta nervosa.* 1–2 feet. Flowers pale blue.

**FALSE DRAGONHEAD**

(*Dracocephalum virginianum*) p. 205

Long known as *Physostegia virginiana,* this tall perennial from moist woods in the eastern U.S. is rather widely grown for its long, terminal, leafy clusters of flowers. Its leaves are oblongish, 3–5 inches long and sharply toothed. Flowers 2-lipped, about

1 inch long, crowded in a leafy, spire-like cluster. **Color:** Purplish red. **Height:** 3–5 feet. **Flowering date:** July–Sept. **Varieties:** Rosy Spire (pink), Summer Snow (white), Vivid (deep pink); and both a tall and dwarf white type. **Culture:** Set purchased plants in Oct. or April, in partial shade or full sun, in any rich garden loam, preferably in a moist but well-drained site. Space 2–3 feet apart.

**DRAGONHEAD** (*Dracocephalum nutans*)                    p. 204
A Siberian perennial not much grown, although it has attractive flower clusters. Leaves oblong or ovalish, 1–2 inches long, the margins toothed. Flowers 2-lipped, the upper lip arched and notched. Flower spike terminal. **Color:** Blue. **Height:** 8–12 inches. **Flowering date:** Aug. **Varieties:** None. **Culture:** Set purchased plants in partial shade, in Oct. or April, in any ordinary garden soil, preferably in a moist but well-drained site. Space 7–10 inches apart.

Related plants (not illustrated):

> *Dracocephalum botryoides.* 4–6 inches. Flowers rose-pink.
> *Dracocephalum ruyschianum japonicum.* 1–2 feet. Flowers blue, shading to white.
> Bell of Ireland (*Molucella laevis*). 2–3 feet. A perennial, its green, swollen calyx corolla-like.

**BEE–BALM** (*Monarda didyma*)                          p. 205
Commonly called Oswego Tea in N.Y., this aromatic native perennial is scattered in many places from Maine to N.C., especially in dry thickets, and is often cultivated, particularly in dry places. It has lance-shaped, stalked, pointed leaves 3–6 inches long, and finely toothed. Flowers showy, fragrant, mostly in a dense, terminal, close cluster, but a few at the leaf joints below this. Flower 2-lipped, ¾–1½ inch long. **Color:** Prevailingly crimson, but see below. **Height:** 1–2 feet. **Flowering date:** July–Aug. **Varieties:** Alba (white), Rose Queen (pink), Cambridge Scarlet (scarlet), Lavender Lady (lavender), Salmon Queen (salmon), Violet Queen (violet). **Culture:** Set purchased plants in April, in full sun, in any ordinary (or even poor) garden soil. Space 15–25 inches apart. A useful plant for hot dry sites.

Related plants (not illustrated):
> Wild Bergamot (*Monarda fistulosa*). 2–3 feet. Flowers lilac to purple.
> Lemon Mint (*Monarda pectinata*). 8–12 inches. Flowers white or pinkish, lemon-scented.

**GERMANDER** (*Teucrium chamaedrys*)                    p. 204

A European woody perennial or undershrub, not hardy for outdoor culture much north of Norfolk, Va., unless protected. It is nearly prostrate or procumbent, with rather woody stems and ovalish, hairy, toothed, evergreen leaves about ¾ inch long. Flowers about ¾ inch long, crowded in a dense cluster, and these arranged in a terminal spike. Corolla 2-lipped, the lower lip much larger than the other. **Color:** Rose-purple, often white-spotted. **Height:** 6–8 inches. **Flowering date:** Aug.–Sept. **Varieties:** None. **Culture:** Set purchased plants in April, in full sun, in any ordinary garden soil, preferably a little sandy, and it must be well drained. Space 6–8 inches apart and cover with a mulch of salt hay or straw anywhere north of Norfolk, and even with protection not reliably hardy north of Philadelphia.

Related plant (not illustrated):
> *Teucrium orientale.* 10–15 inches. Flowers blue.

**SKULLCAP** (*Scutellaria baicalensis coelestina*)          p. 204

A little-grown Asiatic, spreading perennial, attractive for its summer-blooming pale blue flowers. Leaves lance-shaped, finely hairy on the margin. Flowers in many simple, mostly unbranched clusters. **Color:** Pale blue. **Height:** 8–15 inches. **Flowering date:** July–Aug. **Varieties:** None. **Culture:** Set purchased plants in full sun, in April or Oct., in a well-drained sandy loam. Space 6–9 inches apart.

Related plants (not illustrated):
> *Scutellaria alpina.* 8–10 inches. Flowers white and purple.
> *Scutellaria orientalis.* Prostrate. Flowers purplish or yellow.

**RUSSIAN SAGE** (*Perovskia atriplicifolia*)              p. 204

A little-grown Siberian, woody perennial, suggesting a *Salvia,* with aromatic, sage-scented foliage. Leaves nearly lance-shaped,

1½–4 inches long, covered with ashy-white hairs. Flowers small, 2-lipped, in close clusters that are arranged in a long, wand-like spike. **Color:** Silvery blue. **Height:** 3–5 feet. **Flowering date:** Aug.–Sept. **Varieties:** None. **Culture:** Set purchased plants in Oct. or April, in full sun, in any ordinary garden soil, and space 2–3 feet apart. Not reliably hardy north of New York City, but if winterkilled it usually recovers from the base.

**COLEUS** (*Coleus blumei*)                              p. 205
Once so popular as a summer bedding plant this, especially in the Middle West, was called simply the "Foliage Plant." Now it is much less grown, but it remains one of the best plants for colored foliage that can be chosen for summer bedding. It is a somewhat weak-stemmed Javanese perennial, which will stand no frost, and hence usually grown as a long-season annual. Leaves, for which the plant is exclusively grown, are arranged opposite each other, and vary in color from green, yellow, red-purple, orange to white, and some are blotched. All have crispy margins. Flowers more or less negligible, often pinched off for greater profusion of foliage. **Color:** Of flowers, blue or lilac; of foliage, see below. **Height:** 1–2 feet. **Flowering date:** July–Aug. **Varieties:** (all are colored foliage variations), Verschaffelti (crimson, with green-frilled edges), Golden Bedder (yellow), Her Majesty (bronze-red), Crimson King (crimson), Salvador (maroon, with green edges), Sun Ray (blotched reddish purple, yellow, and bronze), Glory (bronze, pink, and apricot, blotched with cream-white). **Culture:** Sow seeds ⅛ inch deep, indoors in Feb. or early March, in a mixture of ¾ garden loam and ¼ sand thoroughly mixed. Set seedlings outdoors only after settled warm weather has arrived, in any rich garden loam, in full sun, and water if dry weather makes it necessary. Space 12–20 inches apart and pinch out flower clusters and unwanted shoots to promote foliage. If wanted for winter pot plants make cuttings in Sept., and bring indoors before cold weather arrives.

# POTATO OR NIGHTSHADE FAMILY
## (*Solanaceae*)

THE huge economic importance of this family (yielding the potato, tobacco, tomato, pepper, tabasco, eggplant, and dangerous drugs like stramonium, belladonna, hyoscyamine, and scopolamine) is scarcely matched by its production of garden flowers, which are few but very popular, especially the Petunia and Butterfly-Flower. The family comprises over 2000 species, mostly tropical shrubs and trees and a handful of garden flowers in the temperate zones. Many of them contain a dangerously poisonous juice (narcotics and medicine). Leaves always alternately arranged. Flowers regular and symmetrical in some, highly irregular and unsymmetrical in others, hence one of the exceptions noted at p. 202. Fruit a dry pod, or a large berry as in the tomato, eggplant, and the peppers (not the spice).

**PETUNIA** (*Petunia* hybrids)                                    p. 205
Tremendously popular summer bedding plants, needing a long growing season, derived mostly from crossing two native species from the Argentine. Stems erect or sprawling, the leaves somewhat sticky and flabby. Flowers typically funnel-shaped, only slightly unsymmetrical, and not 2-lipped, 2–4½ inches wide, and in many modern types double-flowered, fringed, ruffled, or crisped, while some have a starlike center. Now divided into 3 distinct types: an Erect form for bedding; a sprawling or weak-stemmed type used mostly for window boxes (Balcony petunias); and a Dwarf type, also for bedding and useful as an edging plant. **Color:** All but yellow, see below. **Height:** 7–15 inches, in erect types, almost trailing in balcony type. **Flowering date:** July–frost. **Varieties:** ERECT TYPES: Heavenly Blue (blue), Violet Queen (violet), Apple Blossom (fringed and pink), Copper Red (ruffled and copper-red), White Beauty (fringed and white), Pink Glory (single and pink), Crimson Glory (single and red), Irene (single, fringed and red), and many others. BALCONY PETUNIAS: Pink Beauty (pink), Pride of Portland (pink), Balcony Blue (blue), Balcony White (white), Black Prince (deep red),

Blue Wonder (blue), White Wonder (white), and many others.
DWARF TYPES: Cheerful (salmon-pink), Igloo (cream-white),
Bright Eyes (rose-pink), Fire Chief (red), Cream Star (cream
white), Snowball (pure white), Linda (salmon pink), Admiral
(blue), and many others. **Culture:** Easy nearly everywhere;
thrives especially well near the sea. Sow seeds indoors (8–10
weeks before outdoor planting is safe), ⅛ inch deep in boxes or
pots filled with ¾ garden loam and ¼ sand, thoroughly mixed.
Transfer seedlings outdoors only after settled warm weather
has arrived, in full sun, in almost any, even poorish garden soil.
Space 7–10 inches apart. They are apt to persist, especially southward, from self-sown seed, but few come true to type, and it
is better to start with fresh seed annually. They will stand no
frost.

**NICOTIANA** (*Nicotiana alata grandiflora*)                    p. 205
Closely related to true tobacco this garden nicotiana is perhaps
our most night-fragrant flower, the blossoms usually being closed
in sunshine, but opening on cloudy days and toward evening.
From its fragrance often called Jasmine Tobacco. It is a stout
perennial from southern South America, usually grown as a
long-season annual. Leaves alternately arranged (juice poisonous), nearly 4 inches long. Flowers tubular, almost completely symmetrical, nearly 3 inches wide. **Color:** Prevailingly
white but see below. **Height:** 3–4 feet. **Flowering date:** July–frost.
**Varieties:** Daylight (reputed to flower in sunshine), Crimson
Bedder (crimson), Orange Blossom (white), Crimson King
(crimson). **Culture:** Start seeds indoors (8–10 weeks before outdoor planting is safe). Sow seeds (which are microscopic) in
pots or boxes by scattering them on a soil of finely sifted garden
loam and sand in equal parts. Do not cover seeds, merely press
them in lightly with a board. When settled warm weather has
arrived transfer seedlings outdoors, in full sun, to a rich garden
soil. See that they are watered in droughts, space 2–3 feet apart
and stake if site is windy. Often offered under incorrect name of
*Nicotiana affinis.* Sometimes persistent from self-sown seed,
especially southward.

Related plants (not illustrated):

*Nicotiana sanderae.* Annual, 2–3 feet. Flowers greenish yellow, but ultimately rose-carmine.

*Nicotiana sylvestris.* Perennial, 3–5 feet. Flowers white.

**BUTTERFLY–FLOWER** (*Schizanthus wisetonensis*)    p. 205

A beautiful garden flower of hybrid origin, its parents Chilean, and often called Poorman's Orchid because of its highly irregular, almost orchid-like flowers, which are extremely decorative for cutting and keep better than most. It is an annual, brittle plant, its leaves broadly lance-shaped, but cut into many fernlike segments. Flowers strongly 2-lipped, highly unsymmetrical, about 1½ inches wide, borne in a loose, lax, terminal, many-flowered cluster. **Color:** White, blue, pink, or brownish, the middle of the upper lip streaked yellow. **Height:** 2–4 feet. **Flowering date:** July–Aug. **Varieties:** Several hybrid strains, not well defined, comprising rose, pink, salmon, violet, white, or yellow flowers, all blotched with darker centers. **Culture:** Sow seeds indoors in Feb. or March, ⅛ inch deep, in pots or boxes in a mixture of ¾ finely sifted garden loam and ¼ sand, thoroughly mixed. Transfer seedlings outdoors only when warm weather is sure, in full sun in a rich garden loam. Space 2–3 feet apart and handle carefully, since they are easily broken. Pinching back terminal shoots will delay but much increase the bloom.

**WHITECUP** (*Nierembergia rivularis*)    p. 223

A creeping, mat-forming plant for the rock garden; a native of the Argentine. Leaves rather scattered, oblongish, about 1 inch long and stalked. Flowers mostly near the ends of the twigs, long-tubed and almost symmetrical, broadly cup-shaped at the top 1–1½ inches wide. **Color:** White, the throat golden yellow. **Height:** Prostrate. **Flowering date:** June–Sept. **Varieties:** None. **Culture:** Can be treated as an annual (it blooms from seed the first year) or as a perennial, which in warm regions it really is. As a perennial: set purchased plants in the rock garden in April or Oct., in full sun, and in sandy or gritty well-drained soil. Space 4–7 inches apart; not reliably hardy north of New York City. As an annual: sow seeds ⅛ inch deep indoors (6–8 weeks before out-

# FIGWORT FAMILY
## (*Scrophulariaceae*)

1. **Germander Speedwell** (*Veronica latifolia*)      **p. 228**
   Eurasian perennial, 12–18 inches high, summer-blooming, and of easy culture in any bed or border.

2. **Chinese Houses** (*Collinsia bicolor*)      **p. 227**
   Californian annual, 12–20 inches high. Sow seed early where wanted. It will not tolerate summer heat.

3. **Nemesia** (*Nemesia strumosa*)      **p. 226**
   Tropical African annual, popular in England, but not well known here. Summer-flowering, 8–20 inches high.

4. **Cat's-Tail Speedwell** (*Veronica spicata*)      **p. 228**
   Old-time garden perennial, 12–20 inches high, and flowering in June–July. Easily grown in any border.

5. **Twin-Spur** (*Diascia barberae*)      **p. 227**
   Long-season South African annual, 8–15 inches high and summer-blooming. Start indoors, 6–8 weeks before outdoor planting is safe.

6. **Red Turtlehead** (*Chelone lyoni*)      **p. 227**
   Native woodland perennial, Aug.-flowering and 10–20 inches high. Needs partial shade and rich moist soil.

7. **Linaria** (*Linaria maroccana*)      **p. 226**
   A Moroccan annual, 12–15 inches high, summer-blooming, and worth more cultivation than it gets.

8. **Torenia** (*Torenia fournieri*)      **p. 225**
   A rare and beautiful annual, 8–10 inches high and summer-blooming. Start indoors, 8–10 weeks before outdoor planting is safe.

9. **Snapdragon** (*Antirrhinum* hybrids)      **p. 225**
   Popular florist's flower forced by the millions, but can be grown by the amateur by following directions in the text.

# FIGWORT FAMILY
## (*Scrophulariaceae*)

1. **Purple Mullein** (*Verbascum phoeniceum*)     **p.** 230
   A stiff, erect biennial, 3–5 feet high, blooming in May or June.

2. **Foxglove** (*Digitalis purpurea*)     **p.** 231
   A European biennial, 2–4 feet high, or more in cool regions.
   June-blooming.

3. **Beardtongue** (*Pentstemon unilateralis*)     **p.** 230
   A western perennial, about 2 feet high. Blooms in June or July.

4. **Beardtongue** (*Pentstemon barbatus*)     **p.** 229
   A western perennial, 4–6 feet high. Blooms in May or June.

5. **Erinus** (*Erinus alpinus*)     **p.** 233
   A tiny perennial, 2–3 inches high, suited only to the rock garden.
   Blooms April–June.

6. **Monkey-Flower** (*Mimulus luteus*)     **p.** 232
   A Chilean perennial, often sprawling, sometimes erect and 2–4
   feet high. Summer-blooming.

7. **Kenilworth Ivy** (*Cymbalaria muralis*)     **p.** 232
   A popular prostrate house plant that may become established
   outdoors. Summer-blooming.

8. **Synthris** (*Synthris rotundifolia*)     **p.** 233
   A low perennial from Oregon, 3–5 inches high, worth trying in
   woodsy places. May-blooming.

9. **Culver's-Root** (*Veronicastrum virginicum*)     **p.** 229
   A native summer-blooming perennial, 4–6 feet high, suited to
   shady wild garden.

door planting is safe), in boxes or pots filled with a mixture of
⅔ garden loam and ⅓ sand, thoroughly mixed. Transfer seedlings outdoors when trees leaf out, in full sun, in a sandy loam,
spacing them 4–7 inches apart. Often called Cup-Flower.

## ANGEL'S–TRUMPET (*Datura Metel*)                              p. 205

A little-known, long-season annual from India with a dangerously
poisonous juice, grown for its large trumpet-shaped flowers. It
is a weedy plant, closely related to the equally poisonous Jimson-
Weed, with ovalish leaves 5–8 inches long, with a few blunt teeth.
Flowers 7–9 inches long, the end of the corolla with 5 weak
prickles that are ¾–1½ inches long. **Color:** Cream-white.
**Height:** 3–5 feet. **Flowering date:** July–Sept. **Varieties:** Ivory
King (double-flowered). **Culture:** Sow seeds indoors (5–7 weeks
before outdoor planting is safe), ¼ inch deep, in boxes or pots
filled with a mixture of ¾ garden loam and ¼ sand. Transfer
seedlings outdoors only after settled warm weather has arrived,
into any ordinary or even poor soil, in full sun. Space 3–4 feet
apart. Children should be warned about its poisonous juice, that
from wilted foliage being deadly.

## BROWALLIA (*Browallia speciosa*)                              p. 205

A popular South American annual grown for its attractive, steel-
blue flowers that are slightly unsymmetrical. Leaves ovalish but
pointed at the tip. Flowers solitary or in sparse clusters, about
1½ inches wide, the corolla with a suggestion of being 2-lipped,
the upper lip of 2 lobes, the lower lip 3-lobed. **Color:** Blue.
**Height:** 12–18 inches. **Flowering date:** July–Sept. **Varieties:** Sap-
phire (blue with white "eye"). **Culture:** Sow seeds ⅛ inch deep
in boxes or pots indoors (8–10 weeks before outdoor planting is
safe). Fill boxes with ¾ garden loam and ¼ sand, thoroughly
mixed. Transfer seedlings outdoors only when settled warm
weather has arrived, in any ordinary or even poor garden soil,
in full sun. Space 7–10 inches apart. Seeds may be sown directly
outdoors in late May, but such plants will have delayed bloom.
Related plant (not illustrated):

> *Browallia americana.* 12–20 inches. Flowers bluish purple.
> Usually offered under incorrect name of *Browallia elata.*

**WINTER CHERRY** (*Physalis alkekengi*)                    p. 205
A showy Eurasian perennial grown more for its handsome fruits
than for its rather inconspicuous flowers. It is an upright plant,
its leaves oval, 2–3 inches long and hairy on the margin. Flowers
solitary at the leaf joints, followed by a small berry which is
surrounded by a papery, inflated, highly colored husk that may
be 2½ inches long. It is this which suggests its other names of
Husk Tomato and Chinese Lantern-Plant. **Color:** Of flowers,
white; of fruits orange-scarlet. **Height:** 1–2 feet. **Flowering date:**
July–Aug. **Fruiting date:** Oct.–Nov., and holding their color all
winter in the house if picked before frost. **Varieties:** None. **Culture:** Set purchased plants in April, in full sun, in any ordinary
or even poor garden soil and space 10–15 inches apart. Usually
offered under the incorrect name of *Physalis francheti,* and sometimes spreading rampantly.

Left: Painted Tongue (*Salpiglossis sinuata*), p. 224.
Right: Whitecup (*Nierembergia rivularis*), p. 219.

**PAINTED TONGUE** (*Salpiglossis sinuata*)                    p. 223
A Chilean long-season annual, grown for its varicolored, petunia-like flowers, nearly all of which have golden markings in the throat of the corolla. Leaves broadly lance-shaped, the margins bluntly toothed. Flowers almost perfectly symmetrical, funnel-shaped, the throat wide and open, about 2½ inches long and broad. **Color:** Unstable and various, from white, yellow, purple-blue, red to crimson. **Height:** 18–30 inches. **Flowering date:** July–frost. **Varieties:** Several, unnamed, in the colors stated above. **Culture:** Sow almost microscopic seeds indoors (8–10 weeks before outdoor planting is safe), in boxes or pots filled with ¾ finely sifted garden loam and ¼ sand, thoroughly mixed. Scarcely cover the seeds, pressing them in with a board or plate. Transfer seedlings outdoors when warm weather has arrived and handle carefully, since they do not like moving too well. Plant in full sun or partial shade in any ordinary or even poor garden soil and space 1–2 feet apart. Seed can also be sown outdoors in late May, but this delays bloom and seeds may be washed out by normal rainfall. Protect such seeds with cheesecloth covering until they have germinated, in 8–10 days.

# FIGWORT FAMILY
## (*Scrophulariaceae*)

A VERY large family (over 3000 species), scattered throughout the world, containing a few shrubs and trees (*Paulownia*), and such garden favorites as the Snapdragon, Foxglove, Nemesia, Speedwell, Pentstemon, Red Turtlehead, and a few others. Leaves oppositely arranged, or sometimes in clusters of 3 to 4. Flowers rarely solitary, nearly always in clusters, never perfectly symmetrical, often distinctly 2-lipped as in the Foxglove and Snapdragon, and some with a spur. Fruit usually a many-seeded, dry pod.

Although the family is large, there are only 19 garden plants of much interest to the average grower, and for ease of identification they may be separated into 3 groups:

*Plants prostrate, or if erect not over 3–5 inches high. 4 species.*
    *See p. 232.*

*Plants tall, 2–3 feet, or even 4–5 feet high. 6 species. See p. 229.*
*Plants of medium height, often 8–12 inches high, some 12–20*
*inches high. The 9 species immediately below.*

**SNAPDRAGON** (*Antirrhinum* hybrids)                    p. 220
An enormously popular perennial from the Mediterranean region,
nearly always grown as a long-season annual by the home gardener, but millions forced by the florist for bloom throughout
the year. It has somewhat sticky, lance-shaped leaves, 2–3 inches
long. Flowers very showy, pouch-shaped, and the top distinctly
2-lipped, hence highly unsymmetrical, borne in a somewhat
leafy, terminal cluster. **Color:** All but blue. **Height:** 12–20 inches.
**Flowering date outdoors:** July–Sept. **Varieties:** Many are adver-
tised by dealers, but varietal names are in such confusion and
conflict that it is better to order seed by color. A recent race or
strain, the so-called tetraploid Snapdragons are claimed by their
sponsors to be finer than the regular type; the statement needs
confirmation. **Culture:** Sow seeds indoors (8–10 weeks before
outdoor planting is safe). Scarcely cover the fine seeds sown in
boxes or pots filled with ¾ sifted loam and ¼ sand, thoroughly
mixed. Do not let room in which they are started get over 55°.
Transfer outdoors, after potting up individual seedlings, to a
cold frame about April 15, protecting with mats or shades if
freezing night temperatures are likely. Move to the open garden
about May 8–15, in full sun, in any good garden soil, and space
8–10 inches apart. The earlier they can be put in permanent posi-
tion the better as they do not like intense heat. Properly hardened-
off seedlings are always available in the market for those who
do not want to raise their own.

**TORENIA** (*Torenia fournieri*)                    p. 220
A little-grown plant from Cochin-China, used here as a long-
season annual. It has a 4-angled stem, the leaves arranged opposite each other, stalked, ovalish, toothed, and 1½–2 inches
long. Flowers 2-lipped, in stalked clusters at the leaf joints or
terminal. **Color:** Blue, with yellow throat. **Height:** 8–10 inches.
**Flowering date:** July–Aug. **Varieties:** White Wings (white-

rose). **Culture:** Sow seeds indoors (8–10 weeks before outdoor planting is safe), ⅛ inch deep in boxes or pots filled with ¾ finely sifted loam and ¼ sand, thoroughly mixed. Transfer seedlings outdoors when trees leaf out, in partial shade, or full sun, in a reasonably moist (not wet) garden loam. Space 6–8 inches apart. Called by some, without much cogency, Wishbone-Flower.

**NEMESIA** (*Nemesia strumosa*)                                    p. 220
A tropical African annual, much more grown in England than here, but useful for summer bedding. It has a square and grooved stem, the leaves alternate, lance-shaped, and 2–3 inches long. Flowers in terminal clusters, the corolla 2-lipped and spurred. **Color:** White, blue, purple, or yellow, deeply marked on the outside, often with 2 colors in the same flower. **Height:** 8–20 inches. **Flowering date:** July–Aug. **Varieties:** Suttoni (finer, and coming true from seed, which some do not). **Culture:** Sow seeds indoors ⅛ inch deep (8–10 weeks before outdoor planting is safe), in mixture of ¾ fine garden loam and ¼ sand. Transfer seedlings outdoors as soon as possible after last frost; they do not like summer heat. Space 6–8 inches apart and grow in masses for best effect.

**LINARIA** (*Linaria maroccana*)                                    p. 220
A garden annual from Morocco, not much grown here but rewarding for its varicolored flowers. It is an erect plant, closely related to our Butter-and-Eggs, and like it with very narrow slender leaves. Flowers in spikes, highly unsymmetrical, small, 2-lipped, and with long spurs. **Color:** Crimson, gold, pink, mauve, blue, or rose, always blotched with another color on the lip. **Height:** 12–15 inches. **Flowering date:** July–Aug. **Varieties:** None. **Culture:** Sow seeds outdoors when trees leaf out, ⅛ inch deep, in any ordinary garden soil. Space 9–12 inches apart. They may not bloom from seed the first year but will the second. Called by some (without valid reason) Baby Snapdragon — which it is not — and, more correctly, Toadflax, to which it is closely allied.

Related plant (not illustrated):
    *Linaria alpina.* 3–6 inches. Flowers blue and yellow.

**RED TURTLEHEAD** (*Chelone lyoni*)                          p. 220
A native perennial from the mountains of the Carolinas and
Tenn., grown for its curious flowers that suggest a turtle's head.
It is an erect plant, its leaves arranged opposite each other, more
or less ovalish, long-stalked, and with marginal teeth. Flowers
in a dense, packed, spike-like but blunt cluster, the individual
flower about 1 inch long, unsymmetrical and 2-lipped. Only 1
or 2 flowers bloom at a time. **Color:** Pink-purple. **Height:** 10–
20 inches. **Flowering date:** Aug. **Varieties:** None. **Culture:** Set
purchased plants in Oct. or April in partial shade, in a moist but
not wet soil that is rich in humus, but is not acid. Space 7–12
inches apart and leave alone.
   Related plant (not illustrated):
        Turtlehead (*Chelone glabra*). 8–14 inches. Flowers
        white, rarely pinkish.

**CHINESE HOUSES** (*Collinsia bicolor*)                     p. 220
An attractive Californian annual producing masses of bloom from
spring-sown seed, but rapidly failing in the intense heat of
summer. Leaves oppositely arranged, oblongish, 1–2 inches long.
Flowers unsymmetrical, 2-lipped, the upper lip differently
colored from the lower. Flower clusters are huddled at the leaf
joints. **Color:** Upper lip white, lower lip rose-purple or violet.
**Height:** 12–20 inches. **Flowering date:** June–July. **Varieties:**
Candidissima (pure white). **Culture:** Sow seeds (carried mostly
by Californian dealers) ⅛ inch deep, in partial shade or full sun,
in any ordinary sandy loam, as soon as trees leaf out. Speed of
growth is essential for bloom since the plants will not tolerate
summer heat. Space 6–8 inches apart.
   Related plants (not illustrated):
        Blue-Lips (*Collinsia grandiflora*). 8–15 inches. Flowers
        purple or violet and blue.
        Blue-eyed-Mary (*Collinsia verna*). 12–20 inches. Flowers
        lilac and white or blue.

**TWIN–SPUR** (*Diascia barberae*)                           p. 220
A South African long-season annual, not very much grown as
yet, but with a very showy terminal flower cluster that may be 6

inches long. Leaves oppositely arranged, ovalish, 1–1½ inches long, the margins toothed. Flowers about ½ inch long, unsymmetrical, and 2-lipped, the lower lip with 2 spurs. **Color:** Rose-pink, the throat yellow. **Height:** 8–15 inches. **Flowering date:** July–Aug. **Varieties:** None. **Culture:** Sow seeds indoors, ⅛ inch deep (6–8 weeks before outdoor planting is safe), in boxes or pots filled with ¾ finely sifted garden loam and ¼ sand, thoroughly mixed. Transfer seedlings outdoors when trees leaf out, in full sun, in any ordinary garden soil, and space 5–8 inches apart.

**GERMANDER SPEEDWELL** (*Veronica latifolia*)      p. 220
This, the best known of all the speedwells, is often sold under the incorrect name of *Veronica Teucrium,* and is a Eurasian perennial with oblongish, coarsely-toothed leaves, the lower opposite each other, the upper alternate. Flowers almost symmetrical, small, in terminal spike-like clusters. **Color:** Prevailingly blue, rarely white or pinkish. **Height:** 12–18 inches. **Flowering date:** June–July. **Varieties:** Prostrata (nearly prostrate). **Culture:** Easy. Set purchased plants in Oct. or April, in full sun, in any ordinary garden soil. Space 8–10 inches apart.
    Related plants (not illustrated):
        *Veronica incana.* 6–8 inches. Flowers blue.
        *Veronica gentianoides.* 12–20 inches. Flowers blue.
        *Veronica repens.* Prostrate. Flowers blue.
        *Veronica spuria.* 12–20 inches. Flowers blue.

**CAT'S–TAIL SPEEDWELL** (*Veronica spicata*)      p. 220
A characteristic but confusing old-time garden favorite, its long, terminal, curving flower cluster, suggesting a cat's tail. It is a Eurasian perennial, sometimes known as *Veronica longifolia* or *Veronica maritima,* but if it has a correct Latin name it is *Veronica spicata.* It has lance-shaped, toothed leaves that are 1½–2 inches long. Flowers small, crowded in the terminal cluster, which may be 4–7 inches long. **Color:** Blue. **Height:** 12–20 inches. **Flowering date:** June–July. **Varieties:** Rosea (pink). **Culture:** Set purchased plants in Oct. or April, in full sun, in any

ordinary garden soil, and space 8–12 inches apart. For still another related plant, often called *Veronica virginica,* see the next species.

**CULVER'S–ROOT** (*Veronicastrum virginicum*)         p. 221
A tall, woodland perennial of eastern North America, its roots once widely harvested as the source of a cathartic; now little used. Grown mostly for ornament in informal parts of the wild garden. Leaves lance-shaped, 4–6 inches long, arranged in clusters of 3–6, the stem naked between such clusters. Flowers very small, but crowded in dense, forked, terminal spire-like clusters that may be 5–7 inches long. **Color:** White. **Height:** 4–6 feet. **Flowering date:** Aug.–Sept. **Varieties:** None. **Culture:** Set purchased plants (from dealer in wild flowers) in partial or complete shade of trees (no evergreens) in a moist (not wet) site in the wild garden, in a soil rich in humus but not especially acid. It will often grow, also, in partial shade of the open border in good garden loam. Space 2–3 feet apart. A striking plant when few other wild flowers are in bloom. Often offered as *Veronica virginica* and *Leptandra virginica* — both incorrect.

**BEARDTONGUE** (*Pentstemon barbatus*)         p. 221
A stout perennial from Utah to Mexico grown for its showy flowers, but more happy as a cultivated plant in the West than along the Atlantic seaboard. Leaves narrow, arranged opposite each other. Flowers 2-lipped, the lower lip bearded. **Color:** Red to scarlet. **Height:** 4–6 feet. **Flowering date:** June–July. **Varieties:** Coccineus (scarlet), Pink Beauty (pink), Firebird (scarlet), Rose Elf (pink). **Culture:** Not easy in the East. Set purchased plants in April or Oct., in full sun, in sandy or gritty loam which should have a good amount of humus but not be especially acid. It must be well drained. Space 20–30 inches apart. They tend to die out in a year or two if in full sun, but must be grown so to bloom.

    Related plants (not illustrated):
        *Pentstemon torreyi.* 3–4 feet. Flowers scarlet.
        *Pentstemon grandiflorus.* 4–6 feet. Flowers lavender-blue.

*Pentstemon Digitalis.* 3–5 feet. Flowers white.
*Pentstemon hirsutus.* 2–3 feet. Flowers purple.
*Pentstemon spectabilis.* 4–6 feet. Flowers rose-purple.

**BEARDTONGUE** (*Pentstemon unilateralis*)                    p. 221
A perennial from Utah to Wyo. suited chiefly to the rock garden
and not too happy in eastern gardens. It is an erect plant with
narrowly lance-shaped leaves, 3–4 inches long, arranged opposite
each other. Flowers about ¾ inch long, arranged in a 1-sided
cluster, 2-lipped and the lower lip bearded. **Color:** Blue. **Height:**
2–2½ feet. **Flowering date:** June–July. **Varieties:** None. **Culture:** Not easy in the East. Set purchased plants only in the rock
garden, in Oct. or April, in a gritty or sandy soil, with perfect
drainage, in full sun. It will not stand water or winter slush at
its roots. Space 12–15 inches apart. Apt to die out in a year or
two and must be constantly renewed.
    Related plant (not illustrated):
        *Pentstemon gloxinioides.* 2–4 feet. Colors various. Will
        generally bloom from seed the first year.

**PURPLE MULLEIN** (*Verbascum phoeniceum*)                    p. 221
A Eurasian biennial, the stiff erect stem springing from a basal
rosette of leaves that are dark green above but hairy and paler
beneath, the margins with rounded teeth. Flowers in a terminal,
stiffish cluster, which is sometimes branched, the corolla almost
symmetrical and not 2-lipped. **Color:** Usually purple, sometimes
lavender or white. **Height:** 3–5 feet. **Flowering date:** May–June.
**Varieties:** None. **Culture:** Sow seeds ¼ inch deep in Aug. or
early Sept. for bloom the next year, after which the plant dies.
Choose any sandy, well-drained loam (it must not be cold or
wet) and preferably in a partially shaded site. Thin out seedlings
so that those left are 2–3 feet apart. In favorable places it may
persist from self-sown seeds, but may not come true from such
seeds.
    Related plants (not illustrated):
        All biennials, or treated as such.
        *Verbascum olympicum.* 3–5 feet. Flowers yellow.

*Verbascum chaixi.* 2–3 feet. Flowers white.

*Verbascum blattaria.* 2–3 feet. Yellow, marked with purple.

## FOXGLOVE (*Digitalis purpurea*)      p. 221

Medicinally of prime importance from the discovery in an English barnyard in 1785 that its leaves contain an invaluable remedy for certain heart diseases. Digitalis as a drug is grown only by experts, but the Foxglove has been grown for centuries for ornament. It is a European biennial (or best grown as such) and does better along the New England coast and in coastal Wash. and Ore. than in hotter and drier regions. It is an erect plant with its rather rough and oblong leaves arranged alternately, the lower ones 9–12 inches long and 3–4 inches wide, the upper ones smaller. Flowers extremely showy, nodding, in a tall, stiff, 1-sided cluster, the individual flower slightly unsymmetrical and 2–3 inches long. **Color:** Prevailingly purple-spotted, but see below. **Height:** 2–4 feet, much higher in England, Wash., and Ore. **Flowering date:** June. **Varieties:** All with spotted flowers, Alba (white), Maculata Superba (more spotted), Gloxiniaeflora (longer flower clusters and in mixed colors), Shirley Hybrids (mixed colors). **Culture:** Sow seeds ⅛ inch deep in boxes or pots outdoors in Aug. or early Sept. Use ¾ rich garden loam and ¼ sand, thoroughly mixed. Winter in cold frame or other protected place (no heat), and transfer seedlings to permanent site the following spring when trees leaf out. Space 2–3 feet apart in a partially shaded, cool, moist (not wet) site, the soil to be rich in humus but not acid. It is a true perennial but tends to die out; hence best treated as above. Does not like heat and dryness. One of the showiest of all garden plants in favorable climates; almost weedy along English roadsides.

Related plants (not illustrated):

Yellow Foxglove (*Digitalis ambigua*). 2–3 feet. Flowers yellow.

*Digitalis laevigata.* 2–3 feet. Flowers yellow, but purple-spotted.

*Digitalis lutea.* 12–20 inches. Flowers yellowish-white.

**MONKEY–FLOWER** (*Mimulus luteus*)                    p. 221
A Chilean perennial with declining stem in some forms, erect in
others. Leaves nearly oval, about 1 inch long, arranged opposite
each other. Flowers usually solitary at the leaf joints, 2-lipped,
the brownish spots giving the impression of a face (hence
Monkey-Flower). **Color:** Deep yellow, darker-spotted. **Height:**
2–4 feet, in erect forms, lower in declining types. **Flowering date:**
July–Aug. **Varieties:** Many and in considerable confusion, offered under such (doubtful) names as *variegatus* (white with
lines of yellow dots), *tigrinus* (yellow, spotted with purple and
brown), *alpinus* (only 3–12 inches high), *grandiflorus* (large
flowered). **Culture:** Set purchased plants in Oct. or April, in
partial shade (they tolerate open sun) in any ordinary good
garden loam, in a moist but not wet site. Space 2–3 feet apart,
and provide winter mulch of straw or strawy manure. They do
best in moist shade. Not reliably hardy north of New York City.
   Related plants (not illustrated):
       *Mimulus ringens.* 2–4 feet. Flowers violet.
       *Mimulus cardinalis.* 8–12 inches. Flowers red, rarely
       yellow.
       *Mimulus guttatus.* 10–18 inches. Flowers yellow, red- or
       brown-spotted.

**KENILWORTH IVY** (*Cymbalaria muralis*)                    p. 221
A prostrate, perennial, European, vine-like herb, useful as a
house plant, and often escaping to the wild in the eastern U.S.,
where it often persists as far north as New York City in protected places. It has weak, ground-hugging stems and long-
stalked, angular, roundish leaves about 1½–2 inches in diameter.
Flowers about ⅓ inch long, solitary at the leaf joints. **Color:**
Lilac-blue, yellowish inside. **Height:** Prostrate. **Flowering date:**
July–Aug. **Varieties:** Alba (white). **Culture:** Set purchased
plants in partial shade in a protected place, in Oct. or April, in
rich garden loam, preferably fairly moist (not wet). Space 5–7
inches apart, and in a few years it will be a modest ground cover.
Not reliably hardy north of Philadelphia, but often escaping from
gardens northward, and sometimes persistent. Also known as

*Linaria Cymbalaria,* and often called Coliseum Ivy and Climbing Sailor.

**SYNTHRIS** (*Synthris rotundifolia*)                         p. 221
An attractive, but not much grown perennial from Ore., almost stemless, and early-flowering. Leaves all basal, nearly round, heart-shaped at the base, hairy, and about 2 inches long. Flowers small, in a few-flowered cluster, the corolla tubular and almost symmetrical. **Color:** White. **Height:** 3–5 inches. **Flowering date:** April–May. **Varieties:** None. **Culture:** Set purchased plants in Oct., in partial or full shade (evergreens are fine) in a woods soil or rich garden loam with plenty of humus. Space 4–6 inches apart. Does better on Pacific Coast than along eastern seaboard. Not suited to hot and dry regions.

  Related plant (not illustrated):
    *Synthris reniformis.* 6–9 inches. Flowers bluish purple.

**ERINUS** (*Erinus alpinus*)                         p. 221
A delightful but little-known alpine perennial from the mountains of Europe, suited only to the rock garden and to those who give it exacting care. It is tufted and has basal, coarsely toothed leaves about ½ inch long. Flower cluster terminal, about 2 inches long, the corolla slightly unsymmetrical. **Color:** Purple. **Height:** 2–3 inches. **Flowering date:** April–June. **Varieties:** Alba (white), Carmineus (crimson). **Culture:** Set purchased plants in Oct., only in the rock garden, on steep bank, shaded from midday sun, in sandy or gritty soil with perfect drainage, as it will not stand water or winter slush at its roots. Space 3–4 inches apart. Quite unsuited to regions with hot or dry summers.

**MAZUS** (*Mazus reptans*)                         p. 234
A probably Himalayan perennial which spreads by rooting at the joints, thus making a prostrate ground cover. Leaves lance-shaped or elliptic, about 1 inch long and coarsely toothed. Flowers small, in 1-sided clusters, very numerous, 2-lipped, the lower lip with two ridges in the throat. **Color:** Lavender or purplish blue. **Height:** 1–2 inches. **Flowering date:** June–Aug. **Varieties:** None. **Culture:** Set purchased plants in partly shady

or fully sunny place, in Oct. or April, in any ordinary garden loam, moist but not wet. Space 4–7 inches apart. Not reliably hardy north of New York City and not always there without a winter mulch of straw or salt hay.

A Himalayan prostrate ground cover with lavender or blue flowers (*Mazus reptans*), p. 233.

# TRUMPET-CREEPER FAMILY
## (*Bignoniaceae*)

A MEDIUM-SIZED family (about 600 species) of mostly tropical woody vines (trumpet-creeper) and trees (the catalpa and tropical calabash), the only herb of garden interest being the one below and its relatives. Leaves, in those below, finely divided, oppositely arranged. Flower unsymmetrical. Fruit a small more or less curved pod.

**TRUMPET–FLOWER** (*Incarvillea delavayi*)                    p. 236
A Chinese perennial not quite hardy north of Boston, and elsewhere needing winter protection. It is a showy plant with its many-segmented leaves nearly 1 foot long. Flowers trumpet-shaped but distinctly unsymmetrical, 1–2 inches long and as wide.

**Color:** Rosy purple, but the tube yellow. **Height:** 18–24 inches. **Flowering date:** June–July. **Varieties:** None. **Culture:** Set purchased plants in a protected place (from north winds), in Oct. or April, in rich garden loam, somewhat sandy and well drained. Space 15–24 inches apart, in full sun, and provide a winter mulch of straw, strawy manure, or salt hay at least 4 inches thick, removing it in April. Not easy to maintain without considerable protection, and useless north of Boston. Sometimes called Hardy Gloxinia.

Related plant (not illustrated):

*Incarvillea grandiflora.* 10–20 inches. Flowers rosy red.

# GLOBE DAISY FAMILY
## (*Globulariaceae*)

A SMALL family of daisy-like herbs (not over 24 species), mostly Eurasian, the one below and its relatives being the only subjects of garden interest. They differ from the true Daisy Family solely in technical characteristics.

**GLOBE DAISY** (*Globularia trichosantha*) p. 236
Not a true daisy but simulating one, this perennial from Asia Minor is an erect plant, the stem a little woody at the base. Leaves mostly basal, about 1 inch long, the upper leaves smaller. Flowers minute, decidedly 2-lipped, but crowded in a dense, terminal, more or less leafy (bracted) head which is about ½ inch in diameter. **Color:** Blue. **Height:** 6–8 inches. **Flowering date:** May–June. **Varieties:** None. **Culture:** Set purchased plants in Oct. or April, in partial shade, in any good, somewhat sandy garden loam that is well drained. Space 5–8 inches apart.

Related plants (not illustrated):

*Globularia cordifolia.* Prostrate. Flowers blue.

*Globularia repens.* Prostrate. Flowers blue. Often offered as *Globularia nana.*

TRUMPET–CREEPER FAMILY (*Bignoniaceae*), 3
LOBELIA FAMILY (*Lobeliaceae*), 2 and 4
ACANTHUS FAMILY (*Acanthaceae*), 1
GLOBE DAISY FAMILY (*Globulariaceae*), 5
TEASEL FAMILY (*Dipsaceae*), 6
ASTER FAMILY (*Compositae*), 7–9

1. **Bear's-Breech** (*Acanthus mollis*)     **p. 238**
   Bold, striking perennial, 15–30 inches high, with thistle-like
   leaves. Not reliably hardy north of New York City.

2. **Cardinal-Flower** (*Lobelia Cardinalis*)     **p. 239**
   Splendid perennial for moist shady place in the wild garden.
   Summer-blooming, 3–4 feet high.

3. **Trumpet-Flower** (*Incarvillea delavayi*)     **p. 234**
   A perennial 18–24 inches high, needing a winter mulch. Blooms
   in June–July. Not hardy north of Boston.

4. **Edging Lobelia** (*Lobelia Erinus*)     **p. 238**
   Long-season South African annual, and one of the best edging
   plants. Summer-flowering, 3–7 inches high.

5. **Globe Daisy** (*Globularia trichosantha*)     **p. 235**
   Woody perennial, simulating a daisy, 6–8 inches high, flowering
   in May–June. Easily grown anywhere.

6. **Sweet Scabious** (*Scabiosa atropurpurea*)     **p. 240**
   European, long-season annual simulating the Aster Family.
   Flowers July–Sept. Height 12–36 inches.

7. **Mountain Bluet** (*Centaurea montana*)     **p. 244**
   A European perennial, 1–2 feet high, flowering in Aug.–Sept.
   Of easy culture anywhere.

8. **Cornflower** (*Centaurea cyanus*)     **p. 243**
   Extremely popular annual which often persists from self-sown
   seed. Flowers July to frost.

9. **Dusty Miller** (*Centaurea Cineraria*)     **p. 244**
   Attractive grayish foliage often surpasses the flowers in interest.
   Summer-flowering. Height 12–18 inches.

## ASTER FAMILY (*Compositae*)
### (*heads only with disk flowers*)

1. **Tansy** (*Tanacetum vulgare*)                    p. 247
   Aromatic, weedy perennial, 2½–4 feet high, summer-blooming.
   Easy to grow and often escaping to roadsides.

2. **Dusty Miller** (*Artemisia stelleriana*)          p. 246
   A gray-leaved perennial, 12–30 inches high. One of the best
   plants for sandy soils along the seashore.

3. **Cotula** (*Cotula squalida*)                      p. 247
   A low perennial, not over 2 inches high, with fernlike foliage.
   Useful for pavement planting.

4. **Blazing Star** (*Liatris scariosa*)               p. 245
   Native perennial, 3–5 feet high, flowering in Aug.–Sept. Fine
   for sandy soil or dry banks.

5. **Lavender Cotton** (*Santolina Chamaecyparissus*)   p. 247
   Silvery-gray perennial, with dissected foliage, 12–18 inches high.
   Not reliably hardy north of Boston.

6. **Ageratum** (*Ageratum houstonianum*)              p. 245
   A long-season tropical annual, popular everywhere as a summer
   bedding plant. Flowers July to frost.

7. **Globe Thistle** (*Echinops ritro*)                p. 248
   Prickly-foliaged perennial, 2–5 feet high, thistle-like and a bold
   subject for borders. Blooms July–Sept.

8. **Mugwort** (*Artemisia vulgaris lactiflora*)       p. 246
   Aromatic, much cut leaves, the plant 2–3 feet high. Easily grown
   in any ordinary garden soil. Blooms Aug.–Sept.

9. **Mist-Flower** (*Eupatorium coelestinum*)          p. 245
   Native perennial, its flower heads ageratum-like. Useful in reasonably moist places in partial shade. Blooms Aug. to Oct.

# ACANTHUS FAMILY
## (*Acanthaceae*)

A LARGE family (over 2000 species) of mostly tropical herbs, but with some shrubs and vines (see Black-eyed Susan at p. 1). The one below is the only herbaceous plant of much garden interest. Leaves oppositely arranged, or basal. Flowers unsymmetrical, followed by a dry pod.

**BEAR'S–BREECH** (*Acanthus mollis*)                        p. 236
A striking perennial from southern Europe, its foliage providing the chief motif for ornamentation of most Corinthian columns. It is a stout plant, its large, thistle-like leaves deeply cut and almost prickly on the margins, nearly 2 feet long. Flowers decidedly 2-lipped, about 2 inches long, in a dense, terminal spike that may be 18–24 inches long, plentifully beset with small spiny leaflets (bracts). **Color:** White, lilac, or rose. **Height:** 15–30 inches. **Flowering date:** Aug. **Varieties:** Latifolius (leaves larger and plant more hardy than the type, but not so easy to come by). **Culture:** Set purchased plants in April in full sun, in a sandy, perfectly drained loam, since they will not stand water at the roots, nor winter slush. Provide a thick but light mulch of evergreen boughs, straw, or salt hay (no manure) for winter protection. Not reliably hardy north of New York City, and often not so there unless in protected place.

# LOBELIA FAMILY
## (*Lobeliaceae*)

A MEDIUM-SIZED family (about 600 species) of generally tropical shrubs and trees but a few garden herbs of great beauty. Leaves alternately arranged. Flowers always irregular, generally conspicuously 2-lipped, followed by a 2-valved pod.

**EDGING LOBELIA** (*Lobelia Erinus*)                        p. 236
A long-season annual from South Africa and one of the most popular of all edging plants. It is low, compact or trailing (according to variety), with small, ovalish leaves and a profusion

of slender-stalked, 2-lipped flowers that are ½–¾ inch long. **Color:** Blue. **Height:** 3–7 inches. **Flowering date:** July–Sept. **Varieties:** Blue Gown (blue), Crystal Palace Compacta (deep blue), Mrs. Clibran (blue with white eye, Hamburgia (pale blue with white eye), Blue Stone (blue; only 4 inches high), Gracilis (blue and trailing). **Culture:** Sow seeds indoors ⅛ inch deep, in late Jan. or early Feb., in boxes or pots filled with ¾ garden loam and ¼ sand, thoroughly mixed. Carry seedlings in moderately cool room (not over 60°), until warm weather arrives. Set seedlings in full sun, in any ordinary garden soil, and for edging, 3–5 inches apart. They thrive better in cool summers than in hot ones.

**CARDINAL–FLOWER** (*Lobelia Cardinalis*)          p. 236
One of the most beautiful of all our native wild flowers, growing in moist woods throughout eastern North America. It is an erect plant, its oblongish leaves alternately arranged, 3–5 inches long, coarsely toothed, and nearly stalkless. Flowers in a striking, wandlike, terminal, loosely flowered spike, the individual flower conspicuously 2-lipped and 1½ inches long. **Color:** Scarlet. **Height:** 3–4 feet. **Flowering date:** July–Sept. **Varieties:** None. **Culture:** Set purchased plants in Oct. or April, in partial or complete shade of trees (no evergreens) in a moist or wet place, in a rich woods soil (not acid). It will sometimes thrive in ordinary garden soil if the site is moist and shady. Space 18–25 inches apart.

Related plant (not illustrated):
Great Blue Lobelia (*Lobelia siphilitica*). 2–3 feet.
Flowers blue, or bluish purple.

# TEASEL FAMILY
## (*Dipsacaceae*)

AN UNIMPORTANT and small family (about 140 species) of Old World herbs, one of which, the Fuller's Teasel, was once widely used to raise the nap on cloth. The sole garden plant is separated from the Daisy Family only by technical characters.

**SWEET SCABIOUS** (*Scabiosa atropurpurea*)                    p. 236
An attractive long-season annual from Europe apparently
related to the huge Daisy Family in having its small flowers
collected into a dense head. Basal leaves cut into lyre-shaped
lobes. Flower heads terminal, below each head a row of minute
leaflets (bracts). **Color:** Various, see below. **Height:** 12–36
inches. **Flowering date:** July–Sept. **Varieties:** Blue Moon (blue),
Blue Cockade (light blue), Coral Pink (pink), Lavender Moon
(pale lavender), and various unnamed varieties with red, white,
black (deep purplish black), and rose-pink flower heads. **Culture:** Sow seeds ⅛ inch deep indoors in pans or pots (8–10 weeks
before outdoor planting is safe). Fill pots or pans with ¾ garden
loam and ¼ sand. Transfer seedlings outdoors when trees leaf
out, in full sun in any ordinary garden soil, and space 10–15
inches apart.

Related plant (not illustrated):

> *Scabiosa caucasica.* 1½–2½ feet. Colors various. A
> perennial.

# Flowers Daisy-like

## Aster, Daisy, Dahlia, Chrysanthemum, and Zinnia Family

### (Compositae)

THE largest family of plants in the world — and in this book — for it contains more garden flowers than any other. Of over 15,000 species in the family most are herbs in the temperate zones, but some are tropical or subtropical (Dahlia, Zinnia, Cosmos) while in the tropics there are a few shrubs and trees. There are almost no plants of economic importance except those yielding absinthe, artichoke, salsify, lettuce, endive, chamomile, pyrethrum, and a few others.

The family is complex in its flower structure and presents considerable difficulty for the amateur, and for many professionals, in identifying the different sorts. It is quite impossible to identify them without some notion of the basic flower structure of all plants in the family.

The outstanding feature of the family is that many (sometimes 60–100) tiny flowers are crowded into a **head,** common examples of which are the Shasta Daisy, Chrysanthemum, Zinnia, and all others in the family. This crowded head is commonly but quite incorrectly called the "flower" by most of us, although it is actually composed of many flowers, which can easily be seen by picking the head to pieces. Beneath the flower head, and usually closely investing its base, is a series of miniature leaflets, correctly known as bracts.

Flower heads in the family are (in the garden plants below) easily seen to be of two kinds. In one all the tiny flowers in the head are minutely tubular and there are no rays (as there are in the daisy), so that the head appears like a small disk, crowded with tiny flowers. Such are called **disk flowers** and common examples include the garden Ageratum, Mist-Flower, and a few others.

The other, and much larger, group have disk flowers in the center of the head, but in addition there are several to many **ray flowers,** which radiate, starlike around the edge of the disk, a common example being any daisy or single Chrysanthemum. Such heads are said to contain ray flowers. These rays are apt to be quite mistakenly called "petals." Hence, for simplicity and accuracy, all the rest of the plants in this family will be specified as with disk flowers or ray flowers, because such a division is fundamental to an understanding of the Compositae. Ray flowers are, in many horticultural forms (hardly ever in wild plants), much doubled, so that scores or even hundreds of rays may be crowded into a single head, common examples being certain dahlias and chrysanthemums. Much more rarely disk flowers are doubled or modified (and hence appear like rays) as in the Cornflower.

Left: Flower head only with **disk** flowers. Right: Flower head with **ray** and **disk** flowers.

The illustration herewith shows typical examples of this fundamental difference in the flower heads of the family, and it is urged that the reader become familiar with these, and reread what has been already noted *before* trying to identify the plants that follow, for their identity is not quickly grasped. A few plants in this family have already been noted among the Ever-lastings on pp. 54–56. These are the Immortelle, Swan River Everlasting, Strawflower, Pearly Everlasting, Winged Everlasting, Edelweiss, and Blue Succory.

There are over 60 common garden plants in the family, and these may be readily separated into the two main groups already outlined:

*Flower heads with obvious rays (not petals) and also with disk flowers. See p. 248.*

*Flower heads with only disk flowers. This group comprises those immediately below.*

# Heads with Only Disk Flowers

THESE garden plants with only disk flowers, as in so many things in nature, contain exceptions that are confusing. All but 2 of them have unmistakably only disk flowers. But in the first 3 the disk flowers, or some of them, are modified to appear as if with rays. These are the Cornflower, one of the dusty millers, and the Mountain Bluet.

**CORNFLOWER** (*Centaurea cyanus*) p. 236
The national flower of Germany and often called Bachelor's Button, Bluebottle, or Ragged Sailor. It is from southern Europe, one of the most popular of all annuals, and is inclined to sprawl. Leaves narrow, nearly 5 inches long and usually without marginal teeth. Flower heads solitary, or in lax clusters, about 2 inches wide, apparently, but not truly with rays, which are often cut or fringed. **Color:** Prevailingly blue, but see below. **Height:** 12–30 inches. **Flowering date:** July–frost. **Varieties:** Several, but not definite as to name, some double-flowered. Best ordered by color, which includes various shades of blue, white, dark purple, and red. **Culture:** Broadcast seed in full sun, only lightly raking it in, in any ordinary garden soil, when trees leaf out. Space, by thinning out, 8–10 inches apart. Nearly always persistent from self-sown seed.

Related plants (not illustrated):
> Sweet Sultan (*Centaurea moschata*). 12–18-inch annual.
> All colors but yellow.
> *Centaurea imperialis.* 2–4 feet annual. All colors but
> yellow.
> Basket-Flower (*Centaurea americana*). 4–6 feet annual
> Flowers rose-pink.

## DUSTY MILLER (*Centaurea Cineraria*)                         p. 236

Not to be confused with the Cineraria, for which see p. 264. An
Italian perennial, grown as much for its white-felty foliage as
for its flower heads. Leaves parted into blunt segments. Flower
heads large but often plucked to promote foliage growth. **Color:**
Yellow or purple. **Height:** 12–18 inches, but often less as grown
for foliage. **Flowering date:** July–Aug. **Varieties:** None. **Culture:** Set purchased plants in full sun in any sandy loam that is
well drained, in April or Oct. For best development of foliage
pinch off all flower heads. It will not stand winter slush or water
at its roots, and is not reliably hardy north of New York City.

Related plant (not illustrated):
> Dusty Miller (*Centaurea gymnocarpa*). 12–20 inches.
> Flowers rose-purple.

## MOUNTAIN BLUET (*Centaurea montana*)                         p. 236

A European perennial, its foliage white-hairy only when young.
Leaves oblongish or oval, silvery white at first, ultimately green.
Flower heads showy, nearly 3 inches wide, some of the disk
flowers raylike and hence as if with conspicuous rays. **Color:**
Blue. **Height:** 1–2 feet. **Flowering date:** Aug.–Sept. **Varieties:**
None. **Culture:** Set purchased plants in full sun, in Oct. or April,
in any ordinary garden soil and space 9–15 inches apart. Some-
times called Perennial Cornflower.

Related plants (not illustrated):
> *Centaurea babylonica.* 5–8 feet. Flowers yellow.
> *Centaurea dealbata.* 18–24 inches. Flowers red, pink, or
> white.
> *Centaurea macrocephala.* 2–3 feet. Flowers yellow.
> *Centaurea ruthenica.* 2–3 feet. Flowers pale yellow.

**AGERATUM** (*Ageratum houstonianum*) p. 237

A tropical American long-season annual widely grown for summer bedding, and in its dwarf forms for edging. It has somewhat heart-shaped leaves, arranged opposite each other. Flower heads fluffy, somewhat sticky, not over ½ inch in diameter, numerous, all of disk flowers. **Color:** Prevailingly blue. **Height:** 5–7 inches; less in dwarf forms. **Flowering date:** July–frost. **Varieties:** One pink and one white, all the others blue; some dwarf, but of uncertain names. **Culture:** Sow seed indoors ⅛ inch deep (8–10 weeks before outdoor planting is safe), in mixture of ¾ garden loam and ¼ sand. Transfer seedlings outdoors only after warm weather has arrived, in partial shade or full sun, in any ordinary garden soil. Space 5–9 inches apart (less for dwarfs). Seed can also be sown directly outdoors after trees leaf out, but bloom will lag behind those started indoors.

**MIST–FLOWER** (*Eupatorium coelestinum*) p. 237

Often called Hardy Ageratum, this beautiful herb from the woodlands of the eastern U.S. is a perennial, with the leaves ovalish, short-stalked, pointed at the tip, 2–4 inches long and arranged opposite each other. Heads wholly of disk flowers, about ⅓ inch in diameter, but numerous and arranged in forked clusters. **Color:** Blue. **Height:** 18–30 inches. **Flowering date:** Aug.–Oct. **Varieties:** None. **Culture:** Set purchased plants in April, in partial shade or full sun, in any ordinary garden loam that is reasonably moist. Space 1–2 feet apart, as tops tend to spread.

Related plant (not illustrated):

White Snakeroot (*Eupatorium rugosum*). 2–4 feet. Flowers white. Its juice is poisonous. Often offered as *Eupatorium urticaefolium*.

**BLAZING STAR** (*Liatris scariosa*) p. 237

A perennial from sandy soils of Pa. to Ga., very useful for dry open places. It is a hairy-stemmed wandlike plant with numerous oblongish or narrower leaves. Heads button-like, all of disk flowers, mostly in interrupted clusters and hence scattered, the heads about 1 inch in diameter. **Color:** Bluish purple. **Height:**

3–5 feet. **Flowering date:** Aug.–Sept. **Varieties:** Alba (white), September Glory (purple), White Spire (white). **Culture:** Set purchased plants in April, in full sun, in a definitely sandy soil, even on dry banks and space 1–2 feet apart. May be offered as *Lacinaria scariosa.*

Related plants (not illustrated):

> Gay-Feather (*Liatris spicata*). 4–6 feet. Flowers rose-purple.

> Button Snakeroot (*Liatris pycnostachya*). 3–5 feet. Flowers purple.

### MUGWORT (*Artemisia vulgaris lactiflora*)                    p. 237

A Eurasian perennial, closely related to the plant yielding absinthe, with fragrant, much cut leaves that are silvery beneath. Flower heads all of disk flowers, not especially showy but keeping well when cut. The heads are about ⅛ inch in diameter and arranged in clustered spikes. **Color:** White (yellow in true *Artemisia vulgaris*). **Height:** 2–3 feet. **Flowering date:** Aug.–Sept. **Varieties:** Silver King (foliage silvery). **Culture:** Set purchased plants in April in full sun, in any ordinary garden soil and space 1–2 feet apart. Nearly always offered under the incorrect name of *Artemisia lactiflora.*

Related plants (not illustrated):

> *Artemisia frigida.* 9–15 inches. Flowers yellow.

> *Artemisia pontica.* 2–4 feet. Flowers whitish yellow.

> Roman Wormwood (*Artemisia absinthium*). 2½–4 feet. Flowers greenish. The plant yielding an ingredient of absinthe.

### DUSTY MILLER (*Artemisia stelleriana*)                    p. 237

A sea-beach perennial found along the coast of Japan but also common along the dunes from Quebec to Va., perhaps as an escape from cultivation. Also called Beach Wormwood and Old Woman. Leaves densely white-woolly, cut but not dissected, 2½–4 inches long. Flower heads with only disk flowers, about ¼ inch in diameter, crowded in dense clusters but not showy. **Color:** Yellow. **Height:** 12–30 inches. **Flowering date:** Aug.–Sept. **Varieties:** None. **Culture:** Set purchased plants in April, in full sun, in a definitely sandy soil, and space 10–15 inches apart. One of the best of all plants for sandy soils along the seashore.

**TANSY** (*Tanacetum vulgare*)                                    p. 237
A richly aromatic, rather weedy European perennial, its foliage once used to make tansy tea, puddings, and pancakes. It is a rank-growing plant with finely dissected leaves, often growing as a weed in barnyards and along roadsides here. Flower heads small, button-like, entirely without rays, arranged in a flat-topped cluster that is 2–4 inches wide. **Color:** Yellow. **Height:** 2½–4 feet. **Flowering date:** July–Aug. **Varieties:** Crispum (leaves more finely divided and crisped). **Culture:** Easily dug from dooryards or roadsides and planted in full sun in any garden soil. Space 18–30 inches apart. Does better in cool regions than in the South.

**LAVENDER COTTON** (*Santolina Chamaecyparissus*) p. 237
An evergreen perennial from the Mediterranean region, very aromatic and a little woody at the base. Leaves very small, finely dissected, silvery gray, scarcely ⅓ inch long. Flower heads solitary, at the end of naked stalks, entirely without rays, about ¾ inch in diameter. **Color:** Yellow. **Height:** 12–18 inches. **Flowering date:** Sept.–Oct. **Varieties:** None. **Culture:** Set purchased plants in full sun, in April, in sandy, well-drained loam, and space 9–12 inches apart. Can be sheared for foliage effect and used for edging, but its small flower heads are attractive. Not reliably hardy north of Boston, and it is better to provide a winter mulch of salt hay or straw. Often offered as *Santolina incana*.
   Related plant (not illustrated):
   *Santolina virens.* 10–15 inches. Flowers yellow.

**COTULA** (*Cotula squalida*)                                    p. 237
A tiny, prostrate New Zealand perennial grown as much for its fernlike, dissected foliage as for its small heads of flowers. Useful for filling in cracks among stepping stones and as a ground cover in the rock garden. Leaves about 2 inches long. Flower heads scarcely ¼ inch in diameter, solitary on the stalks, entirely without rays. **Color:** Yellow. **Height:** Prostrate, not over 2

inches high. **Flowering date:** July–Aug. **Varieties: None. Culture:** Set purchased plants in partial shades, in April or Oct., in a rich garden loam. Often it is easy to split up the small sodlike clumps and increase the area to be covered. Space 4–6 inches apart, and its trailing stems will soon make a dense mat. May be offered as *Leptinella*.

**GLOBE THISTLE** (*Echinops ritro*)                                p. 237
A bold, handsome Eurasian perennial, with white-felty stems, prickly foliage and flower heads, and steely-blue bloom. Leaves alternately arranged, green above but white-felty beneath, cut into narrow spiny segments and 2–5 inches long. Flower heads entirely without rays, nearly 2½ inches wide, spiny. **Color:** Steely blue. **Height:** 2–5 feet. **Flowering date:** July–Sept. **Varieties:** Taplow Blue (metallic blue). **Culture:** Set purchased plants in full sun, in April or Oct., in sandy or even poorer soil. Space 2–3 feet apart. Apt to die out in 3–4 years and needs replanting then.

Related plants (not illustrated):
> *Echinops humilis*. 3–4 feet. Flowers blue.
> *Echinops sphaerocephalus*. 5–8 feet. Flowers pale blue.

# *Heads with Central Disk and Ray Flowers*

Plants of the family Compositae (see p. 241) which have both a central disk and ray flowers to comprise the head, an example of which is the common white daisy or Shasta Daisy. These rays (commonly mistaken for petals) give most of the color to all the rest of the plants in the family. The central disk is always present and composed of many crowded, tiny, tubular flowers that attract little attention in comparison to the relatively showy ray flowers. As this large group contains all the remaining plants in the family it is fortunate that they can be divided into two main divisions for ease of identification, thus:

*Foliage when crushed not pungently aromatic or spicy; if odorous only mildly so. See p. 256.*

*Foliage when crushed pungently aromatic or spicy. The plants immediately below.*

# FOLIAGE AROMATIC

**CHRYSANTHEMUM** (*Chrysanthemum* hybrids)          p. 252
Of the thousands of forms of the Hardy Chrysanthemum, most seem to be derived, after 3000 years of cultivation, from an unknown race of Chinese perennials, including the florist's Chrysanthemum, which is grown only under glass. Our garden plants have highly aromatic foliage, the leaves alternately arranged, always more or less divided. Flower heads of varying sizes, always with many rays, much doubled in some sorts, single in others. So complex and hybridized has the group become (over 1200 are offered in America), that the experts have divided them into 6 or 7 sections, each of which is split into several subsections. Perhaps an oversimplification of these complexities is to reduce this mass, for the purposes of this book, to 3 main classes:

Pompons: flower heads small, tight, never quilled or fluted. Often called Button Chrysanthemums.

Hardy, large-flowered singles: heads large, never doubled.

Hardy, large-flowered doubles: heads large, never single. (Including "Decoratives.")

**Color:** All but blue. **Height:** 9–30 inches. **Flowering date:** Early July to frost and beyond, according to variety. **Varieties:** An enormous number. Arranged according to the above simplified classification, a fair selection might include the following, together with their expected dates of first blooming.

Pompons: Early Bronze (bronze, Aug. 25), Ruth Hatton (white, Sept. 25), R. Marion Hatton (yellow, Oct. 6), Canary Wonder (canary yellow, Oct. 1), Sept. Gold (golden yellow, Sept. 15), Governor Duff (orange, July 15), Mandalay (bronze, Oct. 6), Irene (white, Oct. 15), Lilian Doty (pink, Sept. 15), Early Wonder (pink, Sept. 20).

Hardy large-flowered singles: Silver Moon (white, Sept. 15),
   Astrid (pink, Sept. 15), Good Morning (yellow, Sept.
   10), Kristina (rose-pink, Oct. 10), Labrador (primrose
   yellow, Oct. 6), Polaris (yellow, Sept. 20).
Hardy large-flowered doubles: Avalanche (white, Sept. 25),
   Betty (pink, Oct. 7), Burma (bronze, Sept. 20), Coura-
   geous (purple, Oct. 12), Lavender Lady (lavender, Oct.
   8), Mrs. Pierre S. du Pont (peach, Oct. 8), Red Velvet
   (crimson, Oct. 4), Barbara Small (rose-pink, Sept. 15),
   Polar Ice (white, Sept. 20), Eugene A. Wander (yellow,
   Oct. 10), Cydonia (orange, Oct. 1), Vivid (red, Oct. 8).
In addition to the types already noted there are others variously
designated as Arcticum, Korean, Anemone-flowered, and Cushion classes, each with many varieties in all colors but blue. One,
called Azaleamum, has a tremendous number of small heads on
compact plants, which look like mounds of bloom. **Culture:** Set
purchased plants in April in full sun, in a rich garden loam (well
manured if the soil is poor) and do not rely upon rainfall to keep
them growing steadily. Water, if there is any prolonged drought.
To ensure bushy plants, pinch off terminal shoots of all straggling branches, up until July 15, otherwise the plants (at least
in some varieties) tend to sprawl. Do not pinch off such shoots
after July 15. For the finest blooms pinch out all but one or two
flower buds on each branch while they are quite young. Space
12–18 inches apart. Easily propagated by inserting shoots in a well-
drained soil almost any time if the cuttings are not allowed to
dry out. There is also a race of annual chrysanthemums that
bloom from seed in a single season. Plant seeds when trees leaf
out, ⅛ inch deep in any ordinary garden soil, and thin to 12–18
inches apart. Less satisfactory than the hardy perennial sorts.

**SHASTA DAISY** (*Chrysanthemum maximum*)                    p. 252
Originally from the Pyrenees, but now much hybridized, the
Shasta Daisy is one of the finer plants for the border, because of
its showy daisy-like heads. Leaves long, narrow, toothed, but not
cut. Flower heads usually long-stalked, solitary, and 2–4 inches
wide. **Color:** White. **Height:** 15–30 inches. **Flowering date:**

June–Aug. **Varieties:** Alaska (white), Mount Shasta (white and double-flowered), Marconi (double, fringed and white), Giant Single (single-flowered and white), Chiffon (double-flowered and white), Mrs. C. Lothian Bell (white, early-flowering), White Swan (white and double-flowered). **Culture:** Although a true perennial, it tends to die out and should be replanted every second or third year. Set purchased plants in full sun, in any good rich garden loam that is well drained, in April or Oct. and space 18–25 inches apart.

Related plants (not illustrated):

Feverfew (*Chrysanthemum Parthenium*). 2–3½ feet. Flower heads white, often button-like and double. Sometimes offered under incorrect name of *Matricaria.*

Paris Daisy or Marguerite (*Chrysanthemum frutescens*). 2–3 feet. Flowers white or pale yellow.

**PYRETHRUM** (*Chrysanthemum coccineum*) p. 252
Also known as Painted Daisy, this perennial is native from the Caucasus to Iran and is a summer-blooming favorite with aromatic foliage. Leaves much divided and fernlike. Flower heads fragrant, showy, 2–3 inches wide, often much doubled, generally solitary. **Color:** All but yellow and blue. **Height:** 1–2 feet. **Flowering date:** June–July. **Varieties:** Robinson's Dark Crimson (crimson), Princess Margaret (pink), Rosy Morn (rose-pink), James Kelway (red), and a white, unnamed variety. **Culture:** Set purchased plants in full sun in April or Oct., in any well-drained garden loam, and pick off faded heads to promote future bloom. It will stand partial shade, and a yearly application of manure will help if spread 2 inches deep and dug in in the spring. Replant every third or fourth year, since the plant tends to die out. It, and one of its relatives, is the source of pyrethrum powder (from dried flower heads).

Related plants (not illustrated):

Ox-Eye Daisy (*Chrysanthemum leucanthemum*). 10–18 inches. Flowers white.

Giant Daisy (*Chrysanthemum uliginosum*). 4–7 feet. Flowers white.

## ASTER FAMILY (*Compositae*)
### (*heads with disk and ray flowers; crushed foliage mostly aromatic*)

1. **Chrysanthemum** (Single-flowered; Silver Moon)    **p. 249**
   A race of garden chrysanthemums, with large rays, but not doubled. See text for many other varieties.

2. **Chrysanthemum** (Pompon; Mandalay)    **p. 249**
   A race of garden chrysanthemums with much-doubled, small heads. See text for many other varieties.

3. **Chrysanthemum** (Hardy, large-flowered [Decoratives]; Lavender Lady)    **p. 249**
   A protean race of garden chrysanthemums, tall, and with very large flower heads. See text for many other varieties.

4. **Shasta Daisy** (*Chrysanthemum maximum*)    **p. 250**
   A perennial from the Pyrenees, 15–30 inches high and summer-blooming. Not persisting unless replanted every two or three years.

5. **Pyrethrum** (*Chrysanthemum coccineum*)    **p. 251**
   Fernlike, aromatic foliage very handsome, 1–2 feet high, and blooming June–July. Not persisting unless replanted every two or three years.

6. **Sneezewort** (*Achillea Ptarmica*)    **p. 254**
   Old garden favorite, 12–20 inches high, with long-lasting flower heads. Of easiest culture anywhere. Blooms June–July.

7. **Golden Marguerite** (*Anthemis tinctoria*)    **p. 254**
   Related to the true chamomile, its foliage highly aromatic. A perennial, 12–30 inches high. Midsummer-bloomer.

8. **German Chamomile** (*Matricaria Chamomilla*)    **p. 255**
   Weedy, but highly aromatic perennial with finely dissected foliage. Height 1–2 feet. Blooms May to Sept.

9. **Blue Daisy** (*Felicia amelloides*)    **p. 254**
   A highly desirable but little-known South African perennial, 1–2½ feet high. Blooms Sept.–Nov.

## ASTER FAMILY (*Compositae*)
### (*heads with ray and disk flowers; crushed foliage not aromatic, except in No. 8*)

1. **Michaelmas Daisy** (*Aster* hybrids; Blue Gem)  **p. 256**
   A fine race of hybrid asters, all perennial, 2–6 feet high, and blooming (according to variety) from Aug. to frost.

2. **Cactus Dahlia** (*Dahlia* hybrids)  **p. 259**
   A race of dahlias with the rays curved toward the center. See text for many varieties.

3. **China Aster** (*Callistephus* hybrids)  **p. 258**
   A race of many varieties of annual asters. See text for types and varieties.

4. **Michaelmas Daisy** (*Aster* hybrids; Beechwood Challenger)  **p. 256**
   See No. 1 and the text for a list of varieties that bloom from Aug. to frost.

5. **Cosmos** (*Cosmos* hybrids)  **p. 261**
   A Mexican weak-stemmed annual, 5–9 feet high, profuse bloomer from July to frost. Stake plants if site is windy.

6. **China Aster** (*Callistephus* hybrids)  **p. 258**
   A race of many varieties of annual asters. See text for types and varieties.

7. **English Daisy** (*Bellis perennis*)  **p. 261**
   Grown as a biennial and one of the most popular of all bedding plants. Height 4–6 inches. Does not tolerate much heat.

8. **African Marigold** (*Tagetes erecta*)  **p. 255**
   A highly aromatic, long-season annual, 18–24 inches high, and flowering from July to Sept.

9. **Decorative Dahlia** (*Dahlia* hybrids)  **p. 259**
   A race of dahlias with large, much doubled heads. See text for many varieties.

**SNEEZEWORT** (*Achillea Ptarmica*)                              p. 252

In its original form this perennial of the North Temperate Zone
is a single-flowered plant scarcely grown in this country, but its
double-flowered varieties are among the most popular of old
garden favorites. Leaves lance-shaped, toothed, or cut into segments, 2–4½ inches long. Flower heads in close clusters, always
double-flowered in the garden forms, very useful for cutting, for
they last well. **Color:** White. **Height:** 12–20 inches. **Flowering
date:** June–July. **Varieties:** Boule de Neige (white), Pearl (pearl
white), Snowball (white), Perry's White (white). **Culture:**
Very easy; set purchased plants in full sun, in any ordinary garden soil, in April or Oct., and space 12–18 inches apart. It tends
to die out unless lifted, divided, and replanted every third or
fourth year.

Related plants (not illustrated):

Yarrow (*Achillea millefolium*). 1–2 feet. Flowers white,
except in the variety Roseum, which is red.

*Achillea tomentosa*. 8–12 inches. Flowers yellow.

*Achillea filipendulina*. 2–4 feet. Flowers yellow.

**GOLDEN MARGUERITE** (*Anthemis tinctoria*)               p. 252

A Eurasian highly aromatic perennial, often called Yellow Chamomile, with daisy-like, yellow flower heads. Leaves twice-cut,
the segments finely dissected. Flower heads solitary, long-stalked,
about 2 inches wide, the rays numerous. **Color:** Yellow. **Height:**
12–30 inches. **Flowering date:** July–Aug. **Varieties:** Kelwayi
(dark yellow), Moonlight (pale yellow). **Culture:** Set purchased
plants in full sun, in April or Oct., in any ordinary garden soil,
and space 15–25 inches apart. To prevent it dying out lift, divide
and replant every third or fourth year.

Related plants (not illustrated):

Chamomile (*Anthemis nobilis*). 8–12 inches. Flowers
white.

*Anthemis biebersteiniana*. 8–12 inches. Flowers yellow;
a rock garden plant.

**BLUE DAISY** (*Felicia amelloides*)                            p. 252

A little-grown but very handsome, late-flowering perennial from

South Africa, often offered under the incorrect name of *Agathea coelestis,* and sometimes called Blue Marguerite. It is a bushy plant with its oppositely arranged leaves elliptic, roughish, and tapering at the base to a winged stalk. Flower heads daisy-like, solitary on each stalk, but numerous, showy, about 1½ inches wide. **Color:** Blue. **Height:** 1–2½ feet. **Flowering date:** Sept.–Nov. **Varieties:** None. **Culture:** Set purchased plants (only from western dealers) in full sun in April, in a warm, well-drained sandy loam, preferably in a place protected from north winds, and space 2–3 feet apart. Not reliably hardy north of the eastern shore of Va. unless protected with a winter mulch of straw or salt hay, and not hardy at all north of Wilmington, Del.

Related plant (not illustrated):

*Felicia bergeriana.* 6–8 inches. Flowers blue; an annual.

**GERMAN CHAMOMILE** (*Matricaria Chamomilla*)      p. 252
A highly aromatic, somewhat weedy Eurasian annual, often called Sweet or False Chamomile, not to be confused with the true Chamomile. It has finely dissected leaves, 1–2½ inches long, and numerous flower heads that are about ½ inch wide and not particularly showy. It is often a weedy escape from gardens to roadsides throughout North America. **Color:** White. **Height:** 1–2 feet. **Flowering date:** May–Sept. **Varieties:** None. **Culture:** Sow seeds ⅛ inch deep, when trees leaf out, in any ordinary garden, or even poor soil. Thin to 12–15 inches apart.

Related plant (not illustrated):

Turfing Daisy (*Matricaria tchihatchewi*). Prostrate perennial. Flowers white.

**AFRICAN MARIGOLD** (*Tagetes erecta*)      p. 253
Sometimes confused with the Pot Marigold (*Calendula*), for which see p. 271, but the latter is scentless, while the African Marigold is highly aromatic. It is a long-season annual from Mexico (long thought to be native in Africa) and is a bushy herb with finely divided leaves. Flower heads solitary on each stalk, 2–4 inches wide, the stalk swollen just beneath the head. **Color:** Yellow or orange. **Height:** 8–24 inches. **Flowering date:** July–Sept. **Varieties:** Badly confused and very numerous, sep-

arated into rather doubtful classes such as dahlia-flowered, chrysanthemum-flowered, carnation-flowered, dwarfs, ball marigolds, etc., each with varying colors from yellow to orange, pink, cerise, and red. Some of these have much doubled or even quilled flower heads, and a few are reputed to have scentless foliage. **Culture:** Sow seeds indoors (7–9 weeks before outdoor planting is safe), ⅛ inch deep in a mixture of ¾ garden loam and ¼ sand, thoroughly mixed, in pots or boxes. Transfer seedlings outdoors only when settled warm weather has arrived, in full sun, in rich garden loam, and space 1–2 feet apart. May also be started from seed sown outdoors when trees leaf out, but bloom will be later.

Related plant (not illustrated):

French Marigold (*Tagetes patula*). 7–12 inches. Flowers red, yellow, or orange; in several varieties.

## FOLIAGE NOT AROMATIC

ALL the above 8 plants and their relatives have highly aromatic foliage (when crushed). Those below, to the end of the book do not have aromatic or spicy foliage, and if odorous at all, only slightly so. The group is a large one and not easily separated, but about half of them almost never have yellow flowers, although they may be of nearly all other colors. Wayward nature usually provides exceptions to any general rule and these will be noted where they occur. To reduce the remainder of the plants in this great family (the Compositae) the following scheme is suggested:

*Flowers prevailingly yellow (shading to orange and red in some forms).* See p. 267.

*Flowers never yellow (except in some forms noted where they occur). This includes the plants immediately below.*

### FLOWERS ALMOST NEVER YELLOW

**PERENNIAL ASTER or**
**MICHAELMAS DAISY** (*Aster* hybrids)                    p. 253
These gorgeous fall-flowering perennials have been derived (mostly from England) by crossing the New England aster, the

New York aster, and one or two other native asters with the Italian aster (*Aster amellus*). As now developed they provide a wealth of varieties (not all satisfactory here, but profuse bloomers in England) which provide a series that bloom from Aug. to frost and are in all colors but yellow. They are stout perennials, often quite tall, and in those below with numerous blooms of showy heads of the single-flowered, daisy-like type. Few plants equal them in profusion of fall bloom. **Color:** All but yellow. **Height:** 1–6 feet, depending on variety. **Flowering date:** Aug.–frost. **Varieties:** Over 150, divided into those derived from the New England aster, New York aster, the Italian aster, and some cushion types that are dwarf and useful for edging. The following list, arranged alphabetically, gives the color, height, and flowering date for the 28 varieties most likely to be hardy here, all generally classed as Michaelmas Daisies, and all available in America.

Barr's Pink (pink, 4–5 feet, Sept.)
Beechwood Challenger (crimson, 18 inches, **Oct.**)
Blue Gem (blue, 5 feet, Sept.)
Blue Gown (blue, 4 feet, Sept.)
Climax (lavender blue, 6 feet, Sept.)
Countess of Dudley (pink, 12 inches, **Sept.**)
Elegans (lavender, 18 inches, Aug.)
Elsa (lilac, 3 feet, Sept.)
Gray Lady (opal-gray, 3 feet, Sept.)
Harrington's Pink (pink, 3 feet, Oct.)
King George (bluish violet, 18 inches, **Aug.**)
Lady Lloyd (rose-pink, 3 feet, Sept.)
Mauve Cushion (mauve, 1 foot, Oct.)
Mount Everest (white, 3 feet, Oct.)
Mrs. J. F. Raynor (crimson, 3 feet, Oct.)
Mrs. R. Wood (rose-pink, 12 inches, **Aug.**)
Nancy (pink, 12 inches, Sept.)
Niobe (white, 8 inches, Sept.)
Palmyra (pink, 3 feet, Oct.)
Queen Mary (blue, 4 feet, Oct.)

Red Cloud (red, 3 feet, Oct.)
Red Rover (red, 4 feet, Oct.)
Robinson (bluish mauve, 4 feet, Sept.)
Royal Blue (blue, 4 feet, Oct.)
Sam Banham (white, 6 feet, Sept.)
Snow Sprite (white, 18 inches, Sept.)
Sunset (pink, 4 feet, Sept.)
Violetta (violet, 4 feet, Sept.)

**Culture:** Set purchased plants in April in full sun in a bed prepared by deep digging in rich garden loam, and if not rich dig in and thoroughly mix ½ pail of manure per plant. Space tall types 2½–4 feet apart and lower kinds 18–30 inches apart. The site should be reasonably moist but not wet. As plants sprout, pinch off all but the two or three strongest shoots. Dig up, divide, and replant every other year, using only the strongest clumps.

Related plants (not illustrated):

*Aster frikarti.* 2–3 feet. Flowers lavender-blue.
*Aster alpinus.* 8–10 inches. Flowers blue; May.
*Aster ericoides.* 2–3 feet. Flowers white.
*Aster subcoeruleus.* 8–12 inches. Flowers blue.

**ANNUAL or CHINA ASTER** (*Callistephus* hybrids)   p. 253
Often called the Garden Aster to distinguish it from the perennial Michaelmas Daisies. All these Annual Asters have been derived by hybridization of the China Aster (*Callistephus chinensis*) which differs from the true *Aster* only in technical characters. It is a true long-season annual with hairy, ovalish leaves and showy, solitary flower heads that are 3–4 inches wide and usually much doubled. **Color:** All but yellow. **Height:** 10–30 inches. **Flowering date:** July–Sept. **Varieties:** Innumerable and in great confusion, due to rival claims of competitive dealers. Sorted out as to types (there are all colors in each, but yellow) there may be distinguished: Giant Branching (late-flowered, the rays incurved), Beauty (late-flowered, the rays incurved), Crego (mid season, the rays twisted and reflexed), Royal (early and single-flowered), King (mid-season, the rays quilled), Comet (mid-season, nearly double-flowered), Astermum (like a Pom-

pon Chrysanthemum head), Peony-flowered (large, double-flowered heads that may be 4½ inches wide). Even these type or class names are not always valid, such is the confusion in the varieties of the garden aster. **Culture:** Sow seeds indoors (7–9 weeks before outdoor planting is safe), ⅟₁₆ inch deep in a mixture of ¾ good garden loam and ¼ sand, thoroughly mixed, in pots or boxes, preferably on a shelf at the kitchen window (no gas stove). Keep in as cool, moist air as possible. Transfer seedlings outdoors when trees leaf out, in full sun, in a rich garden loam (if not, manure it 3 weeks before planting). Space 15–25 inches apart and see that they do not dry out in droughts. One of the best of all flowers for cutting.

**DAHLIA** (*Dahlia* hybrids) p. 253

One of the most popular of all tender perennials and now known in over 2000 named varieties, all derived from a few species found wild in the mountains of Guatemala and Mexico, mostly by hybridization, much of it done in America. They are not winter-hardy over most of the country and their roots must be stored during frosty weather. Leaves oppositely arranged, nearly always divided, or even twice-divided (compound). Flower heads showy, rarely single-flowered, more often much doubled, the rays numerous and quilled, ruffled, crisped, and otherwise modified from the original single-flowered wild type, which has flat rays and a starlike head. **Color:** All, including a few with yellow rays, which is an exception to the group noted at p. 256. **Height:** 2–6 feet, according to variety. **Flowering date:** July–frost, according to variety. **Varieties:** An enormous number, few of which persist over the years. So complicated is dahlia classification that it is here simplified into 6 main types: SINGLES, open-centered heads with a single row of rays; DUPLEX, similar, but the head with 2 rows of rays; PEONY, with not more than 4 rows of rays, but with some incurved rays at the center; DECORATIVE, completely double-flowered, but the rays not recurved; CACTUS, like Decorative, but many of the rays curved toward center of head. POMPON, heads not usually more than 2 inches in diameter. These 6 types include 8 more, which are mere subdivisions favored by the experts. Varieties under some of the most important types might include: **Singles and Duplex** — Orange Gold (orange), Purity (white), Scarlet Lady (scarlet), Snow Princess (white), Garnet Poinsettia (scarlet), Newport Wonder (raspberry), Pequot Yellow (yellow). **Decorative** — Jersey Beauty (pink), Jane Cowl (buff, gold, and rose), Lord of Autumn (yellow), Murphy's Masterpiece (red), Arelda Lloyd (yellow and pink), Betty Cotter (salmon-red), Thomas A. Edison (violet-purple), White Wonder (white), Forest Fire (red), Blue Train (blue), Purple Mist (pinkish purple), Red Sunset (pink). **Cactus** — Coral Cactus (pink), Golden Standard (orange-yellow), Adries Orange (orange), Frau O. Bracht (yellow), Ivory Princess (white), Michigan White (white), Pink Mum (pink), Sarett's Pink Flamingo (pink), Son of Satan (scarlet), Jersey Dainty (white), Lady in Red (red). **Pompon** — Amber Queen (pale yellow), Little Edith (yellow and carmine,) Little David (russet-orange), Bronze Beauty (bronze), Honey (yellow and red), Yellow Gem (yellow), Joe Fette (white), Baby Royal (salmon-pink), Bishop of Llandaff (red). **Culture:** Set purchased tuberous roots in full sun, only after settled warm weather has arrived, about 6 inches deep, the root flat or slightly pointing upward, the "eye" (terminal bud) always pointing upward. The soil must, or should be rich garden loam (manured, if not), and cover the roots with about 4 inches of soil, filling up the hole to ground level, as the shoots grow upward. For all tall varieties provide a stout stake set at planting intervals before the roots are planted, especially in windy sites. Do not let the plants suffer from drought, and for best bloom restrict plant to two or three main shoots. In fall, after first frost cut off all tops to ground level and dig up the collection of joined roots that have matured during the summer. Cut off all stems to within an inch of root and dry the cluster of roots for a few hours in the sunshine (it must be above freezing). Store the root cluster, without dividing, in a cool, frost-free place (no furnace heat), either loose or covered with sand or straw (preferred temperature 35°–45°), and the storage place must not be wet or the roots will mildew. In the spring divide the root cluster by tearing apart, and use for planting only the plumpest roots, being sure that each has an "eye." Space tall varieties 3–4 feet apart, the lower sorts 2–3 feet. For real exhibition blooms, disbud all but a few, and use a cupful of bone meal per plant, raked in near it but not touching the stem, in June or early July, and another in early Aug., none thereafter. If soil is definitely acid apply lime at rate of 1 pound to 25 square feet, raked in before planting time.

**COSMOS** (*Cosmos* hybrids)                                    p. 253
A tall annual, now in many varieties, derived from *Cosmos bipinnatus* from the uplands of Mexico and (in the yellow varieties) from *Cosmos sulphureus* of the same region. They have tall, thin, and weak stems, and a profusion of leaves cut into threadlike segments. Flower heads 1–2 inches wide, solitary or a few on each stalk, but profuse, the rays scarcely, if at all doubled, always slightly toothed at the tip. **Color:** All but blue. **Height:** 5–9 feet. **Flowering date:** July–frost. **Varieties:** Best to order by color and use Early sorts, since Late varieties are apt not to bloom before cut off by frost. Various dealer-named varieties are in much confusion. **Culture:** Sow ⅛ inch deep indoors (6–8 weeks before outdoor planting is safe), in boxes or pots filled with ¾ garden loam and ¼ sand, thoroughly mixed. Transfer seedlings outdoors when settled warm weather has arrived, in full sun, in poor or indifferent soil (rich soil promotes foliage instead of flowers), and stake all tall varieties if in a windy site. The early varieties will bloom steadily from July until frost. Space 2–3 feet apart, and for best bloom pinch out terminal shoot when it is about 18 inches high. A fine flower for cutting.

**ENGLISH DAISY** (*Bellis perennis*)                          p. 253
*The* daisy of history and the poets, but commonly called English Daisy or Bachelor's-Button here. It is a European perennial but grown as a biennial here. The basal leaves are in tufts or rosettes, broadest toward the tip. Flower heads solitary, nearly 2 inches wide, on stiff stalks, the rays numerous, often doubled, and in some varieties quilled. **Color:** All but yellow; prevailingly white.

**Height:** 4–6 inches. **Flowering date:** June–Aug., and sometimes to frost. **Varieties:** Monstrosa (much doubled), Dresden China (blue), Red Monstrosa (red), Rose Monstrosa (pink), Longfellow (white), The Bride (white). **Culture:** Sow seeds ⅛ inch deep in any good garden soil in July for bloom the following summer. Transfer seedlings in early Oct. to cold frame for winter protection. When trees leaf out, set seedlings in full sun or partial shade, in any good garden loam, and space 4–5 inches apart. Fine for summer bedding and as edging. Will bloom nearly to frost if the site is cool, but often stops blooming (or even dies) if heat is intense. Naturalized in the cool lawns of England but seldom here.

**BELLIUM** (*Bellium bellidioides*)                                    p. 268

A tiny perennial from the Mediterranean region suited only to the rock garden or for pavement planting, and not much grown here. Leaves minute, in a basal rosette, from which springs a short stalk crowned with the solitary, pert head of ray flowers about ½ inch wide. **Color:** White, rarely pinkish or bluish. **Height:** 4 inches. **Flowering date:** July–Aug. **Varieties:** None. **Culture:** Set purchased plants in April or Oct. in gritty or sandy, well-drained soil in the rock garden or among cracks in pavements. Space 3–4 inches apart.

Related plant (not illustrated):

> *Bellium minutum.* 2–3 inches. Flowers white; an annual.

**URSINIA** (*Ursinia anethoides*)                                    p. 268

A little-grown South African annual, with wiry stems and its leaves deeply cut into narrow segments. Flower heads numerous but solitary on each stalk, daisy-like, about 1 inch wide, the flower stalk about 8 inches long. **Color:** Orange, but purple at base of rays. **Height:** 8–12 inches. **Flowering date:** July–Aug. **Varieties:** None. **Culture:** Sow seeds ⅛ inch deep, when warm weather has arrived, in full sun in any well-drained garden loam, and thin to 8–10 inches apart. They do not bloom well, and may die in regions of great summer heat.

Related plants (not illustrated):
> *Ursinia anthemoides.* 8–12 inches. Flowers yellow.
> *Ursinia pulchra.* 12–18 inches. Flowers orange.

**VENIDIUM** (*Venidium fastuosum*) p. 268
A little-grown South African long-season annual with showy flower heads that open in the morning and close at night, even when cut for the house, for which they are very attractive. Leaves lyre-shaped, cobwebby when young. Flower heads solitary, 4–5 inches wide. **Color:** Orange, with purplish band at the base of rays. **Height:** 2–3 feet. **Flowering date:** July–Aug. **Varieties:** None. **Culture:** Not easy in the East, far better in Calif. Sow seeds indoors (in the East) in pots or boxes filled with ¾ loam and ¼ sand, thoroughly mixed. Sow seeds ⅛ inch deep (about 8 weeks before outdoor planting is safe). When warm weather comes transfer seedlings outdoors, in full sun, in a rather sandy loam. Do not overwater, since (in the East) the plants are subject to stem rot. In Calif. and similar climates, can be sown directly outdoors, but in the East they do not usually thrive when so treated.

**FALSE CHAMOMILE** (*Boltonia asteroides*) p. 268
A somewhat coarse perennial from the eastern U.S., so profusely blooming that it is often called Thousand-flowered Aster. Leaves lance-shaped, 3–5 inches long, practically without marginal teeth. Flower heads about ¾ inch wide, very numerous, in an open, much branched leafy cluster. **Color:** White, rarely violet or purple. **Height:** 5–8 feet. **Flowering date:** Aug.–Oct. **Varieties:** None. **Culture:** Easy; set purchased plants in April in full sun in almost any garden soil and space 3–4 feet apart. It is a relatively short-lived perennial and should be dug, divided, and replanted every third or fourth year.
Related plant (not illustrated):
> *Boltonia latisquama.* 5–8 feet. Flowers violet-blue.

**STOKES ASTER** (*Stokesia laevis*) p. 268
A showy perennial growing wild from S.C. to La., but hardy far north of this. It has purplish stems covered with white-woolly

hairs and lance-shaped leaves 7–10 inches long. Flower heads
2–4 inches wide, solitary or few, in a branching cluster. **Color:**
Lavender-blue. **Height:** 12–30 inches. **Flowering date:** Aug.–
Sept. **Varieties:** Alba (white), Blue Moon (blue), Rosea (pink).
**Culture:** Set purchased plants in April or Oct. in full sun, in
warm, sandy loam (no clay or heavy loam), and space 10–15
inches apart. It will not stand water at its roots during slushy
winters, and is not reliably hardy north of Boston.

**CINERARIA** (*Senecio cruentus*)                              p. 268
Profuse-blooming tender plants from the Canary Islands, not
possible to grow without a cool greenhouse, but widely used as
a very showy bedding plant in the spring, and for window boxes.
As grown by florists it is a bushy plant, kept so by pinching off
leggy shoots. Leaves long-stalked, often covered with scattered
white-woolly hairs when young. Flower heads 1½–2 inches wide,
in a dense truss that stands above the dome-shaped mass of
foliage; extremely showy, but not staying in flower for long.
**Color:** Prevailingly blue, but in nearly all other colors except
yellow in some of its varieties. **Height:** 15–30 inches. **Flowering
date:** May–June; usually grown for spring bedding. **Varieties:**
Several florist's kinds, but best ordered by color. **Culture:** Impossible (in the East) without a cool greenhouse. For those without one, purchase potted plants to be set in full sun, preferably
still in their pots, plunged to the rim in a good garden soil, and
not before trees leaf out. Such plants, if properly grown by the
florist should be on the verge of blooming, and will provide some
of the most showy color of all bedding plants until really hot
weather arrives. Fine for window boxes or house plants, but
failing if the temperature gets much above 60°.
    Related plants (not illustrated):
        Dusty Miller (*Senecio Cineraria*). Hardy perennial, 15–
        30 inches. Flowers yellow.
        German Ivy (*Senecio mikanioides*). Tender, climbing
        house plant; hardy in the South. Flowers yellow.
        Purple Ragwort (*Senecio elegans*). Long-season annual,
        1–2 feet high. Flowers purple or red.

**TAHOKA DAISY** (*Machaeranthera tanacetifolia*)    p. 268
A recently introduced annual native from S.Dak. to Montana, south to Mexico and Calif., named for the town of Tahoka, Texas. It is a sticky plant the leaves 3–4 inches long, much divided, the segments bristle-tipped. Flower heads about 2 inches wide, the rays slender and pointed. **Color:** Lavender-blue. **Height:** 1–2 feet. **Flowering date:** July–Oct. **Varieties:** None. **Culture:** Sow seeds, which have been kept in the refrigerator for 2 weeks (not in deep freeze), ⅛ inch deep (6 weeks before outdoor planting is safe) in a mixture of ¾ sandy loam and ¼ sand, thoroughly mixed. Transfer seedlings outdoors when trees leaf out, in full sun, in a warm sandy loam. Fine for cutting; the plant will stand extreme heat.

**FLEABANE** (*Erigeron speciosus*)    p. 268
A daisy-like perennial from western North America, widely cultivated for its showy clusters of bloom. Leaves narrow, almost stem-clasping at the base, without marginal teeth. Flower heads about 1½ inches wide, its rays numerous (nearly 100), and pointed. **Color:** Prevailingly violet, but see below. **Height:** 15–30 inches. **Flowering date:** May–July. **Varieties:** Several, but the names are uncertain. They include white, purple, and pink forms. **Culture:** Set purchased plants in full sun, in April or Oct., in any ordinary garden soil, and space 12–18 inches apart.
  Related plants (not illustrated):
    *Erigeron karvinskianus.* 12–18 inches. Flowers pinkish white. Not hardy northward.
    *Erigeron glaucus.* 8–10 inches. Flowers violet or lilac. Not hardy in the East; a Calif. species.
    *Erigeron macranthus.* 15–30 inches. Flowers bluish purple, or violet.
    *Erigeron compositus.* 5–8 inches. Flowers white. A rock garden plant.
    *Erigeron trifidus.* 2–4 inches. Flowers lavender to white. A rock garden plant.

**BLACK SAMPSON** (*Echinacea purpurea*)    p. 268
A kind of coneflower from the central U.S. with a branched stem,

rather coarse foliage, and solitary, not very showy flower heads. Leaves broadly oval, 5–7 inches long, narrowed at the base to a winged stalk. Flower head about 3 inches wide, the central cone (center) nearly 1 inch high. Rays drooping, 2–toothed at the tip. **Color:** Rose-purple. **Height:** 3–4 feet. **Flowering date:** July–Oct. **Varieties:** White Lustre (white). **Culture:** Easy; set purchased plants in full sun in April, in any ordinary, or even poor soil and space 2–3 feet apart. Sometimes offered as *Brauneria purpurea.*

Related plant (not illustrated):

*Echinacea angustifolia.* 1–2 feet. Flowers rose-purple.

**SWAN RIVER DAISY** (*Brachycome iberidifolia*)     p. 269

An Australian long-season annual with a bushy habit and cineraria-like flower heads, low enough to be a valuable edging plant. It has small, much divided leaves, the ultimate segments very narrow. Flower heads solitary, about 1 inch wide, long-stalked. **Color:** All but yellow. **Height:** 6–15 inches. **Flowering date:** July–Aug. **Varieties:** None named; best ordered by color. **Culture:** For early bloom sow seeds indoors (6–8 weeks before outdoor planting is safe), ⅛ inch deep, in boxes or pots filled with a mixture of ¾ garden loam and ¼ sand. Transfer seedlings outdoors when trees leaf out, in full sun, in a warm sandy loam, or ordinary garden soil, and space 6–9 inches apart, closer if used for edging. May also be sown directly outdoors when settled warm weather arrives, but bloom will be delayed.

**AFRICAN DAISY** (*Arctotis stoechadifolia*)     p. 269

The name African Daisy is apt to be confusing, since it is applied also, and not inappropriately, to related plants known as *Dimorphotheca, Gazania,* and *Gerbera* (see each of these just below). *Arctotis* is a long-season, South African annual, with ovalish, white-woolly, toothed leaves that are about 3 inches long. Flower heads showy, solitary, long-stalked, nearly 3 inches wide, much exceeding the foliage. Rays many, usually darker colored near the base. **Color:** Nearly all, see below. **Height:** 30–48 inches. **Flowering date:** July–Aug. **Varieties:** Grandis (an improved form) in nearly all colors, the center of the head usually of a different color from the tips of the rays, the head thus appearing as if with an "eye" or halo. **Culture:** Sow seeds indoors ⅛ inch deep (6–8 weeks before outdoor planting is safe), in boxes or pots, filled with a mixture of ¾ sandy loam and ¼ sand. Transfer seedlings outdoors only after settled warm weather has arrived, in full sun, in a definitely sandy loam or even an indifferent soil. Space 10–15 inches apart. Will stand great heat and considerable drought. Sometimes offered as *Arctotis grandis.*

## FLOWERS USUALLY YELLOW

All the plants between pp. 256 and 267 have flowers that are not usually yellow, although there are some exceptions noted where they occur. From here to the end of the book the flowers are nearly always yellow, except in some forms of the Cape Marigold, gaillardias, *Gazania,* Transvaal Daisy, and Zinnias.

All of these can be separated into 3 not always rigid groups, thus:

*Plants tall, usually 3–6 feet or more. See p. 277.*
*Plants low, usually less than 1 foot high. See p. 276.*
*Plants of medium height; mostly from 12–30 inches. See*
*those immediately below.*

**CAPE MARIGOLD** (*Dimorphotheca aurantiaca*)          p. 269
Also called African Daisy (for others see the next two plants and p. 266). South African perennial, but as it blooms from seed in a single season, best treated as a long-season annual. It is a useful plant for hot, dry places. Leaves mostly basal, a little rough to the touch, narrowly oblong. Flower heads 3–4 inches wide closing at night, the rays curved so that the central disk seems depressed. **Color:** Prevailingly yellow, but see below. **Height:** 12–18 inches. **Flowering date:** July–Sept. **Varieties:** None named satisfactorily, but forms are offered with orange, pink, white, salmon, and red flowers. **Culture:** Sow seeds ⅛ inch deep indoors (6–8 weeks before outdoor planting is safe), in boxes or pots filled with a mixture of ¾ sandy loam and ¼ sand. Transfer seedlings outdoors only after settled warm weather has arrived, in full sun, in a definitely sandy loam, and space 8–12

# ASTER FAMILY (*Compositae*)
### (*foliage generally scentless; if scented,*
### *not spicy or aromatic*)

1. **False Chamomile** (*Boltonia asteroides*)     **p.** 263
   A native perennial, 5–8 feet high, blooming from Aug. to Oct.
   Of easiest culture anywhere.

2. **Bellium** (*Bellium bellidioides*)     **p.** 262
   Not over 4 inches high this Mediterranean perennial is suited
   only to the rock garden or for pavement planting.

3. **Fleabane** (*Erigeron speciosus*)     **p.** 265
   Daisy-like perennial from western North America, 15–30 inches
   high, blooming from May to July. Easily grown.

4. **Cineraria** (*Senecio cruentus*)     **p.** 264
   Magnificent spring bedding plant from the Canary Islands. Possible only for those with a cool greenhouse.

5. **Tahoka Daisy** (*Machaeranthera tanacetifolia*)     **p.** 265
   Recently introduced western annual, 1–2 feet high, and flowering
   from July to Oct. Will stand much heat.

6. **Venidium** (*Venidium fastuosum*)     **p.** 263
   A little-known South African annual, 2–3 feet high, chiefly of
   value for cut flowers.

7. **Stokes Aster** (*Stokesia laevis*)     **p.** 263
   Showy native perennial, 12–30 inches high, flowering Aug.–
   Sept. Prefers sandy loam; not hardy northward.

8. **Black Sampson** (*Echinacea purpurea*)     **p.** 265
   A coarse coneflower-like perennial, 3–4 feet high. Can be grown
   in sandy or even poor soil. Flowers July–Oct.

9. **Ursinia** (*Ursinia anethoides*)     **p.** 262
   A somewhat rare South African annual, 8–12 inches high. Does
   not thrive under great summer heat.

## ASTER FAMILY (*Compositae*)
*(flowers prevailingly yellow; plants usually of medium height)*

1. **Transvaal Daisy** (*Gerbera jamesoni*)     **p. 270**
   A half-hardy African perennial, not hardy north of Washington, D.C.

2. **African Daisy** (*Arctotis stoechadifolia*)     **p. 266**
   A South African long-season annual, 30–48 inches high. Summer-blooming.

3. **Cape Marigold** (*Dimorphotheca aurantiaca*)     **p. 267**
   A South African perennial, best treated as an annual, 12–18 inches high.

4. **African Daisy** (*Gazania longiscapa*)     **p. 270**
   A South African, long-season annual, 8–12 inches high. Summer-blooming.

5. **Annual Blanket-Flower** (*Gaillardia pulchella*)     **p. 272**
   A native annual, 12–20 inches high, of easy culture if seeds are sown where wanted.

6. **Swan River Daisy** (*Brachycome iberidifolia*)     **p. 266**
   An Australian long-season annual, 8–18 inches high. Useful for edging a border or path.

7. **Pot Marigold** (*Calendula officinalis*)     **p. 271**
   A long-season annual, 12–20 inches high, with scentless foliage. Summer-blooming.

8. **Perennial Gaillardia** (*Gaillardia aristata*)     **p. 272**
   Often called Blanket-Flower, and 2–3 feet high. Summer-blooming and profuse.

9. **Golden Aster** (*Chrysopsis mariana*)     **p. 272**
   One of the best native perennials for dry sandy sites. Summer-blooming.

inches apart. A very showy plant for hot, dry climates. Seed may also be planted directly outdoors if the growing season is long and hot, but the bloom will be delayed. A perennial, and winter-blooming in southern Calif.

**AFRICAN DAISY** (*Gazania longiscapa*)                    p. 269
For other African daisies see the preceding plant, the next entry, and p. 266. *Gazania* is less well known than the other 3 African daisies, but is a handsome South African long-season annual, with mostly basal leaves white-felty beneath and short-stalked, solitary flower heads that may be 2–3 inches wide, day-blooming and closing at night. **Color:** Prevailingly yellow, but see below. **Height:** 8–12 inches. **Flowering date:** July–Aug. **Varieties:** Franklin (white), Potsii (deep yellow), Bishop (orange-red), Sunspot (reddish brown), Splendens (pointed rays). **Culture:** Sow seeds ⅛ inch deep, indoors (7–9 weeks before outdoor planting is safe) in pots or boxes filled with a mixture of ¾ sandy loam and ¼ sand. Transfer seedlings outdoors only when settled warm weather arrives, in full sun, in a definitely sandy loam, and space 6–10 inches apart. Not suited to regions of short growing season and cool nights.

**TRANSVAAL DAISY** (*Gerbera jamesoni*)                    p. 269
Also called African Daisy, for which see also the above two entries and p. 266. Also sometimes called Barberton Daisy. This is the most desirable of all the plants usually classed as African Daisy, but the most difficult to grow in the North without a greenhouse. It is a half-hardy perennial from South Africa, not reliably hardy north of Washington, D.C., and to be grown out-doors elsewhere only by following the directions below. Leaves nearly 8 inches long, deeply cut, and white-woolly beneath. Flower heads extremely showy, 3–4½ inches wide, solitary on long stalks that much exceed the foliage. Rays very numerous, slender or even strap-shaped, stiff, the whole head starlike. **Color:** Prevailingly orange, but see below. **Height:** 1–2 feet. **Flowering date:** July–Aug. **Varieties:** Under the name Hybrida are many forms with orange-red, scarlet, yellow, white, pink, salmon, and violet flowers. **Culture:** Not easy in the North without a green-

house. Start seeds indoors in Jan. or early Feb., sowing them
$\frac{1}{16}$ inch deep in boxes or pots filled with a mixture of $\frac{1}{2}$ rich
garden loam and $\frac{1}{2}$ sand, thoroughly mixed. As seedlings
become 2–3 inches high transplant, two to a 3-inch flower pot
filled with mixture $\frac{3}{4}$ rich garden loam and $\frac{1}{4}$ sand. Transfer
potted seedlings outdoors only when settled warm weather has
arrived, in full sun, in a rich garden loam that is a little sandy,
spacing them 12–15 inches apart. North of Washington lift the
plants, repot, and carry them through the winter in the house or
in a greenhouse, since they seldom survive in a cold frame. Unsuited to regions of frosty winters, but a true perennial in warm
regions and one of the best in the family for cut flowers; hence
a very popular florist flower and offered throughout the winter
and spring.

**POT MARIGOLD** (*Calendula officinalis*)         p. 269
A scentless marigold from the Mediterranean region differing
from the African and French Marigolds, both of which have
strongly-scented foliage when the leaves are crushed (see p.
255). The Pot Marigold is a long-season annual, its leaves
oblongish, 2–3 inches long and somewhat stem-clasping. Flower
heads solitary, stalked, $1\frac{1}{2}$–2 inches wide, day-blooming but the
rays night-closing. In some forms the heads are doubled, the
rays quilled and the head dense. **Color:** Prevailingly yellow or
orange, but see below. **Height:** 12–20 inches. **Flowering date:**
June–frost. **Varieties:** After centuries of cultivation there are
many, not always reliably named. Current varieties, of reasonable certainty are: Orange Quills (orange), Golden Giant (golden
orange), Lemon Beauty (lemon yellow), Cream Beauty (white),
Glowing Gold (gold), Orange Fluffy (orange-red), Yellow
Colossal (large yellow heads), Persimmon Beauty (orange).
**Culture:** Sow seeds $\frac{1}{16}$ inch deep indoors (6–8 weeks before
outdoor planting is safe) in boxes or pots filled with a mixture
of $\frac{3}{4}$ garden loam and $\frac{1}{4}$ sand. Transfer seedlings outdoors
when trees leaf out, in full sun, in any ordinary garden soil and
space 6–9 inches apart. May also be sown directly outdoors when
warm weather arrives, but this will delay, and prolong bloom.

For the finest flower heads, pinch off all but the terminal one when in bud.

## PERENNIAL GAILLARDIA (*Gaillardia aristata*)          p. 269

A native of western North America, often called Blanket-Flower. It is a rough-hairy perennial, the leaves lance-shaped, 3–5 inches long, more or less dotted. Flower heads 3–4 inches wide, very showy, the rays notched or fringed. **Color:** Prevailingly yellow or orange, but see below, the center always of different color from the tips of the rays. **Height:** 18–30 inches. **Flowering date:** July–Aug. **Varieties:** Mr. Sherbrook (yellow), Goblin (yellow and red), Burgundy (red), Ruby (red), Sun God (golden yellow), Tangerine (coppery orange). **Culture:** Set purchased plants in full sun, in Oct. or April, in any ordinary garden soil, and space 12–18 inches apart. Of easy culture, but does better if a forkful of manure per plant is dug in each spring. Often offered under incorrect name of *Gaillardia grandiflora*.

## ANNUAL BLANKET–FLOWER

(*Gaillardia pulchella*)                                                p. 269

An annual relative of the above, but lower and found wild from N.C. to Fla. and westward, and now in many fine horticultural forms. **Color:** Prevailingly yellow or orange, but see below. **Height:** 12–20 inches. **Flowering date:** July–Sept. **Varieties:** Many, but not reliably named, some double, single, quilled, and in colors from red, through orange, copper, yellow, and white. **Culture:** Sow seeds outdoors where wanted, in full sun, ⅟₁₆ inch deep in any ordinary garden soil, and thin to 6–9 inches apart. Most varieties, unlike the wild plant, do not thrive if summers are too hot and moist.

## GOLDEN ASTER (*Chrysopsis mariana*)                    p. 269

A somewhat weedy perennial from the sandier parts of the eastern U.S. scarcely worth growing except for its remarkable persistence in the sandiest and poorest sites in the garden. It has chiefly basal, hairy, toothed leaves that are lance-shaped, 3–7 inches long, diminishing in size toward the flower cluster. Heads about 1 inch in diameter, in a few-flowered, close, terminal cluster. **Color:** Yellow. **Height:** 12–20 inches. **Flowering date:**

Aug.–Oct. **Varieties:** None. **Culture:** Set purchased plants in April, in full sun, in any sandy or dry place, and space 6–9 inches apart. Not widely grown but one of the best perennials for sandy places.

Related plant (not illustrated):
> Rosinweed (*Chrysopsis villosa*). 10–18 inches. Flowers yellow.

**LEOPARD'S–BANE** (*Doronicum plantagineum*) p. 284
A spring-blooming European perennial, the foliage of which tends to die down during its summer resting period. Leaves mostly basal, the stalk narrowed into a winged and stem-clasping base. Flower heads solitary, long-stalked, about 3 inches wide, with a single series of rays in the common form, but many-rayed in the varieties. **Color:** Yellow. **Height:** 18–30 inches. **Flowering date:** April. **Varieties:** Excelsum (nearly 3 feet high), Mme. Mason (large-flowered). **Culture:** Set purchased plants in Oct. in partial shade or full sun, in a rich garden loam, preferably in a moist but not wet site. Space 12–18 inches apart, and dig, divide, and replant every third or fourth year. Useful for planting among spring-blooming bulbs.

Related plant (not illustrated):
> *Doronicum caucasicum.* 12–18 inches. Flowers yellow.

**TICKSEED** (*Coreopsis grandiflora*) p. 284
A rampant and often invasive perennial from the prairies of the central U.S., cultivated for its ability to stand abuse and for its "ragged" flower heads. Leaves cut into many narrow segments. Heads few or solitary on long, naked stalks, the tips of the rays toothed or almost fringed, the head not over 2½ inches wide. **Color:** Yellow. **Height:** 12–20 inches. **Flowering date:** July–Aug. **Varieties:** None. **Culture:** Easy; set purchased plants in Oct. or April, in full sun, in any ordinary garden soil, and space 8–10 inches apart. Watch for its invading surrounding beds or even fields, since it spreads quickly and may dominate better plants. This and the ones below may be offered under the incorrect name of *Calliopsis*.

Related plants (not illustrated):
> *Coreopsis lanceolata.* 1–2 feet. Flowers yellow.
> *Coreopsis rosea.* 1–2 feet. Flowers pink.
> *Coreopsis maritima.* 2–3 feet. Flowers yellow.
> *Coreopsis stillmani.* 12–18 inches. Flowers yellow.
> The last two species often offered as *Leptosyne*.

**GOLDEN–WAVE** (*Coreopsis drummondi*)                p. 284
Habitually, but incorrectly offered as *Calliopsis drummondi,* this
Texan long-season annual is an old-time favorite, long cultivated
for its profusion of bloom. Leaves much cut into narrow segments. Flower heads nearly 2 inches wide, the rays notched or
fringed at the yellow tip, brownish purple at the base, the head
thus with a dark center. **Color:** Prevailingly yellow, but see
below. **Height:** 12–20 inches. **Flowering date:** July–Sept. **Varieties:** Crimson King (crimson), Gold Crest (double-flowered
and golden yellow), Golden Crown (yellow and maroon). **Culture:** Sow seeds ¹⁄₁₆ inch deep, indoors (6–8 weeks before outdoor planting is safe), in boxes or pots filled with a mixture of
¾ sandy loam and ¼ sand. Transfer seedlings outdoors when
trees leaf out, in full sun, in a rich, sandy, well-drained loam, and
space 8–12 inches apart.
  Related plants (not illustrated):
> *Coreopsis tinctoria.* 20–30 inches. Flowers yellow, but
>   crimson in a variety.
> *Coreopsis atkinsoniana.* 20–30 inches. Heads yellow,
>   but brownish purple at center.

**OXEYE** (*Bupthalmum salicifolium*)                p. 284
A little-grown European perennial with willow-like, toothed,
and white-hairy leaves about 3 inches long. Flower heads solitary, about 2 inches wide, the center of the head darker than the
yellow-tipped rays. **Color:** Yellow. **Height:** 1–2 feet. **Flowering
date:** July–Aug. **Varieties:** None. **Culture:** Easy; set purchased
plants in April or Oct., in full sun, in any ordinary garden soil.
Space 8–12 inches apart.
  Related plant (not illustrated):
> *Bupthalmum speciosum.* 18–30 inches. Flowers yellow.

**ZINNIA** (*Zinnia* hybrids)                                        p. 284
Attractive and very popular long-season annuals derived from
much hybridizing of two Mexican plants: *Zinnia elegans,* which
has been the parent of the tall varieties, and *Zinnia angustifolia,*
of the lower types. All of them perish at freezing time, but can
be flowered from midsummer to frost by following cultural
directions. Often called Youth-and-Old-Age, and by some Cut-
and-Come-Again, a name better restricted to a variety of Sunflower (see p. 277). The number of named forms is so numerous
that it is impossible to mention even a fraction of them here. But
the types to which they belong are important to the grower and
are listed below under Varieties. **Color:** All but blue, the original type was yellow or orange; but see below. **Height:** Tall
sorts 18–30 inches; low sorts 8–15 inches. **Flowering date:** July–
frost, depending on the variety. **Varieties:** Very numerous, and
in considerable confusion because of rival claims of dealers and
duplication of identical forms under different names. The main
types of zinnia are the following.

GIANT: huge double-flowered heads 4–5 inches wide, the
plants 18–30 inches high. In all colors but blue.

DAHLIA-FLOWERED: even larger, double-flowered heads, sometimes over 5 inches wide and like a Decorative Dahlia.
Plants 18–30 inches high. In all colors but blue.

CACTUS-FLOWERED: heads double-flowered, 4–5 inches wide,
many of the rays quilled as in the Cactus Dahlias. Plants
28–32 inches high. In all colors but blue.

LILLIPUT, DWARF, MINIATURE, BABY, POMPON, CUPID, etc.:
Collective and often confusing terms for low zinnias with
double-flowered heads not usually over 2½ inches wide.
Plants 8–15 inches high. In all colors but blue.

CUT-AND-COME-AGAIN: heads about 2½ inches wide, freely
produced if cut frequently. Plants about 18 inches high.
In all colors but blue.

**Culture:** Sow seeds ¹⁄₁₆ inch deep, indoors (8–10 weeks before
outdoor planting is safe) in boxes or pots filled with a mixture
of ¾ rich garden loam and ¼ sand. When seedlings are 2–3

inches high, transplant them one to a small pot (Lily cups are fine), in the same soil mixture, and grow along until settled warm weather has arrived. Then plant seedlings outdoors in full sun or partial shade, in any ordinary garden soil, although they will thrive better in rich, well-manured garden loam. Space tall kinds 12–20 inches apart, low kinds 8–15 inches apart. Water if there is a drought. For prize blooms, especially of the Giant, Dahlia-flowered, and Cactus-flowered varieties, disbud all but the terminal head.

## *Plants Low, Usually Less Than 1 Foot High; Flowers Yellow*

**"CREEPING ZINNIA"** (*Sanvitalia procumbens*)          p. 284
An unfortunate dealer's name for a Mexican annual that is not a Zinnia, and is an attractive prostrate plant, its foliage covered with short hairs. Leaves ovalish, opposite each other, about 1 inch long. Flower heads numerous, about 1 inch wide, double-flowered, and zinnia-like. **Color:** Golden yellow. **Height:** Prostrate. **Flowering season:** July–Sept. **Varieties:** None. **Culture:** Sow seeds outdoors, ⅛ inch deep, in full sun, in any ordinary garden soil that is well drained. Space 6–9 inches apart. It thrives in dry, hot places and is useful for edging or as a seasonal ground cover.

**GOLDEN–STAR** (*Chrysogonum virginianum*)          p. 284
A native, woodland perennial from Pa. to Fla. and useful for partially shady places, as most of the plants in the family require full sun. Leaves ovalish to circular, few, about 4½ inches long, long-stalked. Flower heads solitary or a few, the rays usually 5 and starlike; not over 1½ inches wide. **Color:** Yellow. **Height:** 6–10 inches. **Flowering date:** April–July. **Varieties:** None. **Culture:** Set purchased plants in Oct. in partial shade (or full sun if necessary) in a sandy, well-drained loam, and space 6–8 inches apart. Not much grown, but its starlike flower heads and woodland habit make it an attractive addition to the Compositae. Does well in dry, hot places.

### Plants Tall, 3–5 Feet, Often More; Flowers Yellow

**SUNFLOWER** (*Helianthus annuus*)                    p. 285
A gigantic annual native from Minn. to Calif., and grown as much for curiosity as for its huge, somewhat blatant flower heads. Leaves ovalish, nearly 1 foot long, hairy on both sides, and mostly alternately arranged. Flower heads enormous, usually solitary and terminal, turning with the sun, and in some of its varieties over 1 foot in diameter. Rays in the wild form in a single series, but doubled and frilled in some cultivated varieties. **Color:** Prevailingly yellow, but see below. **Height:** 8–12 feet. **Flowering date:** Aug.–Oct. **Varieties:** Chrysanthemum-flowered (yellow and double, 6–8 feet high), Red Sunflower (red and yellow, 5–8 feet), Russian Mammoth (single, yellow, 8–12 feet), Cut-and-Come-Again (a dwarf variety with small flower heads that are profuse when cut frequently). **Culture:** Sow seeds outdoors ⅓ inch deep, after trees leaf out, in any ordinary garden soil, and space 3–4 feet apart. Easy to grow and tolerates great heat.

Related plants (not illustrated):
All perennials.
*Helianthus angustifolius*. 5–7 feet. Flowers yellow.
*Helianthus decapetalus*. 3–5 feet. Flowers yellow.
*Helianthus orgyalis*. 3–5 feet. Flowers yellow.
Jerusalem Artichoke (*Helianthus tuberosus*). 8–12 feet. Flowers yellow.

**YELLOW STAR** (*Helenium autumnale*)                    p. 285
Often called False Sunflower or Sneezeweed; a strong-growing perennial native over much of North America. Leaves alternately arranged, lance-shaped or narrower, 2–6 inches long, and faintly toothed on the margin. Flower heads few or many, mostly terminal, the central disk much above the downward-pointing rays. **Color:** Prevailingly yellow, but see below. **Height:** 4–6 feet. **Flowering date:** Aug.–Oct. **Varieties:** Crimson Beauty (red), Gartensonne (yellow), Riverton Beauty (lemon yellow),

Riverton Gem (golden yellow), Rubrum (terra-cotta red),
Mooreheim Beauty (brownish red). **Culture:** Set purchased
plants in Oct. or April, in full sun, in any ordinarily rich garden
soil, preferably a little moist, but not wet. Space 2–3 feet apart,
and dig, divide, and replant every third or fourth year.

Related plants (not illustrated):

*Helenium peregrinum.* 2–3 feet. Flowers red.

*Helenium bigelovi.* 2–4 feet. Flowers yellow.

*Helenium hoopesi.* 2–3 feet. Flowers yellow.

**ORANGE SUNFLOWER** (*Heliopsis helianthoides*)          p. 285
A rather coarse, sunflower-like perennial found wild over most
of North America, its ovalish leaves arranged opposite each
other, 3–5 inches long, and in one form very rough on upper and
lower sides. Flower heads solitary, or a few, about 2½–3 inches
wide, typically with 8–15 rays, but doubled in some varieties.
**Color:** Orange yellow. **Height:** 3–5 feet. **Flowering date:** Aug.–
Sept. **Varieties:** Pitcheriana (deep yellow), Incomparabilis
(golden yellow and double-flowered), Excelsa (yellow, double-
flowered), Gold-Greenheart (double-flowered, yellow, with a
greenish center). **Culture:** Easy. Set purchased plants in full
sun, in April or Oct., in any ordinary or even indifferent garden
soil, and space 2–3 feet apart. It will stand poor soil, heat, and
drought better than many finer plants. Sometimes called False
Sunflower and may be offered (in some of its varieties) as
*Heliopsis scabra.*

**INULA** (*Inula ensifolia*)                              p. 285
A Eurasian perennial, not much grown here, but attractive and
earlier blooming than most of its taller sunflower-like relatives.
Leaves arranged alternately, narrowly lance-shaped, 3–4 inches
long. Flower heads solitary or a few, about 1½ inches wide, the
rays numerous and pointed. **Color:** Yellow. **Height:** 2–3 feet.
**Flowering date:** July–Aug. **Varieties:** None. **Culture:** Set purchased plants in full sun, in Oct. or April, in any ordinary garden
soil that is well drained (no standing water), and space 18–24
inches apart.

Related plant (not illustrated):

Elecampane (*Inula Helenium*). 3–5 feet. Flowers yellow.

**LIGULARIA** (*Ligularia clivorum*)                                    p. 285
A showy perennial from China and Japan grown for its late-blooming flowers. Leaves mostly basal, kidney-shaped or round-ish, 15–20 inches wide, and coarsely toothed. Flower heads soli-tary or in branched clusters, 3–4 inches wide, the rays numerous and strap-shaped. **Color:** Orange-yellow. **Height:** 3–4 feet. **Flowering date:** Aug.–Sept. **Varieties:** None. **Culture:** Set pur-chased plants in full sun or partial shade, in April, in any ordinary soil, and space 2–3 feet apart. Sometimes offered under the old name of *Senecio clivorum*.

**GOLDENGLOW** (*Rudbeckia laciniata hortensis*)                p. 285
A very common, almost weedy derivative of a sunflower-like perennial of the eastern U.S., known in cultivation almost ex-clusively in the double-flowered form and so ubiquitous as to be anathema to many. It has deeply divided leaves, cut into 3–5 lobes, and numerous, somewhat cabbagy, double-flowered heads, 2–3½ inches thick. **Color:** Yellow. **Height:** 5–8 feet. **Flowering date:** July–Aug. **Varieties:** None. **Culture:** Easy; and since plant is invasive, difficult to control. Set purchased plants in full sun, in April or Oct. in any ordinary garden soil, and space 3–4 feet apart.

**CONEFLOWER** (*Rudbeckia speciosa*)                              p. 285
A handsome North American perennial often confused with its close, also native, relative known as *Rudbeckia fulgida*. It is a stout plant with unlobed, alternately arranged leaves that are a little broader toward the tip and 3–5 inches long. Flower heads solitary, or rarely a few, long-stalked, and about 3 inches wide. The central cone of disk flowers stands well above the 10–20 rays that are inclined to droop at their tips. **Color:** Orange-yel-low. **Height:** 3–5 feet. **Flowering date:** July–Aug. **Varieties:** (some may be derived from the closely related *Rudbeckia ful-gida*) The King (crimson), Goldsturm (yellow), White Lustre (white). **Culture:** Set purchased plants in full sun, in April or

Oct., in any ordinary garden soil, and space 2–3 feet apart. As they tend to die out, dig, divide, and replant every third or fourth year.

Related plants (not illustrated):
> Black-eyed Susan (*Rudbeckia hirta*). 18–24 inches. Flowers yellow. A beautiful, weedy, and dangerously invasive biennial.
> *Rudbeckia triloba*. 4–5 feet. Flowers yellow and orange.
> *Rudbeckia subtomentosa*. 4–6 feet. Flowers yellow.

## CUP–PLANT (*Silphium perfoliatum*)                          p. 285

An interesting perennial from the central U.S., not much grown, although it has striking sunflower-like flower heads. It has a square stem and the upper leaves, which are oppositely arranged, form a cuplike depression at the junction with the stem, the leaf blade nearly 12 inches long. Flower heads several or numerous, nearly 3 inches wide, and with 20–30 rays. **Color:** Yellow. **Height:** 5–8 feet. **Flowering date:** July–Sept. **Varieties:** None. **Culture:** Set purchased plants in April or Oct., in full sun, in any ordinary garden soil, and space 3–5 feet apart, since it is a rampant plant. Well suited to warm dry places.

## TEXAS STAR (*Xanthisma texanum*)                          p. 285

A beautiful, starlike annual from prairie and semidesert regions of the central U.S. recently introduced into cultivation for its showy flower heads. It is a wiry-stemmed plant, its alternately arranged leaves narrow and 1½–2½ inches long. Flower heads mostly solitary, long-stalked, about 2½ inches wide, its 18–20 rays pointed and starlike. **Color:** Yellow. **Height:** 2–4 feet. **Flowering date:** July–Aug. **Varieties:** None. **Culture:** Sow seeds ¹⁄₁₆ inch deep in full sun, after warm weather has arrived, in any light sandy loam with perfect drainage, and space 18–24 inches apart. It thrives in places with great heat and sketchy rainfall. Sometimes known as Star of Texas.

# List of
# Reference Books

·

# Finding Lists

*Preferred Habitat*

*Height*

*Season of Bloom*

*Especially Fragrant Flowers*

*Perennial Ground Covers*

*Plants Difficult to Grow*

*80 Annual Plants*

*(Plants arranged by flower color appear
on front and back endpapers)*

·

# Index

# List of
# Reference Books

THE compression of much information here has inevitably crowded out details that would have been helpful if this book could have been twice its size and expense. This is especially true for the *related plants* that follow each species when these other forms are worth attention. Many of them are, and for those seeking more information than could be included here the following will be found helpful:

Bailey, L. H. *Manual of Cultivated Plants,* 2nd ed. New York: Macmillan, 1951.

——. *Hortus II.* New York: Macmillan, 1941.

Everett, T. H. *Flower Garden Guide.* Greenwich, Conn.: Fawcett Publications, 1952.

Foley, Daniel J. *Garden Flowers in Color.* New York: Macmillan, 1943.

Hull, Helen S. *Wildflowers for Your Garden.* New York: Barrows, 1952.

Ortloff, H. S., and Henry B. Raymore. *Color and Succession of Bloom in the Flower Border.* New York: Doubleday, 1935.

Seymour, E. L. D. *Favorite Flowers in Color.* New York: Wm. H. Wise, 1949.

Steffek, E. F. *Wildflowers and How to Grow Them.* New York: Crown, 1954.

# ASTER FAMILY (*Compositae*)
## (*flowers prevailingly yellow; plants moderate-sized*)

1. **Golden-Wave** (*Coreopsis drummondi*)      p. 274
   Texan, long-season annual, 12–30 inches high, flowering from July to Sept. Start indoors; 6–8 weeks before outdoor planting is safe.

2. **Tickseed** (*Coreopsis grandiflora*)      p. 273
   Rampant perennial, easy to grow but hard to prevent its invasive spreading. Height 12–20 inches. Bloom profuse.

3. **Oxeye** (*Bupthalmum salicifolium*)      p. 274
   Rather unknown European perennial, 1–2 feet high, and summer-blooming. Easily grown in any ordinary garden soil.

4. **Zinnia** (*Zinnia* hybrids; Dwarf or Lilliput type)      p. 275
   A race of hybrid zinnias. For details and varieties see the text.

5. **Zinnia** (*Zinnia* hybrids; Cactus-flowered)      p. 275
   A race of hybrid zinnias. For details and varieties see the text.

6. **Zinnia** (*Zinnia* hybrids; Giant type)      p. 275
   A race of hybrid zinnias. For details and varieties see the text.

7. **Leopard's-Bane** (*Doronicum plantagineum*)      p. 273
   Spring-blooming perennial, 18–30 inches, the foliage tending to die down in summer. Prefers moist site.

8. **"Creeping Zinnia"** (*Sanvitalia procumbens*)      p. 276
   A prostrate, Mexican annual, blooming July–Sept. and valuable, since it thrives in hot dry places.

9. **Golden-Star** (*Chrysogonum virginianum*)      p. 276
   Native woodland perennial, 6–10 inches high, flowering in April–July. Useful in dry, sandy, partly shady places.

## ASTER FAMILY (*Compositae*)
### (*flowers prevailingly yellow; plants tall*)

1. **Sunflower** (*Helianthus annuus*)     **p. 277**
   Enormous annual from western North America, 8–12 feet high. Easy to grow and will thrive in great heat.

2. **Yellow Star** (*Helenium autumnale*)     **p. 277**
   Native perennial, 4–6 feet high, flowering Aug.–Oct. Prefers reasonably moist site and rich soil.

3. **Goldenglow** (*Rudbeckia laciniata hortensis*)     **p. 279**
   Perhaps overpopular perennial, almost weedy, but certain to bloom anywhere. Height 5–8 feet. Summer-blooming.

4. **Inula** (*Inula ensifolia*)     **p. 278**
   A summer-blooming Eurasian perennial, not too well known, but easily grown in ordinary garden soil.

5. **Orange Sunflower** (*Heliopsis helianthoides*)     **p. 278**
   Native, sunflower-like perennial, 3–5 feet high, blooming Aug.–Sept. Somewhat indifferent as to site or soil.

6. **Texas Star** (*Xanthisma texanum*)     **p. 280**
   Starlike annual from our prairies, useful for its indifference to heat and drought. Summer-flowering.

7. **Cup-Plant** (*Silphium perfoliatum*)     **p. 280**
   Sunflower-like perennial from the prairies, 5–8 feet high, flowering July–Sept. Stands heat well.

8. **Coneflower** (*Rudbeckia speciosa*)     **p. 279**
   North American perennial, 3–5 feet high and summer-blooming. Easy to grow but tending to die out.

9. **Ligularia** (*Ligularia clivorum*)     **p. 279**
   Showy, Asiatic perennial, 3–4 feet high, with very large leaves. Blooming Aug.–Sept. Easily grown.

Taylor, Norman. *Taylor's Encyclopedia of Gardening,* 3rd ed. Boston: Houghton Mifflin, 1957.

———. *Fragrance in the Garden.* New York: Van Nostrand, 1953.

———. *Color in the Garden.* New York: Van Nostrand, 1952.

———. *Wild Flower Gardening.* New York: Van Nostrand, 1955.

———. *The Everblooming Garden.* New York: Van Nostrand, 1954.

Wilder, Louise B. *Colour in My Garden.* New York: Doubleday, 1927.

———. *The Fragrant Path.* New York: Macmillan, 1932.

There are, of course, many others, but to cite them all is impossible. From those above the seeker may extend his reading beyond what is possible to include here.

# Finding Lists

## Arranged by Preferred Habitat

### A selection of 135 plants for special sites

NOTE: Most of the plants in the book will grow in ordinary garden soil, and have considerable tolerance as between open sunlight or partial shade. The plants below, however, do better if planted in the habitat suggested for them in the following lists. It will be noted that some plants are necessarily in more than one list.

### ACID SOILS

Bearberry, 165
Buckbean, 178
Bunchberry, 139
Feather-Fleece, 47
Fire-Pink, 74
Foam Flower, 111
Heather, 166

Irish Heath, 167
Mitrewort, 111
Shortia, 168
Showy Orchis, 52
Snowdrop Windflower, 82
Spike Heath, 168

Spring Heath, 167
Trailing Arbutus, 165
Twinflower, 196

### RICH WOODLAND SOIL NOT ESSENTIALLY ACID

Bellwort, 34
Black Cohosh, 85
Bloodroot, 97
Blue Cohosh, 90
Bowman's-Root, 114
Cardinal-Flower, 239
Climbing Fumitory, 154
Closed Gentian, 177

Cow-Tongue, 22
Culver's-Root, 229
Hepatica, 85
Jack-in-the-Pulpit, 38
Large-flowered Trillium, 30
Lily-of-the-Valley, 21
Mayapple, 89

Partridge-Berry, 195
Rue Anemone, 88
Twin-Leaf, 90
Yellow Lady's-Slipper, 51
Yellow Trillium, 31

### MOIST OR WET SITES

Bluets, 194
Buckbean, 178
Cardinal-Flower, 239
Closed Gentian, 177
Cowslip, 170

Culver's-Root, 229
English Primrose, 170
False Dragonhead, 213
Globeflower, 82
Glory-of-the-Snow, 21

Japanese Burnet, 114
Japanese Iris, 32
Leopard's-Bane, 273
Loosestrife, 174
Marsh Marigold, 84

Masterwort, 138
Meadow Rue, 88
Oxlip, 170
Polyanthus, 169

Purple Loosestrife, 131
Queen-of-the-Meadow, 113
Red Turtlehead, 227

Rose Mallow, 126
Sea Holly, 138
Tree Mallow, 127
Virginia Cowslip, 193

## DRY SANDY PLACES

Aaron's-Rod, 147
*Artemisia stelleriana,* 246
Bear's-Breech, 238
Bee-Balm, 214
Bellium, 262
Blazing Star, 245
Blue False Indigo, 145
Bush Clover, 147
Butterfly-Weed, 180
Cinquefoil, 115

Flowering Spurge, 122
Frostweed, 133
Genista, 145
Globe Thistle, 248
Golden Aster, 272
Poppy Mallow, 127
Prairie Mallow, 129
Prickly Pear, 134
Prickly Poppy, 96
Purple Rock Cress, 100

Rose-of-Sharon, 131
Sand Verbena, 66
Sandwort, 78
*Sedum sieboldi,* 106
Stone Cress, 102
Sundrops, 135
Tahoka Daisy, 265
Yellow Puccoon, 191

## IN SHADE OR PARTIAL SHADE

Barrenwort, 90
Bloodroot, 97
Bowman's-Root, 114
Brunnera, 193
Bunchberry, 139
Cardinal Flower, 239
Christmas Rose, 83
Climbing Fumitory, 154
Closed Gentian, 177
Coral Bells, 111
Corydalis, 155
Cow-Tongue, 22
Culver's-Root, 229
Dogtooth Violet, 16
False Dragonhead, 213
Globe Daisy, 235

Goatsbeard, 114
Golden-Star, 276
Hardy Begonia, 160
Hepatica, 85
Jack-in-the-Pulpit, 38
Japanese Spurge, 122
Kenilworth Ivy, 232
Large-flowered Trillium, 30
Lily-of-the-Valley, 21
Lithodora, 193
Mayapple, 89
Mist-Flower, 245
Mitrewort, 111
Red Turtlehead, 227
Rue Anemone, 88

Shooting Star, 175
Shortia, 168
Showy Orchis, 52
Siberian Squill, 20
Siberian Wallflower, 99
Snowdrop, 11
Snowdrop Windflower, 82
Trailing Arbutus, 165
Twinflower, 196
Virginia Cowslip, 193
Welsh Poppy, 96
Wild Sweet William, 183
Winter Aconite, 84
Yellow Lady's-Slipper, 51

# *Arranged by Height*
## *A Selection of 258 Different Plants*

### 20 PROSTRATE PLANTS

Bearberry, 165
Bitter-Root, 68
Ceratostigma, 176

Creeping Mint, 212
Crown Vetch, 146
Forget-Me-Not, 187

Germander, 215
Ground Pink, 183
Ice-Plant, 66

Maiden Pink, 73
Mountain Avens, 122
Partridge-Berry, 195
Periwinkle, 178

Rock Jasmine, 175
Rose Moss, 68
Sand Verbena, 66
Snow-in-Summer, 78

Trailing Arbutus, 165
Twinflower, 196
Wall Pepper, 105

## 24 ERECT PLANTS 3-6 INCHES HIGH

Alpine Catchfly, 74
Baby Blue-Eyes, 186
Bunchberry, 139
Christmas Rose, 83
Crested Iris, 32
Crocus, 10
Edelweiss, 55
English Daisy, 261
English Primrose, 170

Erinus, 233
Glory-of-the-Snow, 21
Hepatica, 85
Mazus, 233
Moss Campion, 75
Pearlwort, 80
Prickly Thrift, 62
Purple Rock Cress, 100
Rock Purslane, 68

Sandwort, 78
Siberian Squill, 20
Spring Meadow Saffron, 14
Synthris, 233
Whitlow Grass, 102
Winter Aconite, 84

## 40 PLANTS 7-12 INCHES HIGH

African Daisy (*Gazania*), 270
Alpine Wallflower, 100
Barrenwort, 90
Bellflower (*C. portenschlagiana*), 198
Bellflower (*C. carpatica*), 199
Bloodroot, 97
Bluebell of England, 20
California Poppy, 95
Candytuft, 99
Cream Cups, 97
Daffodil, 17
Dragonhead, 214

Globe Amaranth, 56
Golden-Star, 276
Goutweed, 138
Grass Pink, 73
Houseleek, 106
Iceland Poppy, 95
Irish Heath, 167
Large-flowered Trillium, 30
Lily-of-the-Valley, 21
Love-in-a-Mist, 84
Lungwort, 193
Mariposa Lily, 33
Mayapple, 89
Pasque-Flower, 81

Polyanthus, 169
Rose-of-Sharon, 131
*Saxifraga decipiens,* 110
Shepherd's-Scabious, 200
Shooting Star, 175
Snowdrop, 11
Snowflake, 14
Spike Heath, 168
Spring Heath, 167
Striped Squill, 25
Sweet Alyssum, 98
Thrift, 59
Twin-Leaf, 90
Zephyr Lily, 15

## 90 PLANTS 1-2 FEET HIGH

African Marigold, 255
Annual Phlox, 181
Baby's-Breath, 75
Balloon-Flower, 199
Bear's-Breech, 238
Bee-Balm, 214
Bleeding-Heart, 154
Blue Daisy, 254
Blue Gilia, 184
Blue Lace-Flower, 137

Blue Succory, 56
Browallia, 222
Butterfly-Weed, 180
Cape Marigold, 267
China Aster, 258
China Pink, 73
Chinese Forget-Me-Not, 190
Chinese Houses, 227
Chrysanthemum, 249

Clarkia, 136
Closed Gentian, 177
Cockscomb, 57
Coleus, 216
Coral Bells, 111
Cornflower, 243
Cranesbill, 117
Evening Campion, 79
Fleabane, 265
Flowering Spurge, 122

Four-O'Clock, 65
Garden Sage, 210
Geranium
   (*Pelargonium*), 161
Gladiolus, 49
Golden Cup, 96
Golden Marguerite, 254
Golden-Wave, 274
Guinea-Hen Flower, 34
Hardy Amaryllis, 24
Hardy Begonia, 160
Hardy Carnation, 72
Honesty, 58
Jack-in-the-Pulpit, 38
Japanese Anemone, 81
Jonquil, 18
Lavender Cotton, 247
Masterwort, 138
Mist-Flower, 245
Musk Mallow, 128
Nemesia, 226
Oxeye, 274

Painted Tongue, 223
Perennial Gaillardia, 272
Perennial Phlox, 182
Plantain-Lily, 33
Poet's Narcissus, 17
Poppy Mallow, 127
Pot Marigold, 271
Prairie Lily, 132
Pyrethrum, 252
Red Turtlehead, 227
Rockfoil, 107
Rose Campion, 79
Sea Holly, 138
Sea Lavender, 62
Shasta Daisy, 250
Showy Orchis, 52
Siberian Tea, 110
Snapdragon, 225
Sneezewort, 254
Snow-on-the-Mountain,
   121
Stonecrop, 105

Summer Cypress, 58
Sweet Scabious, 240
Sweet William, 72
Sweet William Catchfly,
   74
Tahoka Daisy, 265
Tall Bearded Iris, 31
Ten-Weeks Stock, 101
Tickseed, 273
Transvaal Daisy, 270
Trumpet-Flower, 234
Tufted Pansy, 150
Tulip, 27
Twin-Spur, 227
Virginia Cowslip, 193
Welsh Poppy, 96
Wild Sweet William, 183
Winter Cherry, 223
Yellow Lady's-Slipper, 51
Zinnia, 275

## 38 PLANTS 2-3 FEET HIGH

Alkanet, 187
Amsonia, 179
Asphodel, 43
Astilbe, 112
Blackberry Lily, 43
Blue Cohosh, 90
Camass, 37
Copper-Tip, 50
Dame's-Rocket, 100
Daylily, 40
Foxglove, 231
Garden Balsam, 160
Gas-Plant, 120

Goat's-Rue, 146
Japanese Burnet, 114
Japanese Iris, 32
Ladybell, 201
Lantana, 206
Loosestrife, 174
Maltese cross, 79
Meadow rue, 88
Mexican Fire-Plant, 123
Monkey-Flower, 232
Mugwort, 246
Oriental Poppy, 94
Peach Bells, 198

Pentstemon, 229
Peony, 83
Prickly Poppy, 96
Purple Loosestrife, 131
Red Valerian, 197
Stokes Aster, 263
Strawflower, 54
Summer Hyacinth, 23
Sundrops, 135
Tansy, 247
Tiger-Flower, 43
Venidium, 263

## 46 PLANTS 3 FEET HIGH OR MORE, OFTEN MUCH MORE

Aaron's-Rod, 147
Adam's-Needle, 46
Angel's-Trumpet, 222
Beardtongue, 229
Black Cohosh, 86
Black Sampson, 265
Blue False Indigo, 145

Blue Sage, 211
Bush Clover, 147
Canna, 48
Cardinal Flower, 239
Castor-Oil-Plant, 121
Climbing Fumitory, 154
Cosmos, 261

Culver's-Root, 229
Cup-Plant, 280
Dahlia, 259
False Chamomile, 263
False Dragonhead, 213
Feather-Fleece, 47
Foxtail Lily, 41

Globe Thistle, 248
Goatsbeard, 114
Goldenglow, 279
Hollyhock, 126
Larkspur, 152
Ligularia, 279
Lily, 39
Michaelmas Daisy, 256
Monkshood, 153

Montbretia, 42
Nicotiana, 218
Orange Sunflower, 278
Plume Poppy, 95
Purple Mullein, 230
Queen-of-the-Meadow, 113
Rose Mallow, 126
Rosemary, 207

Russian Sage, 215
Spiderflower, 103
Sunflower, 277
Sweet Pea, 143
Tree Cypress, 184
Tree Mallow, 127
Wild Senna, 148
Yellow Star, 277

## *Arranged by Season of Bloom*
## *A Selection of 257 Different Plants*

### WINTER

Christmas Rose, 83

Snowdrop, 11

Winter Aconite, 84

### MARCH TO APRIL I

Crocus, 10
Glory-of-the-Snow, 21

Siberian Tea, 110

Snowflake, 14

### APRIL

Bluebell of England, 20
Crested Iris, 32
Grape Hyacinth, 20
Hepatica, 85

Leopard's-Bane, 273
Siberian Squill, 20
Spring Adonis, 85

Spring Meadow Saffron, 14
Striped Squill, 25
Whitlow Grass, 102

### LATE APRIL OR MAY

Alpine Wallflower, 100
Bleeding-Heart, 154
Bloodroot, 97
Blue Cohosh, 90
Brunnera, 193
Bunchberry, 139
Confederate Violet, 151
Cowslip, 170
Cow-Tongue, 22
Creeping Buttercup, 89
Crown Imperial, 37
Daffodil, 17
Dogtooth Violet, 16

English Primrose, 170
Erinus, 233
Fire-Pink, 74
Foam-Flower, 111
Globeflower, 82
Gold-Dust, 98
Grass Pink, 73
Ground Pink, 183
Hyacinth, 22
Jack-in-the-Pulpit, 38
Jonquil, 18
Large-flowered Trillium, 30

Lily-of-the-Valley, 21
London Pride, 110
Lungwort, 193
Maiden Pink, 73
Mayapple, 89
Mitrewort, 111
Moss Campion, 75
Oxlip, 170
Poet's Narcissus, 17
Polyanthus, 169
Rock Jasmine, 175
Rue Anemone, 88
Saxifrage Pink, 78

Shooting Star, 175
Showy Orchis, 52
Snowdrop Windflower, 82
Spring Heath, 167

Sweet William, 72
Tall Bearded Iris, 31
Tulip, 27
Twin-Leaf, 90
Virginia Cowslip, 193

Wall Cress, 103
Wall Pepper, 105
Yellow Lady's-Slipper, 51

## JUNE AND EARLY JULY FLOWERS

Aaron's-Rod, 147
Alkanet, 187
Alpine Catchfly, 74
Baby's-Breath, 75
Bearberry, 165
Bitter-Root, 68
Bluets, 194
Borage, 194
Buckbean, 178
Camass, 37
Candytuft, 99
Columbine, 152
Coral Bells, 111
Corydalis, 155
Cranesbill, 117
Creeping Forget-Me-Not, 190
Creeping Mint, 212
Daylily, 40
Douglasia, 176
Dropwort, 113

Edelweiss, 55
English Daisy, 261
Evening Campion, 79
Everlasting Pea, 143
Flowering Spurge, 122
Foxglove, 231
Garden Heliotrope, 196
Genista, 145
Globularia, 235
Goatsbeard, 114
Goutweed, 138
Hardy Carnation, 72
Iceland Poppy, 95
Japanese Iris, 32
Ladybell, 201
Maltese Cross, 79
Mountain Avens, 116
Nasturtium, 159
Oriental Poppy, 94
Peony, 83
Perennial Phlox, 182

Periwinkle, 178
Plume Poppy, 95
Prairie Lily, 132
Rose-of-Heaven, 80
Sand Verbena, 66
Shortia, 168
Siberian Wallflower, 99
Sneezewort, 254
Stone Cress, 102
Sweet Pea, 143
Thrift, 59
Tree Cypress, 184
Trumpet-Flower, 234
Tufted Pansy, 150
Twinflower, 196
Wallflower, 99
White Mariposa Lily, 33
Wild Sweet William, 183
Winged Everlasting, 55

## SELECTED MIDSUMMER FLOWERS

African Daisy (*Arctotis*), 266
African Daisy (*Gazania*), 270
African Marigold, 255
Ageratum, 245
Annual Blanket-Flower, 272
Annual Phlox, 181
Baby Blue-Eyes, 186
Balloon-Flower, 199
Bee-Balm, 214
Betony, 212
Black Cohosh, 85
Black Sampson, 265
Blue False Indigo, 145

Blue Gilia, 184
Blue Lace-Flower, 137
Blue Succory, 56
Butterfly-Flower, 219
Butterfly-Weed, 180
California Bluebell, 186
California Poppy, 95
Canna, 48
Cape Marigold, 267
China Aster, 258
Chinese Forget-Me-Not, 190
Chrysanthemum, 249
Cinquefoil, 115
Clarkia, 136
Cornflower, 243

Dahlia, 259
Dame's-Rocket, 100
Dragonhead, 214
Evening Primrose, 135
Flax, 119
Four-O'clock, 65
Foxtail Lily, 41
Fuchsia, 155
Garden Balsam, 160
Garden Sage, 210
Garden Verbena, 203
Gas-Plant, 120
Geranium (*Pelargonium*), 161
Germander Speedwell, 228

## FALL-BLOOMING FLOWERS

### *August 15 — September*

### *September to Frost*

## *34 Especially Fragrant Flowers*

Hardy Amaryllis, 24
Hardy Carnation, 72
Heliotrope, 191
Hyacinth, 22
Iceland Poppy, 95
Lavender, 208
Lily-of-the-Valley, 21
Mignonette, 104
Nicotiana, 218

Night-blooming Gladiolus, 50
Night-scented Stock, 101
Poet's Narcissus, 17
Pot Marjoram, 209
Prairie Lily, 132
Red Valerian, 197
Rosemary, 207
Royal Lily, 39

Saffron Crocus, 10
Sand Verbena, 66
Sweet Marjoram, 209
Sweet Scabious, 240
Thyme, 208
Trailing Arbutus, 165
Tuberose, 47
Wall Cress, 103

## *15 Perennial Ground Covers*

Bearberry, 165
Bugle, 212
Cotula, 247
Creeping Buttercup, 89
Creeping Mint, 212

Crown Vetch, 146
Gold-Dust, 98
Goutweed, 138
Ground Pink, 183
Japanese Spurge, 122

Maiden Pink, 73
Mazus, 233
Periwinkle, 178
Snow-in-Summer, 78
Wall Pepper, 105

## *15 Plants Difficult Enough to Grow to Require Patient or Expert Care*

Bearberry, 165
Bunchberry, 139
Erinus, 233
Foxtail Lily, 41
Heather, 166

Irish Heath, 167
Mountain Avens, 116
New Zealand Bur, 116
Rock Jasmine, 175
Spike Heath, 168

Spring Heath, 167
Trailing Arbutus, 165
Transvaal Daisy, 270
White Mariposa Lily, 33
Wood Sorrel, 119

## *80 Annual Plants, or Best Grown as Such*

African Daisy, 270
Ageratum, 245
Angel's-Trumpet, 222
Annual Blanket-Flower, 272
Annual Forget-Me-Not, 190
Annual Lupine, 144
Annual Phlox, 181
Anoda, 129
Baby Blue-Eyes, 186

Blue Gilia, 184
Blue Lace-Flower, 137
Borage, 194
Browallia, 222
Butterfly-Flower, 219
California Bluebell, 186
California Poppy, 95
Candytuft, 99
Cape Marigold, 267
Castor-Oil-Plant, 121
China Aster, 258

Chinese Forget-Me-Not, 190
Chinese Houses, 227
Cockscomb, 57
Coleus, 216
Cornflower, 243
Cosmos, 261
Cream Cups, 97
"Creeping Zinnia," 276
Edging Lobelia, 238
Four-O'clock, 65

*(See front and back endpapers for plants arranged by flower color)*

# Index

ALL ITEMS are alphabetically arranged. Many cross references have been inserted to facilitate finding the wanted item: thus, African Daisy is listed under "African" and "Daisy." Latin names of plants are in *italic* type, while English or vernacular names are in roman type. Page numbers in **boldface** type refer to a colored illustration of the plant.

*(Plants Arranged by Flower Color — continued from front endpapers)*

Rose Campion, 79
Satin-Flower, 136
Scarlet Sage, 210

Spring Heath, 167
Tiger-Flower, 43
Tree Cypress, 184

## *22 Prevailingly* Purple *Flowers*

Alpine Wallflower, 100
Black Sampson, 265
Blazing Star, 245
Chinese Houses, 227
Dame's Rocket, 100
Erinus, 233
Fireweed, 135
Germander, 215
Meadow Rue, 88
Moss Campion, 75
Night-scented Stock, 101

Poppy Mallow, 127
Purple Loosestrife, 131
Purple Rock Cress, 100
Red Turtlehead, 227
Showy Orchis, 52
Spiderflower, 103
Spring Meadow Saffron, 14
Synthris, 233
Thyme, 208
Trumpet-Flower, 234
Ursinia, 262

## *10 Prevailingly* Orange *Flowers or Orange - Yellow*

Blackberry Lily, 43
Butterfly-Weed, 180
California Poppy, 95
Copper-Tip, 50
Ligularia, 279

Siberian Wallflower, 99
Transvaal Daisy, 270
Venidium, 263
Wallflower, 99
Yellow Puccoon, 191

## *49 Prevailingly* Yellow *Flowers*

Aaron's-Rod, 147
African Marigold, 255
Asphodel, 43
Barrenwort, 90
Bladder-Pod, 102
Corydalis, 155
Cotula, 247
Cream Cups, 97
"Creeping Zinnia," 276
Cup-Plant, 280
Dogtooth Violet, 16
Douglasia, 176

Edelweiss, 55
English Primrose, 170
Frostweed, 133
Globeflower, 82
Gold-Dust, 98
Golden Aster, 272
Golden Cup, 96
Goldenglow, 279
Golden Marguerite, 254
Golden-Star, 276
Golden-Wave, 274
Inula, 278